Infusing Technology
in the 6-12 Classroom

A Guide to Meeting Today's Academic Standards

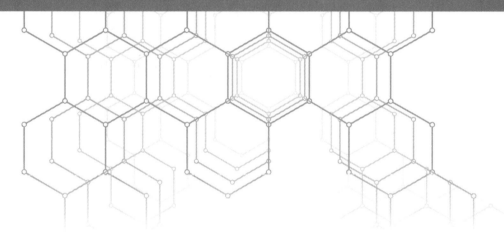

VALERIE MORRISON, STEPHANIE NOVAK, TIM VANDERWERFF

International Society for Technology in Education

PORTLAND, OREGON • ARLINGTON, VIRGINIA

Infusing Technology in the 6–12 Classroom
A Guide to Meeting Today's Academic Standards
Valerie Morrison, Stephanie Novak, and Tim Vanderwerff

Editor: *Emily Reed*
Copy Editor: *Karstin Painter*
Proofreader: *Corinne Gould*
Indexer: *Wendy Allex*
Book Design and Production: *Jeff Puda*
Cover Design: *Edwin Ouellette*

Library of Congress Cataloging-in-Publication Data
Names: Morrison, Valerie, author. | Novak, Stephanie (Stephanie M.), author. | Vanderwerff, Tim, author.
Title: Infusing technology in the 6-12 classroom : a guide to meeting today's academic standards / Valerie Morrison, Stephanie Novak, and Tim Vanderwerff.
Description: Portland : International Society for Technology in Education, [2019] | Includes bibliographical references and index.
Identifiers: LCCN 2019018800 (print) | LCCN 2019980773 (ebook) | ISBN 9781564847416 (pbk.) | ISBN 9781564847393 (epub) | ISBN 9781564847409 (pdf) | ISBN 9781564847386 (mobi)
Subjects: LCSH: Middle school education–Computer-assisted instruction. | Education, Secondary–Computer-assisted instruction. | Educational technology–Study and teaching (Middle school) | Educational technology–Study and teaching (Secondary) | Blended learning.
Classification: LCC LB1028.5 .M6375 2019 (print) | LCC LB1028.5 (ebook) | DDC 371.33–dc23
LC record available at https://lccn.loc.gov/2019018800
LC ebook record available at https://lccn.loc.gov/2019980773

First Edition
ISBN: 978-1-56484-741-6
Ebook version available.
Printed in the United States of America
ISTE® is a registered trademark of the International Society for Technology in Education.

About ISTE

The International Society for Technology in Education (ISTE) is the premier non-profit organization serving educators and education leaders committed to empowering connected learners in a connected world. ISTE serves more than 100,000 education stakeholders throughout the world.

ISTE's innovative offerings include the ISTE Conference & Expo, one of the biggest, most comprehensive edtech events in the world—as well as the widely adopted ISTE Standards for learning, teaching, and leading in the digital age and a robust suite of professional learning resources, including webinars, online courses, consulting services for schools and districts, books, and peer-reviewed journals and publications. Visit iste.org to learn more.

Related ISTE Titles

Integrating Technology in the Classroom, Second Edition: Tools to Meet the Needs of Every Student (2019), by Boni Hamilton

To see all books available from ISTE, please visit iste.org/Books.

About the Authors

 **Valerie Morrison** graduated with an elementary education degree from Northern Illinois University (NIU) and began her career as a classroom teacher. She became interested in teaching with technology early on and was a computer teacher for two years at a K–8 private school. Morrison then switched to the public school system, where she obtained a master's degree in instructional technology with an emphasis in media literacy from NIU, and is currently pursuing a doctoral degree from National Louis University in Advocacy, Policy, and Curriculum. She gained fourteen years of experience as a technology director/technology integration specialist and technology coach. Morrison worked closely with teachers and students to plan and differentiate lessons and projects that integrate technology. She taught technology workshops and classes for teachers and oversaw the technology program at her school. (She loves working with kids, teachers, and technology!) Like her coauthor Tim Vanderwerff, Morrison regularly served on her district's technology committee and was involved with integrating current state and district standards with the latest educational technologies. She presented at various conferences, including a presentation in Springfield, Illinois, to state legislators, where she and coauthor Stephanie Novak briefed legislators on how schools use technology. Morrison has switched career paths and is now teaching education classes at the college level; she enjoys using technology to teach the next generation of teachers. She also uses her time to write, which allows her to further educate the current generation of teachers.

 **Stephanie Novak** knew from a very young age that teaching and working with kids was the right career path for her. She graduated from Northern Illinois University with a master's degree in education and earned a reading specialist certificate from National Louis University. Novak started teaching at the middle school level but eventually settled in the elementary school system. As a classroom teacher for twenty-seven years, and an extended-learning teacher and coach for the last seven years of her career, she has always felt learning should be fun and meaningful. Novak was on her school district's technology committee for many years and regularly tried new technology in her classroom. As an instructional coach, she

encouraged teachers to help students grow in their learning at a pace that allowed for the most intellectual and personal growth. For the last two years of her career, Novak guided Grades 1–5 teachers through the Common Core State Standards, teaching them how to blend these standards with rigorous curriculum and prepare students for the digital age. After many years in education, Novak retired in 2014. She now applies her years of experience in lesson development by writing and publishing a blog depicting current instructional practices in the field of education and technology.

 **Tim Vanderwerff** has an extensive background in teaching and technology that began in the 1970s. Although writing was a new experience, trying out new experiences in education are second nature to him. After graduating from Illinois State University and then earning a master's in educational administration from Northern Illinois University, Vanderwerff saw many federal and state initiatives come and go in his thirty-three years of teaching. Starting as a classroom teacher in Grades 2–5, he was on his school district's technology committee for many years and regularly tried new technology in his class during that time. Vanderwerff eventually moved to the library and media center at his elementary school. He was the librarian and the technology teacher, and he provided tech support for the building for many years. In 2010, he was asked to be a teaching coach in his school district where he worked extensively with Valerie Morrison and Stephanie Novak; advising grade-level team meetings, finding resources for the standards, supporting individual teachers and teams in the classroom (with both technology and the newest educational strategies), and coaching new teachers. Vanderwerff is now retired, allowing him to devote more time to writing and advocating for the field about which he is so passionate.

Acknowledgments

We are grateful for the contributions of our friends, teammates, colleagues, and assistants with whom we worked throughout the years and who helped us come up with ideas for the books in this series. Working with so many talented people, we appreciate the collaboration and teamwork that allowed us to learn a great deal about coaching and technology.

We would also like to thank our families for all of their amazing support during the writing of these books. During the time we spent meeting, editing, and struggling to write, their unwavering support was truly appreciated.

Also, we would like to thank the editors and staff at ISTE for their insight, guidance, and patience. Their ongoing support has been much appreciated.

Dedications

To my husband, Glenn, and for my three daughters—Allana, LeeAnn, and Annaleese— who motivate me to inspire educators for the sake of children. —Valerie Morrison

To my husband Bill—thank you for your advice and patience while working on this book; to Helene, Estin, Jacob, Wyatt, and Abby—I wish great things for you in school and your future. —Stephanie Novak

To my ever-patient wife, Kim; my children Eric, Michael, and Kristina; and my grandson, Tyler, who motivate me every day to make our future the best that it can be. —Tim Vanderwerff

Contents

CHAPTER 10
Practical Ideas for Eighth Grade

CHAPTER 11
Practical Ideas for Grades 9-10

CHAPTER 12
Practical Ideas for Grades 11–12 217

Introduction

Have you ever found yourself sitting in a meeting wondering, "How am I ever going to cover all these standards and get to everything I'm supposed to be teaching this year?" At that moment, you also realize your district wants you to integrate the latest digital technology, and that may have you asking yourself, "Where will I get the technology I need? Who will help me learn and implement the technology?"

All of this might seem overwhelming—what is a teacher to do? First, you might turn to your teammates and colleagues for help and support. Perhaps your district provides current technology development for staff on a regular basis and has instructional coaches to help teachers chart this new territory, planning new lessons, bringing in resources, and infusing technology. In reality, most districts don't have all of this support. Yet teachers are especially in need of technology when considering their clientele: students.

We have an important role in helping you and your students implement technology into the standards. Our hope is that you are in a place that regularly provides high-quality professional learning experiences to help teachers understand the state standards and supports you with the latest in equipment and software. Professional development, along with this book and its resources, will help guide your instruction using the standards with technology, and it will support you in transferring new knowledge and skills to the classroom. It is a large task, but focusing on specific goals for student learning utilizing the state standards with technology will have a positive effect on student achievement. This will improve your teaching.

What Are My State Standards?

Until 2010, every state was doing their its thing when it came to state standards. The Common Core State Standards (CCSS) initiative was a state-created drive that sought to bring diverse state curricula into alignment by following the principles of standards-based education reform. Despite the public perception that it was a federal program, CCSS was sponsored by the National Governors Association Center for Best Practices (NGA Center) and the Council of Chief State School Officers (CCSSO), and a vast majority of the fifty U.S. states are members of the initiative. So, even if you're in a state that did not adopt Common Core, there is a high likelihood your curriculum looks very similar to CCSS.

As of the writing of this book, there are forty-six states that use CCSS in some form. Please see the map (Figure 0.1) to check if your state is one of them. But even the four states that never adopted Common Core have standards that are similar to them. Thirteen states adopted and subsequently, over the next several years,

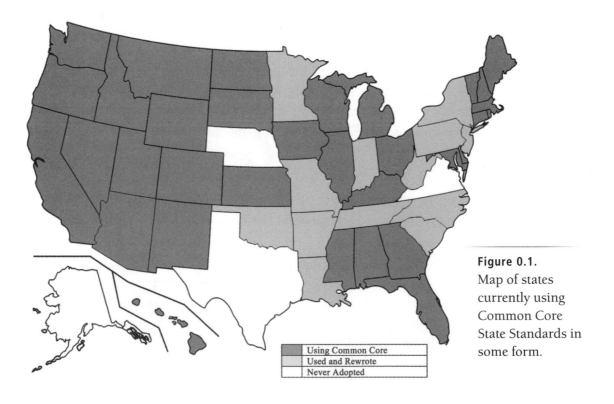

| Using Common Core |
| Used and Rewrote |
| Never Adopted |

Figure 0.1. Map of states currently using Common Core State Standards in some form.

rewrote the Common Core standards as their own. States have also renamed them, with the most popular alternate title being College and Career Readiness Standards (CCRS), and there are many others names used. According to an *Education Week* article about states' rewrites,

> [N]early 70 percent of the changes that were made in either math or language arts across all grades were simply wording or format clarifications, . . . Another 25 percent of the changes added a standard or a concept to an existing math or reading standard. In only 6 percent of the math or reading changes did states delete a standard, and none lessened their rigor. (Sparks, 2017)

Many articles have been written about the demise of CCSS, but a vast majority of states still have CCSS in place. In fact, most states would have problems getting textbooks and resources for their own standards, if they did not adhere to, or closely resemble, CCSS.

Why? Because most publishers, lesson creators, and online purveyors write for, and align to, the CCSS. Recently the assessments have come under fire; several states have changed, opted out, or created their own assessments for students, but the Common Core (or its close approximation) remains.

If you would like to explore the history behind CCSS, review the Common Core State Standards Initiative's "About the Standards" page **(tinyurl.com/26f7amp).**

What Is in This Book?

This is the second book in a two-book series designed to help teachers connect technology to CCSS in their K–12 classrooms. Although we refer to "standards," "CCR standards," and "CCSS" often in this book, we mean Common Core State Standards. We have reviewed the CCSS and selected those specific standards that implicitly or explicitly refer to technology. In other words, we do not cover every standard, only those that direct teachers to use technology as part of their instruction and assessment. Here is what you will find in this book.

- We address some of the issues that your students face and discuss how important it is to tailor their learning experiences.

- We give you ways of engaging and educating parents about the standards and assessments.

- We discuss the equipment you need to teach the standards.

- We show you how to address the roadblock that stand between you and this technology.

- We explain how the CCSS are organized and list the specific standards with the technology aspect in bold for the grade level you teach.

- We show you how to offer several classroom-tested lesson ideas by grade level from Chapter 8 through the end of the book. This ensures that your students are satisfying the tech-related benchmarks outlined in the CCSS.

Who Is This Book For?

Our intentions for this book, and the first book in this series, is that it be used as a resource for K–12 teachers, administrators, school librarians, and homeschool providers in the United States. Additionally, we believe the books will greatly benefit college instructors of elementary, middle school, and high school teachers. Really, any educator who is responsible for developing and delivering instruction to students in the United States and its territories will love this book.

We intend you to use this book as your technology coach when you need support for your lessons, especially when you are working with the standards. We experienced firsthand how to do this when teaching together and working as technology coaches. We have more than eighty-five years of combined teaching experience. As a team, we worked with teachers, students, administrators, and parents to integrate technology in our district. We hope that you will view this book as your own individual technology support because we can't be with you personally. Please consult this book often, especially if you're in a school, district, or state that does not provide enough professional development in this area. We hope to show you how to integrate the embedded tech related language found within the standards into your everyday curriculum.

How Can We Keep This Book up to Date?

We realize that technology is constantly changing and that digital tools come and go. To make certain that you continue to have the most current resources at your fingertips, visit our website, Infusing Technology in the Classroom **(tinyurl.com/ y9dfltpr).** The website password for the 6–12 book is: ITITC612. There, you will find an updated list of the apps, software, and websites mentioned in this book.

Book Website

We should also mention that, although we are sharing many tools and resources with you, we are not affiliated with any company. The programs, apps, and websites listed in this book are simply those that we feel support the CCSS. There are many other wonderful digital tools available that are not included due to space and time constraints. If you come across a particularly good or new resource that fits a specific standard, we hope you will visit our website and share that resource.

Let's begin by taking a closer look at today's generation of tech-savvy students and the skills they bring to the classroom.

1 Today's Students

A two-year-old taking a selfie? Seven-year-olds tweeting? No doubt about it, today's students come to school knowing more technology than ever before. New educational research suggests that offering a variety of learning opportunities, including lots of technology options, may be the best way to engage today's generation of learners. Educators must respond to this generation and address its unique learning needs. We believe this so passionately that we think a chapter about this subject is a must in any book about teaching children in the digital age. Technology must be made available to students. Technology must become ubiquitous.

The CCSS are designed to upgrade our school system's standards to meet the needs of prospective high school graduates who want to get into a good college or land a great job. They are designed with the tech-savvy child in mind. More specifically, the standards are designed with students' future workplaces in mind. That is the driving force behind the technology we see in the standards, and it is why teaching to your students' future needs is extremely important. Please keep this mind as you read this chapter.

Who Are Your Students?

Today's students grew up using digital technology and mass media. According to Debra Szybinski, executive director at New York University's Faculty Resource Network, **(tinyurl.com/y22s3kzo),** this generation is:

> generation characterized by some as self-absorbed, short attention spanned digital addicts who disrespect authority and assume that they can control what, when, and how they learn, and by others as smart, self- assured, technology

wizards, who follow the rules, and who are on their way to becoming the pow-
erhouse generation. Clearly, this is a generation like no other, and that has
posed an entirely new set of challenges both in and out of the classroom for
faculty members and administrators alike. (2016)

This current generation is ever changing. New technologies and new media are constantly invented and refined, creating pressure on schools to evolve. Most students
entering school now are completely immersed in technology outside of school.

Ironically, at many schools, there is a disconnect from students' real lives and their
way of learning. Schools are often islands of twentieth-century thinking in what is
now a digital age. Schools must do a better job of reaching the current generation
of students; making technology available to students at school helps educators
respond to and address students' unique learning needs.

What Does This Generation Know and Do?

Most students entering kindergarten now have access to desktop computers, smartphones, tablets, and laptops at home. These children begin using most of these
devices by the time they are three years old. Whether you go to playgroups, parks,
or other places frequented by young children, you're likely to see them working
on their parents' tablets or smartphones (or begging to use them!). These students
come to us with skills that include (but are not limited to) swiping to work an
app; navigating a mouse to play computer games; operating their own electronic
devices, such as children's learning tablets, handheld learning devices, and interactive video games; and hunting and pecking on the keyboard to send emails. Also,
our tech-savvy students can take videos and photos using a tablet or smartphone,
as well as converse with someone by texting, blogging, and messaging. Most have
been exposed to the internet and understand that they can find almost any information there.

Because they have so much information at the touch of a button, and constant stimulation around them, this generation often attempts to multitask. It makes sense
to them to watch TV, send a text, and find out what the weather will be all at the
same time!

Being social is very important to the students in this tech-savvy generation. They are certainly the "in touch" generation, with immediate access to texts, emails, social networking sites, and even the sound of a human voice at the other end of the line. This generation is lost when their smartphones or tablets break; they feel "cut off from the world" when they don't have instant access to the internet.

Some say that the current generation has hovering parents and a sense of entitlement. While this may be taken as a negative, having parents who are involved with their children and their children's school is a good thing, as it strengthens the home–school connection. Students with parents who are involved in their academic lives can be better students, and they are less afraid to try new things. Educators need to recognize these traits and use them to help students reach their maximum potential.

How Has Technology Affected Students' Minds?

By the time they're in their twenties, today's students will have spent thousands of hours surfing the internet and playing video games. This vast amount of screen time seems to be shortening their attention spans. At a time when their brains are particularly sensitive to outside influences, excessive screen time affects the way they learn and absorb information.

Furthermore, this generation does not read books to find information. Online search engines are prevalent in providing all of the information they need quickly, without having to go through a book from cover to cover. With access to an over-abundance of information, they need to be skilled hunters who know how to sift through data quickly and efficiently. This new type of learner doesn't necessarily read from left to right or from beginning to end. Visuals help today's students absorb more information than they do from straight text. Thus, students become better scanners, a useful skill when confronted with masses of online information in a world that's full of noise and multiple stimulations. So, most modern students have learned to block out distractions while they focus on the task at hand.

How Has Technology Affected Behavior?

There is less and less face-to-face communication taking place because of constant technology use. We have seen instances of parents and children sitting next to one another without speaking at a restaurant. Instead, they simply sit and quietly engage with their individual tablets or smartphones.

There are many debates about how technology helps or harms the development of a student's thinking. Of course, this depends on the specific technology used, as well as how and with what frequency it is used in school. Our duty as educators is to decide what technology to use in the classroom and when, because technology influences students' thought processes. We must be aware of this effect to guide students as digital-age learners.

How Do We Move beyond the ABCs?

Education has gone through a monumental transformation in the last twenty years. Some changes have greatly improved the way teachers educate, while others are still under evaluation. Great educational debates, such as teacher-directed versus self-directed learning, are cases in point. What we have found during our years of experience is that to progress in the classroom, teachers must adapt to the times, adopting new techniques while using time-tested methods. Success in teaching a new generation of students isn't based solely on what educators are teaching students but *how* educators are teaching them.

Distance learning

We have seen our share of success stories and our share of students who struggled for reasons that are completely preventable. For these highly activity-scheduled and gadget-oriented students, traditional one-size-fits-all teaching is no longer effective. Sitting behind a desk, listening to the teacher talk, and reading from a textbook are completely ineffective. This generation of students needs to be engaged in active and interactive learning to enhance their knowledge. They do not want technology just because it is "cool." They need technology because it drives their world (now and in the future). They are looking for something dynamic to make learning come alive—to make it different and interesting every day. Being connected accomplishes that goal.

How Can Educators Succeed in the Digital Age?

Thinking of technology as a new toy that will go away or doesn't have a place in education is no longer an option. Educators need to embrace technology and tap into what our students are already coming to us with, using it to advance their learning. But this technology cannot just be digital worksheets!

This is not always easy, especially when students know more about how to use the technology than many teachers. Therefore, it is our duty to catch up and make sure we know what our students know. This can be done in many different ways; however, the easiest way is to do what they do: pick up tablets or smartphones and start using apps that they use! Once we have the background skills to know what our students know, we can move forward. We simply need to remember that technology is a tool. And we can use these tools like anything else we use in education—like manipulatives in math, novels in reading, and microscopes in science, to name a few.

Of course, this new reality being imposed on and by the current generation has implications for you as a teacher. It used to be that students conducted research by using books that were from credible publishers, and those books had been rigorously edited and fact-checked. This generation uses the internet almost exclusively. If your students get all of their information from the internet, then you must teach them media literacy skills. This skill set has become extremely important in an information age where children need to discern fiction from fact on the internet when, sometimes, adults have trouble differentiating it for ourselves.

You need to tap into what your students are experiencing every day and use it to your advantage. Many of your current students will work in very social settings but in a different way than previous generations. Let them work often as partners or in groups to create multimedia presentations or digital videos. Because they love to send texts and video chat, let them text, instant message, or video chat with students around the world! This generation is good at multitasking. Allow them to do more things at once, such as collaborate with others while taking notes on a research paper. Students all know how to use a smartphone, so when on a field trip, let them record a video of what they are seeing. They are used to constant noise and stimulation. Do not make them work quietly at their desks; rather, they should work with hands-on activities like live apps, green-screen technology, or maker labs. Students know at a very young age how to navigate the internet. Let them use a computer when they have a question instead of asking you for the answer.

We know this new generation of children, teenagers, and young adults can be challenging because of how digital technology has changed their way of learning and behaviors. The following chapters will further address some of these issues and how learning must be specialized, giving more examples of how to integrate technology with the CCSS. These standards keep this new generation of students in mind, and so will we.

CHAPTER 2

Parent Education

The past decade has been financially difficult for schools. States across the country have had to slash education budgets due to economic downturns. If your district's budget was unaffected by financial cuts, it is among the few. As for the rest of us, we have had to achieve more with less. To make matters more challenging, we had to implement new standards that ask schools to immerse students in technology—a very expensive task. Having parents on your side in this budget struggle can be very helpful.

In the years since the CCSS were written and adopted by most states, some attitudes toward the standards have changed. More recently, parents and community members have questioned them. So it is important, as a teacher, to be proactive in getting the word out about what is going on in your classroom. Work with parents and the community to educate them about standards in your state, district, and school. Parents only want what is best for their children, and a little reassurance from you can go a long way.

This reassurance begins with listening to parents. Ask them about their concerns. Answering their questions with facts will help them to better understand why your state adopted the standards. The following topics cover a few of the technology concerns that have been raised about CCSS recently. Knowing about these and other controversial issues allows you to defuse concerns before they become major issues.

Why Do Parents Need to Know about Technology Standards?

You don't need technology to read or do math—civilizations have been doing both for centuries. Nevertheless, technology does help in both areas. If we were still at the turn of the last millennium (1000 CE), we would be hand-copying books. The printing press brought books to the commoner and education to those who wanted to learn. The abacus is fine but cannot compete with a calculator or computer. Technology marches on so that we can advance, learn more, and pass that knowledge along to the next generation.

The computer revolution of the last century is finally hitting the classroom with the encouragement of the CCR standards. Before these standards, computers were for schools with money or those won grants. Even so, many schools that were considered advanced had not integrated technology into everyday learning. These were the first set of widely recognized standards to do that. There are several reasons for parents to know about CCSS.

First, keeping students versed in the fundamentals of technology will enhance your teaching tremendously, and students' parents can help with this at home. Survey parents to see how many students have internet access at home. What kind of equipment do they use—do they have cameras or video capabilities? What do they allow their children to use? Knowing what your students have at home improves equitable access in the classroom. Encourage parents to teach their children how to properly use tablets, computers, smartphones, and other mobile devices so students come to school more prepared.

Second, learning doesn't happen only at school. You need to educate parents because they are the main support system for learning outside of school. Consistent, clear standards now put forward by CCR standards enable more effective learning. Knowing what technology and what software will be used to master these standards greatly assists parents and, in turn, their children. Look at the Global Family Research Project (**tinyurl.com/hguh777**) for the latest research and insights on how to get students' parents involved.

Third, technology can instantly link parents to what their children are learning. Knowing assignments, communicating with teachers, and understanding what is expected are all improved with today's technology. There is even a principal out there who tried "flipping" parent communication, which you might try too (DeWitt, 2013). Whatever you implement is a win-win for you and your students. Take advantage of technology in communication; don't shun it. It will make your life easier.

Finally, we are becoming a smaller, more codependent world. To have a world-class education that keeps our nation and civilization moving forward, all students need to be well versed in the newest technologies. That is what the CCR standards are all about! The CCSS Initiative's mission statement affirms, "The standards are designed to be robust and relevant to the real world, reflecting the knowledge and skills that our young people need for success in college and careers" (National Governors Association Center for Best Practices & Council of Chief State School Officers, 2010). In other words, the CCSS are designed for your students' success as adults in the workplace, of which technology is an integral part.

Even so, parents must be a part of this endeavor or their children will struggle to succeed. Involving them is as important to you, as a teacher, as is any other aspect of your students' learning. Do not think of parent education in the standards as an add-on, a resource to be used if you have time. Investing in your students' parents and having them on your team benefits you and lessens your load. In a synthesis of studies done on families, communities, and schools, Henderson and Mapp stated, "Efforts to improve children's performance in school are much more effective if they encompass their families. Regardless of income level or education background, all families can—and often do—support their children's success" (2002, p. 208).

What Issues Do Parents Have with Technology in the Standards?

Parents may ask you about some of the controversial things they hear related to the standards. One controversy involves a misunderstanding about standards and curriculum. Standards describe what students should know; curriculum is how they get there. For example, even though there is no standard for cursive writing or keyboarding, that doesn't mean it won't be in your school's curriculum. Curriculum is still developed locally. Educate parents who are concerned that they have no control over their child's curriculum—they still have the ability to contribute to how it is taught in their local school.

Another controversy centers on decreased test scores from 2015 and 2017 National Assessment of Educational Progress. Although it may or may not be true in your district, scores quite often decrease when the format of the test changes. One example is when students go from paper-and-pencil tests to digital assessments. According to Swanson (2013), if your school changed tests, then a result might be decreased scores until students become familiar with the new format. The best way to combat this is to have other digital tests in the classroom throughout the year, to familiarize students with the new format. Also, the NAEP tests are still in trial stages, even four years after implementing the standards. Some states have changed their tests to new assessments. Cumulative results from standards-based teaching and assessment will tell more as parents, teachers, administrators, and policy makers look at the data and adjust the test accordingly.

A common concern we have heard is that the federal government will be able to collect the data of individual students because of these digital tests. This has been a particularly heightened apprehension recently. The U.S. Congress (2010) passed laws that prohibit the creation of a federal database with students' personally identifiable information. Although the law is in place, you should still be vigilant about keeping this sensitive data secure. You are the first line of defense and need to have procedures in place. Please go over your district's privacy policy. If there is none, push hard to make one.

How Can Parents Help with Assessment Technology?

Teachers should help parents and community members understand the types of questions and problems that students are asked to solve on the new digital assessments. During parent nights, open houses, and/or in newsletters, introduce parents to the kind of testing their son or daughter will be experiencing. The Partnership for Assessment of Readiness for College and Careers (PARCC), **(parcconline.org)** and Smarter Balanced Assessment Consortium **(smarterbalanced.org)** websites still the most commonly used assessments. If your state is using a different format, choose questions from these tests. You can download sample questions to show to parents; it can also be helpful to put new assessment questions next to old assessment questions so everyone can directly observe the shift.

If your state is going to use the Smarter Balanced test, have parents use the sample questions on the PARCC site to test their children at home. The sample Smarter Balanced test can also be used to prepare for the PARCC test. Both tests' questions are similar, based on the CCR standards, and can be used prepare students for state written tests.

Don't forget the basics. Make sure parents know what kind of equipment the students will be using for the test, and have them use similar equipment at home if possible. This will make the device a secondary concern so your students can focus on the test's content. Send home a sample question weekly so parents can become familiar with changing assessments. Make sure some of the sample test questions you send home require students to use technology to answer the question, as this will be included on the assessments.

How Can Parents Help Students Meet Technology Standards?

Parents need to see the value of having technologies at home that can help their children achieve more. At the same time, home technology helps you accomplish these new curriculum tasks that, as we teachers know, are daunting, to say the least.

A poll by the Leading Education by Advancing Digital (LEAD) Commission found that parents and teachers believe students who lack home access to the internet are at a significant disadvantage (2013, p. 23). Home access to broadband is viewed as important to learning and succeeding in school for the following reasons:

- It greatly exceeds anything that your students could ever bring home in their backpacks.

- It allows parents to be more involved in their child's schoolwork and allows for more effective communication between parents and schools, thus promoting greater student success.

- It vastly expands the time your students can learn and explore.

- It leads to greater collaborative work engaging students in online group homework. (This last point dovetails perfectly with many of the CCR technology initiatives.)

Home access requires your active support. At the beginning of the year, run a workshop for parents about the kinds of technology you will be using and why. Teach them how to monitor their children for internet safety. You may want to call on your library media specialist or tech specialist to help, if they are available in your school. Of course, you may teach in an area where parents do not have the funds for broadband access or technology at home. Following are a few ways to address the issue.

- For homes that have broadband but no computers/tablets, start a program that allows students to check out resources from the school.

- Have after-school clubs or homework help where technology is available.

- Open the school in the evenings for parents and students, providing them access to teachers and technology.

- Apply for one of many grants available from different levels of government, foundations, and companies to help with your school community's access to technology.

- Ask parents to allow their children to use their smartphones that have cellular access.

Wherever you teach, parent education is the key to student success with the state standards. Lack of information is one of the main reasons parents have been opposed to the CCR standards. Being a proactive partner will defuse most objections that arise—from parents and others in the community—and actually create proponents of what is going on in your classroom. Having parents as partners can only help when you are faced with technology needs, such as lack of hardware and software, lack of assistance, and gaps in your students' tech knowledge.

However, parent education is only part of the puzzle; you must first educate yourself about the standards and technology before you can effectively educate others. To address this, we have included a chapter on staff development (Chapter 4). But before we explore your professional development options, let's take a closer look at the roadblocks you may encounter on your journey to get technology into your classroom.

CHAPTER

3 | Roadblocks to Technology

U nless your school or district has unlimited funding and gives you completely free reign on your purchases, you have hit roadblocks in your quest for classroom technology. Chances are that you do not have the student technology to become a fully stocked digital-age learning environment, but you are not alone. In this chapter, we provide ideas to use and manage the equipment and software/apps you already have, and we explore ways to add more. It is our hope that when we come to the later chapters on practical ways to integrate your technology with the CCR standards and your curriculum, you will be better prepared to maximize your resources.

What Are the Roadblocks to Accessibility?

If it is not possible to provide all of your students with tablets or laptops, providing them to half the class is the next best thing. This allows you to work with small groups or pairs of students. Another option is to share technology with the classroom next door to gain at least some time with a full class set of laptops or tablets.

Lack of Funding for 10–12 Tablets/Laptops per Classroom

One option is to have each grade level share a cart of fifteen laptops or tablets in addition to a mobile lab that any classroom can access. We suggest department-level sharing of technology with no more than three sections, as more sections are likely to be too limiting. If there are four or more sections in a department or subject area, add more mobile labs. This will allow the subject area class to have access to at least half of a class set. When you need a full class set, use the mobile cart to fill in the gaps. Another way to share additional mobile devices is to divide the fifteen laptops or tablets into sets of five for each of three classes and then have teachers share devices when necessary. You could also place all fifteen laptops or tablets on a cart and provide a signup sheet for as-needed use.

Only 4–6 Laptops/Tablets per Classroom

You can have half the class double up on the tablets at one time or you can share with other classes near you to get more. To accomplish the latter, you have several options: look for other subject areas that can share their laptops or tablets for that period; arrange certain days when each class has all of the devices; or teachers can request them informally. The key is easy accessibility for your students.

Computer Lab Limitations

A computer lab with enough computers for all of your students is another great resource, especially if it includes a tech or media center teacher or assistant. This is great because everything is in a set location and there is another knowledgeable teacher available. The down side is that teachers have to schedule certain times, and everyone must work on the computers at the same time. If you have access to tables in the lab or a nearby learning space, you have the opportunity to do other things with students who finish their work early, forming smaller work groups as in a traditional classroom.

1:1 Initiatives

Many districts are moving to a 1:1 device initiative for tablets or laptops. If this is not the case in your district, then you will be more limited. More than likely, you will not have a full class set to yourself. If you are able to get a set to share, the easiest arrangement is to schedule times to use the devices. However, with such limited class time and many students per class, splitting up a class set so teachers get four to five devices per class may be a better option. It will take more planning on your part to outline how your students will divide their technology time.

At high school, and even middle school level, enlisting students' smartphones is another option. Many students have them and bring them to school. Your district should discuss how to use these resources to their advantage while not interfering with the learning process. Some states are already using student-owned devices in their schools and have begun writing policies for them. For an interesting look at cell phone issues in schools, see Derrick Meador's article, "The Pros and Cons of Allowing Cell Phones in School" **(tiny.cc/0ajq3y).**

Additional Equipment

How do you choose additional technology to better equip your classroom when your budget is already tight or inadequate? Aside from laptops and tablets, it is imperative to have a multimedia projector so that all students can see lesson materials, projects, resources, and so on. Other valuable equipment includes:

- **Document cameras:** You will use these every day to display written books, worksheets, student work, and the like. Once you have one, you won't know how you got along without it!

- **Interactive whiteboards:** These are great for engaging students, especially during whole-group instruction.

With so many new websites that can turn laptops, tablets, or smartphones into interactive technology, buying interactive response systems is no longer necessary.

Free interactive websites may offer upgrades for an affordable fee, including: Socrative **(socrative.com),** AnswerPad **(theanswerpad.com),** AnswerGarden **(answergarden.ch),** Quizlet **(quizlet.com),** and Annotate **(annotate.net).**

Keeping Up with Students' State Assessments

Different groups developed PARCC and Smarter Balanced to test for college and career readiness beginning in Grade 3. As of 2018, twenty-three states use one of these two tests to assess their students in Grades 6–8. The rest use state-created or other tests to assess students. In high school fifteen states use PARCC or Smarter Balanced, twenty-one use ACT or SAT testing, and the rest use state or other exams for student assessment. Your students may be tested more than once a year depending on their grade level and what test is given in your state. Many of these assessments are computerized and have certain technology requirements, but they allow traditional paper-and-pencil versions when necessary. (Teachers should be aware that traditional versionsmay be phased out eventually.)

We will not address the specifics of network requirements; just know that your school or district will need to meet certain operating system and networking specifications whether they are using the Smarter Balanced, PARCC, or state-created assessment.

Additionally, your network must be able to address security requirements to keep student information safe. Following are the informational sites to help you find what you will need.

- **PARCC** technical requirements: **(tinyurl.com/y8vknzrk)**

- **Smarter Balanced** technical requirements: **(tinyurl.com/yddyof89)**

- **ACT** technical requirements: **(tinyurl.com/y8dae3ob)**

How Do We Overcome Software and Hardware Roadblocks?

You cannot benefit from technology if you don't have it. It is also difficult to share it if you don't have enough of it. You need it on time and easily accessible if you truly want to use it seamlessly. This may be the biggest roadblock. We discussed how you might use different configurations of new or existing hardware in your school. The more pervasive the technology, the easier it is for you to achieve the goals set forth by the standards.

Sources of Funding

If you don't have enough equipment and/or software, apply for grants. While there are more grants available for economically disadvantaged districts, some are accessible to all districts. State and federal grants are available, especially if you can link your needs to the standards. The Bill & Melinda Gates Foundation and big companies like Google, Target, and Staples give to schools. Ask your Parent Teacher Association (PTA) or Parent Teacher Organization (PTO) for money. Many districts have foundations that fund grants for teachers. You could even do a fundraiser for new technology. Following is a list that is by no means complete but offers a great place to start.

GOVERNMENT

- **21st Century Community Learning Centers (tinyurl.com/7nx37vb):** This funding is designed to get parents and the community to actively support your work in the classroom.

- **Individuals with Disabilities Education Act (IDEA), (tinyurl.com/y5ue5o6d):** These funds are for students with disabilities.

- **Grants.gov (tinyurl.com/k8fybkt):** Search this site for all available federal grants. These grants include:

- **Every Student Succeeds Act (ESSA):** This funding replacing the No Child Left Behind Act is designed to create equitable funding, support for the standards, and grow innovation in the classroom.

- **Investing in Innovation Fund (i3):** This program provides competitive grants to schools demonstrating improved student achievement and innovative practices.

- **Grants Funding Forecast (tinyurl.com/hkcrx74):** This resource offers an annual list of funding opportunities.

- **Computers for Learning (computersforlearning.gov):** This government program encourages agencies to transfer their used computers and related peripheral equipment directly to schools.

- **State Government (tinyurl.com/y9dfltpr):** Look for your state's educational website in this online index.

FOUNDATIONS

Many private foundations offer grants. Following are just a few.

- **Bill & Melinda Gates Foundation (tinyurl.com/odwcrra):** This is the largest private foundation in the world. Its primary aim in the United States is to expand educational opportunities and access to information technology.

- **The Foundation Center (foundationcenter.org):** This independent, nonprofit, information clearinghouse collects information on foundations, corporate giving, and related subjects.

- **Foundations.org (tinyurl.com/7sf3c):** This online resource provides an A–Z directory of foundations and grant makers.

- **The NEA Foundation (tinyurl.com/or2qc56):** This teacher association gives grants in several areas.

COMPANIES

Many of the companies that manufacture the products we use every day have educational initiatives that offer grants for public schools. Following are just a few.

- **Target (tinyurl.com/cdt25kz):** Target offers grants in many areas, including: education, the arts, and public safety.

- **Toshiba (toshiba.com/taf/612.jsp):** Toshiba offers math and science grants for 6–12.

- **Google (tinyurl.com/pm9gar4):** Google has several sites dedicated to corporate giving. Google for Nonprofits is a good place to start your search.

- **Microsoft Corporate Citizenship (tinyurl.com/p62et7u):** These grants are available for after-school programs.

- **Staples Foundation (tinyurl.com/yaysgbpo):** Staples educational giving teaches, trains and inspires people from around the world by providing educational and job skill opportunities.

- **CenturyLink Clarke M. Williams Foundation's Teachers and Technology Program (tinyurl.com/otej8rl):** These grants are designed to help fund projects that advance student success through the innovative use of technology. Teachers in public or private PK–12 schools in CenturyLink's residential service areas are eligible to apply for a Teachers and Technology grant.

OTHER RESOURCES

Microfunding through school- and classroom-specific grants can yield substantial results. Often donors are willing to fund projects whose impact they can directly observe.

- **Donors Choose (donorschoose.org):** A crowd-sourced educational funding site that works with donors funding specific projects of various types.

- **ClassWish (classwish.org):** Crowd-sourced educational funding that lets you raise money for any classroom project in the country.

- **Adopt-a-Classroom (adoptaclassroom.org):** Facilitates individual donations to help teachers get the supplies they need.

- **National Charter School Resource Center (tinyurl.com/ph2ytng):** This resource website has many links to funding opportunities.

- **eSchool News (eschoolnews.com):** This is a great grant resource for K–12 and higher education.

- **Internet@Schools (tinyurl.com/nnh5n9d):** This online magazine for education provides a vast list of free resources, grants, and funding.

- **Scholastic (tinyurl.com/nd3t97t):** This educational mainstay has many great grant resources, too.

Free Software and Apps

Software and app purchases are a challenging roadblock, especially if your district or school doesn't provide enough funding. Fortunately, there are many free resources. Search app stores for free apps. Free sites, such as Google Docs, are also great places to start. In addition, there are entire sites with free services geared toward the standards.

If you are in a small district or a private school, or if you live in a state where funding is limited, follow the money. Go to websites in states and at schools that do have the funds. Look at websites in wealthier school districts near you. Do they have lessons, activities, and technology ideas that match your standards and are free to anyone on the internet?

Many states have CCSS resources posted for free! Take advantage of them. For example, New York has many helpful suggestions at EngageNY.org **(tinyurl.com/ npc7q58).** Utah has also published a very resourceful standards site that can be found at the Utah Education Network (UEN), **(tinyurl.com/l2e532).**

Free software and apps are also available from private companies. These sites usually have ads, or they may want you to purchase add-ons; you and your district will have to judge their value for yourselves. More examples of free applications and websites are given in the Practical Ideas chapters (8–12) of this book.

What Other Roadblocks Must We Solve?

Systemic educational roadblocks can take many forms, which are often unintended or unavoidable. Here are three common challenges teachers face.

Misguided Policies

Some districts or schools require that all departments have the same apps or software. They don't allow teachers to choose what they prefer, and this can be frustrating. If your district wants all software to be the same, you might try explaining why each department and each teacher would benefit from using different software, apps, and equipment appropriate to their students' needs.

Some districts implement policies that do not allow teachers to use technology as a tool. Instead, they force teachers to use technology when other mediums or tools make more sense. For example, we discovered a district that required teachers to teach with a tablet 85% of their instructional time. This district even required students to bring tablets to gym class and physical education teachers to use tablets in every class period. School leaders who enforce this kind of policy know very little about infusing technology into the classroom. It would be better to achieve higher technology use through staff development and individual coaching (e.g., through the use of this book) than by generating untenable policies that don't actually affect meaningful student learning.

To counter these policies, speak to your principal, go to a technology meeting, or attend a board meeting! Explain that technology is a tool and that meeting the CCSS does not require you to use technology every second of the day. There is a time and place for technology just as there is a time and place for math manipulatives, a calculator, a book, and even a pencil. Balance is the key. If anything is overused, it (and your effort) is set up for failure.

Parents

Parents will ask the question, "Why do we need new or more technology?" Have a discussion at open house nights and board meetings about what you will be doing or would like to do with technology. Explain that your state's standards require everyone to integrate technology, and this is important for today's students. Please refer to the chapter on parent education (Chapter 2), which has specific suggestions about many of the issues that become parental roadblocks.

Staff Development

Teacher training is so important. You need to have professional development in the area of technology for yourself as well as for your students. If you have a technology or instructional coach, great! Spend a lot of time with this coach—set up weekly meetings. A coach can help you as well as model or co-teach with you. There are many professional development opportunities online as well as off-site in the area of technology. Refer to Chapter 4 to learn how to get staff development outside your district and how best to get around these roadblocks!

How Do You Get the Help You Need?

One of the key components of using technology is getting help. It is easier for middle and high school students to work independently with technology and follow directions. However, it may still be very difficult to manage a class of students who are all trying to use technology at the same time. This is also the case when teachers try to work with a small group while the rest of the class is doing something else on tablets. Inevitably, something goes wrong with someone's computer, so many high school districts use student technology assistants.

It is extremely helpful to have another set of hands. If you have assistants who come to help on a regular basis to help, this is a great resource. You can call on these assistants when you need them, which allows greater freedom to work with the whole class—if you have enough equipment.

If you do not have access to assistants, middle school teachers might try using parent volunteers. The worst part of using volunteers is inconsistent attendance. However, if you can find a parent or two who are willing to come in on a regular basis, they can be a great help. You will need to find time to train your volunteers of course, but once you do, most will be savvy enough to pick up what they need to do in class.

Make sure that you have class passwords where it is easy for you to find them. Forgotten passwords are an annoying occurrence, so having them easily accessible will help you manage the situation comfortably.

Another option is to work with your fellow teachers. Consider arranging your schedules so that you each take extra students while the other uses technology with a smaller group. Overseeing fewer students makes technology use much easier to manage.

Create peer groups that have a mix of tech-savvy students and those who struggle with technology. This is especially effective at the high school level. Making the most of available technology is all in the management of it. We know several high schools that have their technology departments employ students and train them to help throughout the high school all year long.

Although there can be many roadblocks that prohibit you from using classroom technology the way that you would like, there are ways to overcome these challenges. By using the suggestions given in this chapter, we hope you will overcome any roadblocks that lie in your way and that you have most everything you need at your fingertips.

4 Staff Development

> When technology integration is at its best, a child or a teacher doesn't stop to think that he or she is using a technology tool—it is second nature. And students are often more actively engaged in projects when technology tools are a seamless part of the learning process.
>
> —"What Is Successful Technology Integration?" (Edutopia, 2007)

Without a doubt, today's students come to school with strong backgrounds and understandings of technology. This generation of tech-savvy students is interested, motivated, and even driven by technology. As you will see, College and Career Readiness standards have explicit technology standards within grade levels. But technology, as a tool, needs to be infused in all other CCR standards as well. Having a tech savvy classroom for today's students is the best way to create a digital age learning environment.

Truly integrated technology is ever present but invisible. You can use technology as a tool for instruction—as a way to vary the way you present information. You also can provide technology options for students as a way for them to engage in content skills. Students in your class should be given opportunities to create and share their new learning with a myriad of technology tools. The CCSS are not just about presenting information to students; today's students need to be able to plan, reason, analyze, evaluate, and create. Technology integration in today's classroom will do just that—it will not only allow your students to become more engaged in the learning process but empower them to gain a deeper understanding of their learning.

A plethora of articles have been written about how to succeed with CCR standards and how good professional development for teachers and staff is a significant key to its success. Technology plays a very valuable role in guiding and fostering this effective professional development, as well as helping to boost current professional-development resources and practices. And technologies that make tools available to teachers on an ongoing basis present a solid jumping-off point for successful classroom integration.

Research has found that sending teachers to workshop-based professional development alone is not very effective. Approximately, 90–100% of teachers participate in workshop-style or in-service training sessions during a school year and through the summer. While workshops can be informational and timely, teachers need opportunities to implement new teaching techniques, not just learn about them. Thus, professional development needs to be ongoing and meaningful to your own professional circumstances. The most effective professional development also uses peer coaches, educational coaches, and mentors to implement new learning in class.

How Do You Create a Technology Plan?

You need lots of support and tools to utilize and sustain technology in your classroom. If you do not have a district or school technology director or coach, how do you develop a plan to get yourself (as well as your fellow colleagues) what is needed? You can be the pioneer to get the technology ball rolling.

Following are suggestions to help you begin the journey of infusing technology in your classroom. Although this should not be your task alone, sometimes it falls to a single individual to blaze the trail. Fortunately, there are many online resources that can assist you with creating a technology plan. Edutopia is a well-known place to start, offering (among other things) "Ten Steps to Effective Technology Staff Development" by Barbara Bray **(tinyurl.com/oesjsmn).**

The first step is to put together a technology committee with as many representatives from different departments and grade levels as you can find. It would be great to include administration staff, as well as a district office representative. Parents, students, and outside technology experts can only enhance your committee.

Next, come up with some ways to show how you and your students can use technology in the classroom. Providing specific examples of students working with technology to address the ISTE Standards and the CCSS would be powerful!

Develop a detailed questionnaire for teachers to express their classroom needs, frustrations, and fears. This questionnaire can also serve as a place for teachers to describe what they hope to learn from professional development, including technology goals they would like students to pursue in class.

Ask students to describe the ideal state of technology in their classroom in one year, two years, five years, and so on. Then place the ideas from this brainstorming session in a public document, so everyone on the committee and in the community can see and refer to it.

Lastly, conduct a teacher survey using the **ISTE Standards for Educators** (Figure 4.1) as a guide **(iste.org/standards).** These standards outline what educators should know and be able to apply in order to teach effectively and grow professionally. ISTE has organized them into the following seven categories.

1. **Learner:** Educators continually improve their practice by learning from and with others and exploring proven and promising practices that leverage technology to improve student learning.

2. **Leader:** Educators seek out opportunities for leadership to support student empowerment and success and to improve teaching and learning.

3. **Citizen:** Educators inspire students to positively contribute to and responsibly participate in the digital world.

4. **Collaborator:** Educators dedicate time to collaborate with both colleagues and students to improve practice, discover and share resources and ideas, and solve problems. Educators:

5. **Designer:** Educators design authentic, learner-driven activities and environments that recognize and accommodate learner variability.

6. **Facilitator:** Educators facilitate learning with technology to support student achievement of the ISTE Standards for Students.

7. **Analyst:** Educators understand and use data to drive their instruction and support students in achieving their learning goals.

Each standard has performance indicators that provide specific, measurable outcomes. You can use them to ascertain teachers' technology comfort level, attitude, and integration use in your school. Answers could be on a scale, such as "proficient

Figure 4.1. ISTE Standards for Educators

enough to teach someone else," "able to hold my own," "a little knowledge," or
"scared to death to even try." It may even be helpful to have teachers identify three-
to-five areas that they feel are most important to improving technology within the
year. Providing a space for them to write an explanation is also important, as they
may not be able to rank themselves on a scale when they can't quantify what they
don't know. Writing a paragraph about where they stand with technology might
be easier for them. The data you gain from this survey should be shared with your
building, other participating schools, the administration, and the district office.
And you may want to consider repeating this comfort-level survey several times
throughout the year.

Once you've determined the proficiency of staff members, you can enlist their help
to create a digital folder of suggested lesson plans, activities, and projects for all

to access and use. Your colleagues will be able to implement the folder's learning opportunities in their classrooms and add to the folder as they try new things. Something you may want to consider having is a reflection page to accompany any lesson, activity, or project posted. This will help others learn from and refine the ideas as they implement them on their own.

Additionally, your meetings, questionnaires, and survey results will identify teachers, staff members, parents, and administrators who have expertise in specific technology areas. Talk to your principal or district administrators to see if funding is available to pay for the planning time and workshops your experts may wish to lead. (As a general rule, every hour of professional-development class time takes at least two hours of planning.) Opportunities also need to be offered to your experts to advance their professional development. Perhaps you can even find a way to tap into the technology expertise of students, parents, and/or community members by having them lead some of your professional development workshops. Perhaps you can build in this professional development/collaboration time at least once a week. Carrying on conversations about the workshops at team meetings, staff meetings, even lunch, is a great way to foster and gain interest in what you and your committee are doing.

Even if you are not willing or able to head up a technology committee, there are many things you can do to prepare your classroom for digital age learning.

What Are Some Staff Development Ideas?

Be creative in your pursuit of ongoing staff development. If you are pressed for time, observe other teachers who use technology in their classrooms. (Ask your principal, department head, or coach to find someone to cover your classroom so you can do this.) If you are fortunate enough to have a coach or staff-development person in your building or district, ask them to set up a weekly meeting with you to work on technology goals. If you do not have a coach, partner up with another teacher or two. Peer coaching, team teaching, peer modeling, or even just conferring with other teachers is a great way to advance your goals, objectives, and outcomes.

There are many conferences and workshops offered throughout the year. Check to see if your district will cover the expenses and provide substitutes so you and your colleagues can attend. Check out the Bureau of Education & Research (BER), **(ber.org);** it is a sponsor of staff-development training for professional educators in the United States and Canada, offering many technology workshops and seminars about how to implement technology with the CCSS. There are also many technology grants offered by businesses. The magazines *Innovation & Tech Today* **(inno-techtoday.com)** and *Tech & Learning* **(techlearning.com)** are good places to look for these opportunities, as well as our "Sources of Funding" section in Chapter 3.

Ask your principal to provide grade-level/departmental time for teachers to review standards and plan how technology can be used. As a group, develop activities, projects, and lessons that include technology; come up with management strategies for using technology; and (perhaps most important) decide how you are going to assess and evaluate students' learning. This team time is important for you to brainstorm, share and develop ideas, and gather materials. Summer is also a good time for you and your colleagues to collaborate and develop projects. Check with your district to see if they will provide paid time for your summer work.

Don't forget to share your successes and those of others. Share disappointments as well so that others can learn from them. Take pictures, write press releases, post on your school's website as well as to social media—both the school and your own accounts—and include what you are doing in your parent newsletters and emails. If possible, make a short presentation at a school board meeting. Who knows? You may gain the moral and financial support you're looking for! Share your successes any way you can!

Because needs continually change, keep planning and reevaluating where you are and where you want to be. Encourage teachers to reach for the stars with their technology needs. Ask students how they feel about using technology and how it has affected their learning. These suggestions will help you and your colleagues get the technology you need.

Where Can You Learn about Staff Development?

There are a multitude of professional-development opportunities out there for technology, either in the workshop/conference format or online (accessible from the comfort of your home or classroom). Some opportunities are free, and some come with a membership fee to use the website or attend organization events. Others are priced per event. Following are a few suggestions.

- **ISTE (iste.org)** has several fantastic staff-development resources, including its Professional Learning Networks (PLNs), which allow you to instantly connect with experts in your field from around the globe **(community.iste.org/home).** There are many different networks to join (depending on your professional interests) where you can ask questions, learn from colleagues, and get access to exclusive events and professional learning opportunities. ISTE also offers free Strategic Learning Programs with partners like NASA and Verizon, which can be brought to your school or district **(bit.ly/1PeJ97t).** In addition, ISTE may have affiliate organizations in your area that provide professional development at seminars and conferences **(iste.org/affiliates).**

- **EdTechTeacher (edtechteacher.org)** is another organization that provides help to teachers and schools wishing to integrate technology to create student-centered, inquiry-based learning environments. They offer keynote presentations, hands-on workshops, online courses, and live webinars for teachers, schools, and school districts—all from your computer! What is nice about EdTechTeacher is that they understand teachers and students because the people leading the professional development have been or still are in the classroom.

- **Education World (educationworld.com)** is a complete online resource that offers high-quality lesson plans, classroom materials, information on how to integrate technology in the classroom, as well as articles written by education experts—a great place for you to find and share ideas with other teachers.

- **Discovery Education (discoveryeducation.com)** supplies a plethora of digital media that is immersive and engaging, bringing the world into the classroom to give every student a chance to experience fascinating people, places, and events. All of its content is aligned to standards that can be adjusted to support your specific curriculum and classroom instruction, regardless of what technology you have in your room. Discovery Education can help you transition to a digital age environment and even replace all of your textbooks with digital resources, if that is your ultimate goal.

Because you are reading this book, you have already started your technology journey! And you are not alone in this nationwide endeavor. Kristi Meeuwse, an Apple distinguished educator, offers sage advice at her blog, iTeach with iPads **(iteachwith-ipads.net)**, as you begin your exciting learning adventure. You can also read about "How Kristi Meeuwse Teaches with iPad" at Apple.com **(tinyurl.com/ybv9esou)**. Following is just a taste of her guidance:

> Wherever you are in your classroom journey, it's important to reflect on where you are and where you've been. It's important to celebrate your successes, no matter how small, and then be willing to move forward and try new things. Daring to imagine the possibilities and being willing to change is not just transforming to your own teaching, it will transform your classroom in ways you never thought were possible. Today we will do exciting new things. Let's get to it."
> (Meeuwse, 2013)

We provide additional resources for staff development in the Practical Ideas chapters (8–12) of this book. To learn about staff development in grades other than 6–12, look for the K–5 title in this series. Before we dive into lesson ideas for your specific grade and subjects, however, we will discuss how to effectively read, understand, and use the CCSS in the next three chapters.

5 Organization of the Standards

When discussing standards in this section, we will be focusing on the CCSS Initiative, which is the basis for the CCR standards in this book, and we will be referring to Common Core State Standards as CCSS.

While reading this chapter, you might want to explore "Read the Standards" on the CCSS website **(tinyurl.com/p9zfnwo)** as we discuss the details.

How Are the ELA Standards Organized?

The English language arts (ELA) standards for Grades 6–12 are divided into seven parts (see Figure 5.1), five of which are comprehensive K–12 sections (grey boxes). Then there are two content area sections specific to Grades 6–12 (white boxes): one set for literacy skills in history/social studies and one set for science/technical subjects. The CCSS website's introduction to the ELA standards has its own "How to Read the Standards" section **(bit.ly/1ZgEHIa)** that gives more information about organization as well as three appendices of supplemental material.

Each section is divided into strands. At the beginning of each strand is a set of CCR anchor standards, which are the same across all grades and content areas. Take, for example, the first anchor standard illustrated in Figure 5.2. It is the same in Grade 6 as it is for a high school senior, but the grade-level standard is refined to what the student at each grade level is expected to accomplish within the anchor standard.

ELA 1 Anchor Standard: Read closely to determine what the text says explicitly and to make logical inferences from it; cite specific textual evidence when writing or speaking to support conclusions drawn from the text.

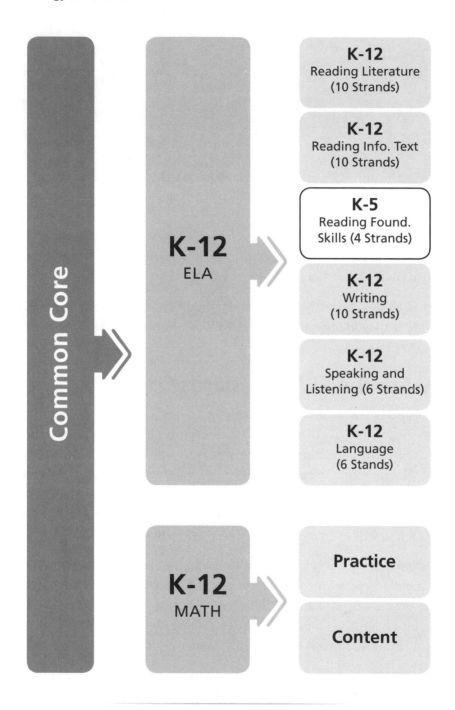

Figure 5.1. The CCSS ELA standards

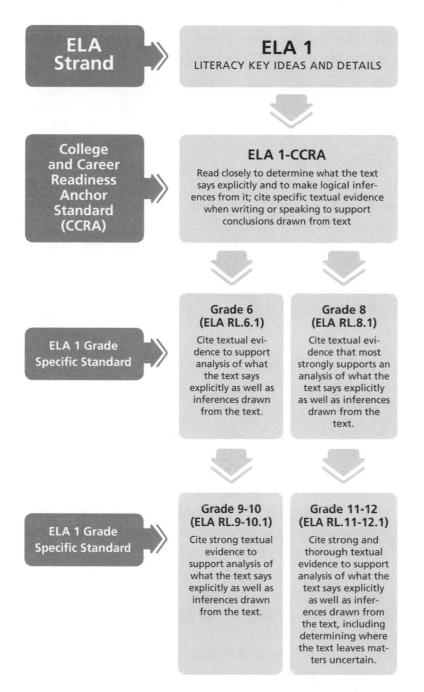

Figure 5.2. College and Career Readiness (CCR) anchor standard ELA 1 (CCSS.ELA- Literacy.CCRA.R.1) with grade-specific standards for Grades 9–12

ELA 1 Standard in Grade 6: Cite textual evidence to support analysis of what the text says explicitly as well as inferences drawn from the text.

ELA 1 Standard in Grade 8: Cite textual evidence that most strongly supports an analysis of what the text says explicitly as well as inferences drawn from the text.

ELA 1 Standard in Grade 9 and 10: Cite strong and thorough textual evidence to support analysis of what the text says explicitly as well as inferences drawn from the text.

ELA 1 Standard in Grades 11 and 12: Cite strong and thorough textual evidence to support analysis of what the text says explicitly as well as inferences drawn from the text, including determining where the text leaves matters uncertain.

These anchor standards complement the specific grade-level standards and define the skills and knowledge base that students should have by the end of each grade. The CCR standards are broad, while the grade-level standards are specific.

ELA standards focus on the following four areas:

1. Reading

2. Writing

3. Speaking and Listening

4. Language

The reading standards focus on text complexity (the difficulty of what students read), as well as the growth of their comprehension skills. Along with fictional stories and informational text, the CCSS focuses on poetry and dramas, too. The writing standards delve into specific text types, reading response, and research. Some writing skills, such as the ability to plan, revise, edit, and publish, can be applied to most types of writing. Other writing skills are more specific: opinion and argumentation, informational explanatory texts, and narratives. Speaking and listening standards deal with collaboration and flexible communication. In this area, students acquire and refine their oral communication and interpersonal skills, perhaps through formal presentations.

The language standards concentrate on vocabulary, conventions, and effective use. This strand not only incorporates the essential "rules" of standard written and spoken English but also helps students to understand how language functions in different contexts. Making effective choices in meaning and style leads to better comprehension when reading and listening. The vocabulary part of this strand clarifies and/or determines the meaning of unknown and multiple-definition words and phrases by using the appropriate context clues and/or reference materials as needed. This strand also helps students demonstrate an understanding of figurative language, word relationships, and nuances in word meanings. In addition, students will be able to acquire and accurately use a range of general and domain-specific words and phrases in any academic area. (We'll talk more about domains later in this chapter, in the math standards section.)

With the organization in mind, let's learn how you, as an individual teacher, use the CCSS in ELA.

How Do You Find ELA Standards by Subject and Grade?

Since most middle and high school teachers teach just one or two subjects, the standards are organized so you can focus on your specific area, but it is very helpful to put your grade-level curriculum in context. Look back at the grade level before the one you teach, and look ahead to the standards that come next. (If you would like to review a grade not included in this book, please refer to the other title in this series.)

Using the main "English Language Arts Standards" page on CCSS website is probably the most efficient way to find your grade- and subject-level standards (**tiny.cc/ w1vn3**). If you know what you are looking for, the corresponding reference numbers are useful. Here is a quick introduction:

All standards that relate to literature, informational text, writing, speaking, listening, language, history/social studies, and science and technical begin with "CCSS. ELA-Literacy." The difference comes at the end, with the letter/numbering system.

Let's use the following as an example.

- CCSS.ELA-Literacy.RL.7.1

    ○ CCSS is the abbreviation for Common Core State Standard.

    ○ ELA-Literacy identifies this as an English language arts standard.

    ○ RL stands for "reading literature."

    ○ 7 is the grade range.

    ○ 1 is the strand.

- CCSS.ELA-Literacy.RH.11-12.5

    ○ CCSS.ELA-Literacy represents the same information as in the previous example.

    ○ RH means "reading history."

    ○ 11–12 is the grade range.

    ○ 5 is the strand.

But there are standards within standards that are not easily apparent at first glance. For instance, there may be a reading standard that uses historical or science text, or a speaking and listening standard that has a technology component. This book focuses on where technology is required in the CCSS, and there is plenty of technology to discuss in ELA and math!

You may be wondering how you will be able to keep all of this straight. After all, we haven't even started talking about math! We invite you to view the math standards online **(tiny.cc/wrvn3y)** as you read this next section.

How Does the Organization of Math Standards Differ?

When you look at the math standards, you will see immediately that they were written by a different group of individuals; they do not integrate other subjects like the ELA standards. Even the technology standard is separate. And the system of organization is different too. The authors of the math standards also state that the grade-level order can be changed. After the following overview, we will help you sort it all out.

Long before CCSS was implemented, it was widely reported that math curricula in the United States was not even close to being on the same level as math education in high-performing countries. The consensus: U.S. math education needed to be substantially more focused and coherent to improve. To solve this, the CCSS were written to be clear, specific, and rigorous. Not only do the Common Core math standards stress conceptual understanding of key ideas but they continually return to the main organizing principles (place value and properties of operations) to structure those ideas. It is important to note that these standards address what students should understand and be able to do in their study of mathematics. But asking a student to understand something also means asking a teacher to assess whether a student understands it. Therefore, we need to break apart these standards to enhance readability and to gauge what Common Core math comprehension looks like—so your students will be able to understand and you will be able to assess.

First, you need to understand that CCSS provide a solid foundation before high school. They cover whole numbers, addition, subtraction, multiplication, division, fractions, and decimals. In grades 6–8, the major math focus is on the study of ratios, proportions, and algebra. The standards require students in grades 9–12 to apply mathematical thinking to real-world problems. What this means to you and your students is that instead of covering a myriad of topics, your students will be required to immerse themselves in deep comprehension by applying mathematics to problems they have not encountered previously.

The CCSS for math begin with eight Standards for Mathematical Practice (SMP), **(tiny.cc/wrvn3y),** which apply to all grades, K–12. These standards represent ways in which students will engage with math content, processes, and proficiencies— longstanding, important practices. The eight SMP are:

1. Make sense of problems and persevere in solving them.

2. Reason abstractly and quantitatively.

3. Construct viable arguments and critique the reasoning of others.

4. Model with mathematics.

5. Use appropriate tools strategically.

6. Attend to precision.

7. Look for and make use of structure.

8. Look for and express regularity in repeated reasoning.

For kindergarten through eighth grade, there are also grade-specific standards. Each contains a number of domains. Domains are larger groups of related standards that are sometimes broken into clusters. Clusters are summarized groups of related standards that fall under the main standard (see the cluster that follows the standard in Table 5.1). Due to the connected nature of math, you may see closely related clusters in other domains as well. You can read more about this on the "How to Read Grade-Level Standards" page **(bit.ly/1sPykwd)** of the CCSS website's math standards introduction.

- The grade-specific domains for Grades 6-8 are the following:
- Ratios and Proportional Relationships (6 and 7 only)
- The Number System (6-8)
- Expressions and Equations (6-8)
- Functions (8 only)
- Geometry (K-8)
- Statistics and Probability (6-8)

At the high school level, the standards outline the mathematics expected of all students to be "college and career ready" (i.e., the CCR anchor standards in ELA, as discussed earlier). These high school standards also include additional mathematics for students who choose to take advanced-level courses. Standards at the high school level are organized by "conceptual categories" (versus grades), with each providing "a coherent view of high school mathematics." The six categories are:

- Number and Quantity
- Algebra
- Functions

- Modeling

- Geometry

- Statistics and Probability

Here is an example of how domains are used to organize the math standards in middle school:

- CCSS.Math.Content.8.EE.A.1

  - CCSS is the abbreviation for Common Core State Standards.

  - Math.Content identifies that this is a math standard.

  - 8.EE is the domain (Grade 8—Expressions and Equations).

  - A.1 is the identifier for a related standard (or cluster) under the main standard—in this case "Expressions and equations work with radicals and integer exponents" (see Table 5.1).

Here is an example of how domains are used to organize the math standards in high school:

- CCSS.Math.Content.HSN.CN.C.7

  - CCSS is the abbreviation for Common Core State Standard.

  - Math.Content identifies that this is a math standard.

  - HSN.CN is the domain (High School: Number and Quantity—The Complex Number System.

  - C.7 is the identifier for a related standard (or cluster) under the main standard—in this case "Use complex numbers in polynomial identities and equations" (see Table 5.2).

Now that you know how to identify a high school math standard and its numbering system, let's look at the following tables to see the way in which these standards are actually presented in these domains.

The standards in Tables 5.1 and 5.2 define what your students should know and be able to do after you taught and assessed that standard. Reading and familiarizing yourself with the standards will go a long way in helping you teach the standards later.

Example of a standard in the eighth-grade domain of Expressions and Equations		Table 5.1
DOMAIN	STANDARD	CLUSTER
Grade 8 EXPRESSIONS AND EQUATIONS	**Expressions and equations work with radicals and integer exponents.**	CCSS.Math.Content.8.EE.A.1: Know and apply the properties of integer exponents to generate equivalent numerical expressions. For example, $3^2 \times 3^{-5} = 3^{-3} = 1/3^3 = 1/27$. CCSS.Math.Content.8.EE.A.2: Use square root and cube root symbols to represent solutions to equations of the form $x^2 = p$ and $x^3 = p$, where p is a positive rational number. Evaluate square roots of small perfect squares and cube roots of small perfect cubes. Know that $\sqrt{2}$ is irrational. CCSS.Math.Content.8.EE.A.3: Use numbers expressed in the form of a single digit times an integer power of 10 to estimate very large or very small quantities, and to express how many times as much one is than the other. For example: estimate the population of the United States as 3 times 10^8 and the population of the world as 7 times 10^9, and determine that the world population is more than 20 times larger. CCSS.Math.Content.8.EE.A.4: Perform operations with numbers expressed in scientific notation, including problems where both decimal and scientific notation are used. Use scientific notation and choose units of appropriate size for measurements of very large or very small quantities (e.g., use millimeters per year for seafloor spreading). Interpret scientific notation that has been generated by technology.

	Table 5.2
Example of a standard in the high school domain of Number and Quality—The Complex Number System	

DOMAIN	STANDARD	CLUSTER
High School NUMBER AND QUANTITY— THE COMPLEX NUMBER SYSTEM	**Use complex numbers in polynomial identities and equations.**	CCSS.Math.Content.HSN.CN.C.7: Solve quadratic equations with real coefficients that have complex solutions. CCSS.Math.Content.HSN.CN.C.8: Extend polynomial identities to the complex numbers. CCSS.Math.Content.HSN.CN.C.9: Know the Fundamental Theorem of Algebra; show that it is true for quadratic polynomials.

There are also SMPs that are part of the CCR anchor standards of the ELA. These standards are not overtly assessed but are necessary for you to include in your instruction. SMPs will not be the focus of this book except when they involve technology.

As you can see, math and ELA standards are written and organized very differently. We have tried our best to guide you through these differences, but we do recommend that you explore the resources we have provided here as well as others that we have referenced on our website **(tinyurl.com/y9dfltpr)**. Here are two great resources that will explain the standards of mathematical practices:

- State of California CCSS Mathematics Resources: **tinyurl.com/l3zzsae**

- ASCD's Implementing the Common Core Mathematical Practices: **tinyurl. com/ybfdgtwr**

In the next chapter, we discuss technology and how it relates to the CCSS.

6 Technology in the Common Core

This chapter focuses on the CCSS in ELA and math that have technology-related components written into them, first identifying and then analyzing these standards. This will prepare you for the later chapters, where we offer practical examples of how you can integrate the standards into your curriculum.

As instructional coaches, we know that there are those of you who are excited about technology, those of you who think it is an annoyance, and those of you who fear it. These standards affect all of you because they force your districts and you, as teachers, to use technology more pervasively. Schools feel pressure to address areas that may have been avoided in the past due to cost or apprehension. If you are a fan of technology, you welcome this focus; if you are not, you still need to become proficient. You simply cannot avoid technology in your classroom.

Where Is Technology in the ELA Standards?

The CCSS are designed to prepare students for college, the workforce, and a technology-rich society. And as you learned in the last chapter, the ELA standards have the CCR anchor standards—reading, writing, speaking and listening, and language—at their core. Following is a summary of those CCR standards that are embedded with technology in Grades 6-12.

ELA Standards (Grades 6–12) in Which Technology Appears

READING (6–12)

- CCR Reading (R) Standard 7 **(tinyurl.com/h9n9ek9)**

  - Reading Literature (RL)

  - Reading Informational Text (RI)

  - Reading History (RH)

  - Reading Science and Technical (RST)

- CCR Reading Science and Technical (RST) Standard 9 **(tinyurl.com/jylor72)**

Note: While reading language (RL) and reading informational text (RI) are in all grades, reading history (RH) and reading science and technical (RST) are in Grades 6–12 only. We will get into more detail about this and related anchor standard R.9 later in this chapter.

WRITING (6–12)

- CCR Writing (W) Standard 2 **(tinyurl.com/zt6kysv)**

  - Writing, History, Science, and Technical Subjects (WHST) Standard 2

- CCR Writing (W) Standard 6 **(tinyurl.com/zmxfdp8)**

  - Writing, History, Science, and Technical Subjects (WHST) Standard 6

- CCR Writing (W) Standard 8 **(tinyurl.com/jercjbv)**

  - Writing, History, Science, and Technical Subjects (WHST) Standard 8

Note: Writing is an anchor standard throughout students' K–12 education, but an added strand of history, science, and technical subjects (WHST) is included from Grades 6–12.

Speaking and Listening (6–12)

- CCR Speaking and Listening (SL) Standard 2 **(tiny.cc/slvy3y)**.
- CCR Speaking and Listening (SL) Standard 5 **(tiny.cc/2lvy3y)**.

Language (6–12)

- CCR Language (L) Standard 4 **(tinyurl.com/hmu54nx)**.

Where Is Technology in the Math Standards?

As mentioned in Chapter 5, the math standards are written differently, and the technology standard in math (yes, only one standard) is separate from the rest of the math standards. However, this technology standard is meant to be used ubiquitously. Though many math standards do not overtly say that technology is required, if there is a need for a calculator or statistical analysis using a computer then that is what students should use. In math, the understanding is that these technology tools are used across grade levels and throughout the math standards even though there is only one written standard. (Note: This math standard is presented in detail after the grade-specific ELA standards at the end of this chapter.)

What about Using Technology in All Subjects?

Because technology is integrated throughout the CCSS, we should discuss in more depth what this actually means as you go about implementing the curriculum day to day. Though the standards give you specific language, the use of technology has been left wide open. They use terms like "digital tools," "other media," and "both print and digital" to let you choose what is appropriate to the lesson. The new standards are trying to infuse technology into everyday classroom use, as opposed to having a separate period in a computer lab. Technology must become like the pencil: simply another tool to choose when students need to find the most appropriate one to complete the task at hand.

CCSS strongly encourages project-based lessons and are designed to be cross-curricular. Also, the standards are looking for higher-level thinking, learning, and application. All of these things lead to technology as the most appropriate tool in many situations. They fit very well into the Partnership for 21st Century Learning (P21) Framework for 21st Century Learning **(tinyurl.com/nzvwyen)** and the ISTE Standards for Students **(iste.org/standards).** If you have been working for some time on lessons that integrate technology and you think you will have to begin again, you will be relieved to know that the technology-embedded standards are not so different.

How Do You Put ELA Technology Standards into Context?

When you look at the patterns of technology use in the standards, you improve your integration planning and learning achievement with these standards. Let's take a quick look at the technology patterns in the related Grade 6–12 standards.

R.7: This is the main technology standard in reading, but the CCSS does not expect students to use technology until Grade 2. The standard then continues to develop in subsequent grades, integrating and evaluating content in various technology formats that support the meaning of a story or literary work.

RL.7: This standard begins in kindergarten, comparing illustrations and text, and then grows through the grades, using all types of media to compare, support, and analyze the story's meaning. Essentially, the purpose of the standard is to get meaning from more than the text. Meaning can also come from all the accompanying media and even the format of the story.

RI.7:
RH.7 These are similar to RL.7 but refer to informational text, history, science, and technical subjects. Thus, you must keep in mind informational graphics—maps; photographs; diagrams; charts; and other media in history, technology, and science—and the way in which they augment information or help to solve a problem.

RST.9: This standard begins in Grades 6–8 with specific technology suggested, and it implies technology use in Grades 9–12. Students are asked to compare science and technical information they have studied with what they experience through experiments, simulations, videos, and other media, to build knowledge.

W.2: From drawing, writing, and telling about a topic in kindergarten, this standard evolves into producing a thesis in high school. It is your basic research paper that now includes an expectation to use any and all media that is appropriate to conveying the information.

W.6: This is one of the few anchor standards that is solely technology-driven. From kindergarten through high school, students are required to use technology to collaborate with others when writing. Of course, this requires keyboarding skills, but they are not mentioned in the standard until Grade 3.

W8: The use of technology in this standard is expected from Grade 3 through high school. It keys in on the gathering of information, the analysis of information, and the avoidance of plagiarism using multiple sources—digital as well as text—when writing informative or explanatory works. This standard works in tandem with standard W.2 and will probably be taught jointly.

WHST.2: These Grade 6–12 writing standards are similar to their W.2, W.6, and
WHST.6 W.8 anchors, but the focus is on history, science, and technical subjects
WHST.8 and the use of multimedia tools.

SL.2: This standard expects the use of technology from kindergarten through Grade 12. It is a listening standard, but in today's world, all kinds of diverse media are constantly available. Students need to be able to analyze and make decisions about this content.

SL.5: Beginning with the use of pictures when speaking in kindergarten, this standard builds to making strategic use of digital media for presentations in high school. Learning to use media in presentations is critical for college and career readiness.

L.4: This is a very straightforward standard that clarifies the meaning of words at all grade levels. Starting in second grade, students need to know how to find word meanings using not just print but digital dictionaries, glossaries, and thesauruses.

What about Assessment?

You don't begin a trip without an end in mind, and the end that must always be kept in mind with the CCSS is the standardized test your state administers. Whether it is the PARCC or Smarter Balanced assessment, SAT, or some other assessment your state is developing, it will certainly involve technology. The tests will require some level of competence in selecting and highlighting text, dragging and dropping text, and moving objects on the screen. In the math areas of the test, tools that might be needed for the exam (calculators, rulers, a slide rule) will be available on the screen. Students may need headphones and a microphone to interact during the speaking-and-listening sections, and other multimedia may be used in other parts of the test.

The best way to prepare students is to know in advance the scope of technology they will need to master. Many things about the tests that your state is using are continually changing. The changes mean your students may not be as fully prepared as you would like them to be. However, your preparation—giving students opportunities to use a myriad of technology as often as possible—will help them to be as ready as they can be for the assessments.

What Are the ELA Standards with Technology?

The following is a listing of where technology appears in the CCSS. The first section contains the anchor standards, and the second section has the more specific grade-level standards. The standards are ordered by level, so that you can find those related to the grade you teach more quickly. The part of the standard that pertains to technology is in boldface type. It is always helpful to look at the standards above and below your level to see where the students have come from and where they are going on their educational journey. Please refer to the first book in this series if you would like to see other grade levels.

Reading
CCSS.ELA-Literacy.CCRA.R.7

> **R.7:** Integrate and evaluate content presented in diverse media and formats, including visually and quantitatively, as well as in words.
>
> Note **R.9** as well: Analyze hoinw two or more texts address similar themes or topics in order to build knowledge or to compare the approaches the authors take.

The R.9 anchor standard does not have any multimedia but does overtly include technology in its science and technical strand concerning the use of simulations, videos, and multimedia sources in Grades 6–8 (RST.6-8.9). Thus, when discussing sources for this standard in high school, digital sources (like those just mentioned) are implied.

Writing

CCSS.ELA-Literacy.CCRA.W.6 and CCSS.ELA-Literacy.CCRA.W.8

W.6: Use technology, including the internet, to produce and publish writing and to interact and collaborate with others.

W.8: Gather relevant information from multiple print and digital sources, assess the credibility and accuracy of each source, and integrate the information while avoiding plagiarism.

Note: Anchor standard **W.2** does not have multimedia but does include technology in that standard's strand starting in Grade 4 (**W.4.2.a**). This book focuses on **W. 2.a**, **W. 6**, and **W. 8**.

Speaking and Listening

CCSS.ELA-Literacy.CCRA.SL.2 and CCSS.ELA-Literacy.CCRA.SL.5

SL.2: Integrate and evaluate information presented in diverse media and formats, including visually, quantitatively, and orally.

SL.5: Make strategic use of digital media and visual displays of data to express information and enhance understanding of presentations.

Even when your grade does not have a technology standard included in these main anchor strands (**R.7, W.2, W.6, W.8, SL.2, SL.5, L.4**), it is implied that it be used. We have listed here only those that state a technology use.

What Are the ELA Grade-Level Standards with Technology?

Following is where ELA grade-level standards appear in the CCSS (listed by grade). Note the following abbreviations: reading literature (RL), reading informational text (RI), writing (W), speaking and listening (SL), and language (L). We are including Grade 5 to give the technology standards some context. Please refer to the other book in this series to get a sense of the full scope of technology standards Grades K–12. (*Note:* as in the preceding section, the part of the standard that pertains to technology is in boldface type.)

Grade 5

RL.5.7: Analyze how visual and **multimedia elements** contribute to the meaning, tone, or beauty of a text (e.g., graphic novel, **multimedia presentation** of fiction, folktale, myth, poem).

RI.5.7: Draw on information from multiple print or **digital sources**, demonstrating the ability to locate an answer to a question quickly or to solve a problem efficiently.

W.5.2.a: Introduce a topic clearly, provide a general observation and focus, and group related information logically; include formatting (e.g., headings), illustrations, **and multimedia** when useful to aiding comprehension.

W.5.6: With some guidance and support from adults, **use technology, including the internet**, to produce and publish writing as well as to interact and collaborate with others; demonstrate sufficient command of **keyboarding skills** to type a minimum of two pages in a single sitting.

W.5.8: Recall relevant information from experiences or gather relevant information from print and **digital sources**; summarize or paraphrase information in notes and finished work, and provide a list of sources.

SL.5.2: Summarize a written text read aloud or information presented **in diverse media and formats**, including visually, quantitatively, and orally.

SL.5.5: Include **multimedia components (e.g., graphics, sound) and visual displays** in presentations when appropriate to enhance the development of main ideas or themes.

L.5.4.c: Consult reference materials (e.g., dictionaries, glossaries, thesauruses), both print and **digital**, to find the pronunciation and determine or clarify the precise meaning of key words and phrases.

Grade 6

RL.6.7: Compare and contrast the experience of reading a story, drama, or poem to listening to or viewing an **audio, video**, or live version of the text, including contrasting what they "see" and "hear" when reading the text to what they perceive when they listen or watch.

RI.6.7: Integrate information presented in **different media or formats** (e.g., visually, quantitatively) as well as in words to develop a coherent understanding of a topic or issue.

RH.6-8.7: Integrate visual information (e.g., in charts, graphs, photographs, **videos**, or maps) with other information in print and **digital texts**.

RST.6-8.9: Compare and contrast the information gained from experiments, **simulations, video, or multimedia sources** with that gained from reading a text on the same topic.

W.6.2.a: Introduce a topic; organize ideas, concepts, and information, using strategies such as definition, classification, comparison/contrast, and cause/effect; include formatting (e.g., headings), graphics (e.g., charts, tables), and **multimedia** when useful to aiding comprehension.

W.6.6: Use **technology, including the internet**, to produce and publish writing as well as to interact and collaborate with others; demonstrate sufficient command of **keyboarding skills** to type a minimum of three pages in a single sitting.

W.6.8: Gather relevant information from multiple print and **digital sources**; assess the credibility of each source; and quote or paraphrase the data and conclusions of others while avoiding plagiarism and providing basic bibliographic information for sources.

WHST.6-8.2.a: Introduce a topic clearly, previewing what is to follow; organize ideas, concepts, and information into broader categories as appropriate to achieving purpose; include formatting (e.g., headings), graphics (e.g., charts, tables), and **multimedia** when useful to aiding comprehension.

WHST.6-8.6: Use **technology, including the internet**, to produce and publish writing and present the relationships between information and ideas clearly and efficiently.

WHST.6-8.8: Gather relevant information from multiple print and **digital sources**, using search terms effectively; assess the credibility and accuracy of each source; and quote or paraphrase the data and conclusions of others while avoiding plagiarism and following a standard format for citation.

SL.6.2: Interpret information presented in **diverse media and formats** (e.g., visually, quantitatively, orally) and explain how it contributes to a topic, text, or issue under study.

SL.6.5: Include **multimedia components (e.g., graphics, images, music, sound) and visual displays** in presentations to clarify information.

L.6.4.c: Consult reference materials (e.g., dictionaries, glossaries, thesauruses), both print and **digital**, to find the pronunciation of a word or to determine or clarify its precise meaning or its part of speech.

Grade 7

RL.7.7: Compare and contrast a written story, drama, or poem to its **audio, filmed**, staged, or **multimedia version**, analyzing the effects of techniques unique to each medium (e.g., lighting, sound, color, or camera focus and angles in a film).

RI.7.7: Compare and contrast a text to an **audio, video, or multimedia** version of the text, analyzing each medium's portrayal of the subject (e.g., how the delivery of a speech affects the impact of the words).

RH.6-8.7: Integrate visual information (e.g., in charts, graphs, photographs, **videos**, or maps) with other information in print and **digital texts**.

RST.6-8.9: Compare and contrast the information gained from experiments, **simulations, video, or multimedia sources** with that gained from reading a text on the same topic.

W.7.2.a: Introduce a topic clearly, previewing what is to follow; organize ideas, concepts, and information, using strategies such as definition, classification, comparison/contrast, and cause/effect; include formatting (e.g., headings), graphics (e.g., charts, tables), and **multimedia** when useful to aiding comprehension.

W.7.6: Use **technology, including the internet**, to produce and publish writing and link to and cite sources as well as to interact and collaborate with others, including linking to and citing sources.

W.7.8: Gather relevant information from multiple print and **digital sources**,
WHST.6-8.8 using search terms effectively; assess the credibility and accuracy of each source; and quote or paraphrase the data and conclusions of others while avoiding plagiarism and following a standard format for citation.

WHST.6-8.2.a: Introduce a topic clearly, previewing what is to follow; organize ideas, concepts, and information into broader categories as appropriate to achieving purpose; include formatting (e.g., headings), graphics (e.g., charts, tables), and **multimedia** when useful to aiding comprehension.

WHST.6-8.6: Use **technology, including the internet**, to produce and publish writing, and present the relationships between information and ideas clearly and efficiently.

SL.7.2: Analyze the main ideas and supporting details presented in **diverse media and formats** (e.g., visually, quantitatively, and orally) and explain how the ideas clarify a topic, text, or issue under study.

SL.7.5: Include **multimedia components and visual displays** in presentations to clarify claims and findings, and emphasize salient points.

L.7.4.c: Consult general and specialized reference materials (e.g., dictionaries, glossaries, thesauruses), both print and **digital**, to find the

pronunciation of a word or to determine or clarify its precise meaning or its part of speech.

Grade 8

RL.8.7: Analyze the extent to which a **filmed** or live production of a story or
drama stays faithful to or departs from the text or script, evaluating
the choices made by the director or actors.

RI.8.7: Evaluate the advantages and disadvantages of using different mediums (e.g., print or **digital text, video, multimedia**) to present a particular topic or idea.

RH.6-8.7: Integrate visual information (e.g., in charts, graphs, photographs,
videos, or maps) with other information in print and **digital texts**.

RST.6-8.9: Compare and contrast the information gained from experiments,
simulations, video, or multimedia sources with that gained from
reading a text on the same topic.

W.8.2.a: Introduce a topic clearly, previewing what is to follow; organize
ideas, concepts, and information into broader categories; include
formatting (e.g., headings), graphics (e.g., charts, tables), and **multimedia** when useful to aiding comprehension.

W.8.6: **Use technology, including the internet**, to produce and publish
writing and present the relationships between information and ideas
efficiently as well as to interact and collaborate with others

W.8.8: Gather relevant information from multiple print and **digital sources**,
WHST.6-8.8 using search terms effectively; assess the credibility and accuracy of
each source; and quote or paraphrase the data and conclusions of
others while avoiding plagiarism and following a standard format for
citation.

WHST.6-8.2.a: Introduce a topic clearly, previewing what is to follow; organize
ideas, concepts, and information into broader categories as appropriate to achieving purpose; include formatting (e.g., headings),
graphics (e.g., charts, tables), and **multimedia** when useful to aiding
comprehension.

WHST.6-8.6: **Use technology, including the internet**, to produce and publish writing and present the relationships between information and ideas clearly and efficiently.

SL.8.2: Analyze the purpose of information presented in **diverse media and formats** (e.g., visually, quantitatively, orally) and evaluate the motives (e.g., social, commercial, political) behind its presentation.

SL.8.5: Integrate **multimedia and visual displays** into presentations to clarify information, strengthen claims and evidence, and add interest.

L.8.4.c: Consult general and specialized reference materials (e.g., dictionaries, glossaries, thesauruses), both print and **digital**, to find the pronunciation of a word or to determine or clarify its precise meaning or its part of speech.

Grades 9–10

RL.9-10.7: Analyze the representation of a subject or a key scene in two different **artistic mediums**, including what is emphasized or absent in each treatment (e.g., Auden's *Musée des Beaux Arts* and Breughel's *Landscape with the Fall of Icarus*).

RI.9-10.7: Analyze various accounts of a subject told in different mediums (e.g., a person's life story in both print and **multimedia**), determining which details are emphasized in each account.

RH.9-10.7: Integrate quantitative or technical analysis (e.g., charts, research data) with qualitative analysis in print or **digital text**.

RST.9-10.7: Translate quantitative or technical information expressed in words in a text into **visual form** (e.g., a table or chart) and translate information expressed visually or mathematically (e.g., in an equation) into words.

RST.9-10.9: Compare and contrast findings presented in a text to those from **other sources** (including their own experiments), noting when the findings support or contradict previous explanations or accounts.

W.9-10.2.a:
WHST.9-10.2.a Introduce a topic; organize complex ideas, concepts, and information to make important connections and distinctions; include formatting (e.g., headings), graphics (e.g., figures, tables), and **multimedia** when useful to aiding comprehension.

W.9-10.6:
WHST.9-10.6 **Use technology, including the internet**, to produce, publish, and update individual or shared writing products, taking advantage of technology's capacity to **link to other information** and to **display information flexibly and dynamically**.

W.9-10.8:
WHST.9-10.8 Gather relevant information from multiple authoritative print and **digital sources**, using advanced searches effectively; assess the usefulness of each source in answering the research question; integrate information into the text selectively to maintain the flow of ideas, avoiding plagiarism and following a standard format for citation.

SL.9-10.2: Integrate multiple sources of information presented in **diverse media or formats** (e.g., visually, quantitatively, orally) evaluating the credibility and accuracy of each source.

SL.9-10.5: Make strategic use of **digital media (e.g., textual, graphical, audio, visual, and interactive elements)** in presentations to enhance understanding of findings, reasoning, and evidence, and to add interest.

L.9-10.4.c: Consult general and specialized reference materials (e.g., dictionaries, glossaries, thesauruses), both print and **digital**, to find the pronunciation of a word or to determine or clarify its precise meaning, its part of speech, or its etymology.

Grades 11–12

RL.11-12.7: Analyze multiple interpretations of a story, drama, or poem (e.g., **recorded** or live production of a play or recorded novel or poetry), evaluating how each version interprets the source text. (Include at least one play by Shakespeare and one play by an American dramatist.)

RI.11-12.7: Integrate and evaluate multiple sources of information presented in **different media or formats** (e.g., visually, quantitatively) as well as in words in order to address a question or solve a problem.

RH.11-12.7: Integrate and evaluate multiple sources of information presented in **diverse formats and media** (e.g., visually, quantitatively, as well as in words) in order to address a question or solve a problem.

RST.11-12.7: Integrate and evaluate multiple sources of information presented in **diverse formats and media** (e.g., quantitative data, **video, multimedia**) in order to address a question or solve a problem.

RST.11-12.9: Synthesize information from a range of sources (e.g., texts, experiments, **simulations**) into a coherent understanding of a process, phenomenon, or concept, resolving conflicting information when possible.

W.11-12.2.a: Introduce a topic; organize complex ideas, concepts, and information
WHST.11-12.2.a so that each new element builds on that which precedes it to create a unified whole; include formatting (e.g., headings), graphics (e.g., figures, tables), and **multimedia** when useful to aiding comprehension.

W.11-12.6: **Use technology, including the internet**, to pro- duce, publish, and
WHST.11-12.6 update individual or shared writing products in response to ongoing feedback, including new arguments or information.

W.11-12.8: Gather relevant information from multiple authoritative print
WHST.11-12.8 and **digital sources** using advanced searches effectively; assess the strengths and limitations of each source in terms of the task, purpose, and audience; integrate information into the text selectively to maintain the flow of ideas, avoiding plagiarism and overreliance on any one source and following a standard format for citation.

SL.11-12.2: Integrate multiple sources of information presented in **diverse formats and media** (e.g., visually, quantitatively, orally) in order to make informed decisions and solve problems, evaluating the credibility and accuracy of each source and noting any discrepancies among the data.

SL.11-12.5: Make strategic use of **digital media** (e.g., textual, graphical, **audio, visual, and interactive elements**) in presentations to enhance understanding of findings, reasoning, and evidence and to add interest.

L.11-12.4.c: Consult general and specialized reference materials (e.g., dictionaries, glossaries, thesauruses), both print and **digital**, to find the pronunciation of a word or determine or clarify its precise meaning, its part of speech, its etymology, or its standard usage.

What Is the Math Standard with Technology?

The Standards for Mathematical Practice (SMP) are skills that all of your students should look to develop. As you learned in Chapter 5, there are eight SMP, which are designed to overlay the math content standards. In other words, the math practice standards apply to every one of the math content standards. So, although **MP5** is the only standard that includes technology, it actually means that every math content standard should use the appropriate tools, including tools that use technology.

Following is **MP5,** taken verbatim from the CCSS website. As in the preceding two sections, any text that pertains to technology is in boldface type.

CCSS.Math.Practice.MP5

MP5: Use appropriate **tools** strategically.

Mathematically proficient students consider the available tools when solving a mathematical problem. These tools might include pencil and paper, concrete models, a ruler, a protractor, **a calculator, a spreadsheet, a computer algebra system, a statistical package, or dynamic geometry software.** Proficient students are sufficiently familiar with tools appropriate for their grade or course to make sound decisions about when each of these tools might be helpful, recognizing both the insight to be gained and their limitations. For example, mathematically proficient high school students analyze graphs of functions and solutions generated using a **graphing calculator.** They detect possible errors by strategically using estimation and other mathematical knowledge. When making mathematical models, they know that **technology** can enable them to visualize the results of varying assumptions, explore consequences, and compare predictions with data. Mathematically proficient students at various grade levels are able to identify relevant external mathematical resources, such as **digital content located on a website,** and use them to pose or solve problems. They are able to use **technological tools** to explore and deepen their understanding of concepts.

It is important to note the standard's emphasis on using technology pervasively. Keep technology in mind, not only when teaching the standards but in the assessment as it creates a learning advantage for your students.

We hope you have taken away important information on where technology can be found in the CCSS. In the next chapter, we discuss practical strategies and offer helpful resources to assist you can begin teaching the CCR standards with technology right away.

CHAPTER 7
Implementing Practical Ideas

Our world and education are changing rapidly. Without question, one size does not fit all in teaching. We know you work hard to personalize the learning in your classroom to reflect the individual needs, capabilities, and learning styles of your students so they have opportunities to reach their maximum potential. With this in mind, why not create tech-savvy classrooms for today's students?

In this chapter, we address practical ways to use new technology ideas within your classroom. Most of your students already come to school with a strong background in, and understanding of, technology. They are interested, motivated, and even driven by technology. Having a tech-savvy classroom for today's students is the best way to create a digital age learning environment.

How and Where Do I Begin?

Whether you are a new teacher, a teacher in the middle of a career, or a veteran teacher with only a few years before retirement, you will begin at the same place in respect to technology. To bring technology into your classrooms and your students into the digital age, you must give up your role at the front of class and let technology be a primary source of information. This journey calls for no longer teaching in the way you've been teaching and instead becoming facilitators of your classroom and the information presented there. Embrace all of the devices you have ignored or struggled to keep out of your classroom. Introduce yourself to new concepts that may not have existed when you were in school.

First, sign up for as many technology teaching blogs and websites as you can find. One website definitely worth a look is PowerMyLearning **(powermylearning.org).**

There are many free activities for you to explore, and you can search for lessons by standard. This website also allows you to build classes, assign and monitor student work, and customize playlists for your classroom.

Blogs are becoming an increasingly pervasive and persistent influence in people's lives. They are a great way to allow individual participation in the marketplace of ideas around the world. Teachers have picked up on the creative use of this technology and put the blog to work in the classroom. The education blog can be a powerful and effective tool for students and teachers. Edutopia has a wonderful technology blog **(tinyurl.com/p33sd7b)**. Scholastic also offers a blog for teachers PK–12 **(tinyurl.com/oaaycar)** and on a wide variety of educational topics.

Edmodo **(edmodo.com)** is a free and easy blog for students and teachers to communicate back and forth. We have given you links to all of these resources on our website **(tinyurl.com//y9dfltpr)**. Teachers can post assignments, and students can respond to the teacher, as well as to each other, either in the classroom or at home. Students have the ability to also post questions to the teacher or one another, if they need help.

What Strategies Can I Use?

Get a routine going. Engage students in independent and self-directed learning activities. This is a great way to begin integrating technology in your classroom. All activities can be tied to your curriculum targets, and a couple of them can be technology based. There are a plethora of computer-based games that you can bring to an educational center or learning station rotation. Two programs that support 6–12 CCR standards and can be used on computers or tablets are **IXL (ixl.com/math)** and **MathPickle (mathpickle.com)**.

Differentiated math meets the needs of all learners. It consists of whole-group mini-lessons, guided math groups, independent learning stations with a wide variety of activities, and ongoing assessment. Independent learning is a great way to infuse technology into lessons. For more information on how to set up a guided math classroom, check out the book *Guided Math: A Framework for Mathematics Instruction* (2009) by Laney Sammons, or view her guided math slide presentation online **(tiny.cc/5btg2y)**.

For ELA instructors, having students work in small groups or independent practice that involves reading, writing, or vocabulary are opportunities to use technologies. All activities can be tied to your curriculum targets and can be technology based. Instead of having students writing in a journal, have them blog. Instead of students reacting or reviewing another student's work (using paper and pencil), have them use interactive response systems or Google Forms. Programs and apps such as Google Docs, Prezi, Edmodo, and Explain Everything are just a few resources you can use to meet standards and bring writing into your ELA curriculum. Your students are using technology to be creative!

Flipping the classroom is another great way to integrate technology into your classroom. This teaching model, which uses both online and face-to-face instruction, has been transforming education for the last several years. Flipping is an educational strategy that provides students with the chance to access information within a subject outside of the classroom.

Instead of students listening in class to content and then practicing that concept outside of the school day, that traditional practice is flipped. Students work with information whenever it best fits their schedule, and as many times as necessary for learning to occur. Inside the flipped classroom, teachers and students engage in discussion, practice, or experiential learning. By creating online tutorials of your instruction, using some of the tools mentioned in this book, you can spend valuable class time assisting students with homework, conferencing about learning, or simply being available for student questions.

Pick an app or program you are interested in bringing into your classroom. Play and explore. See what the possibilities are for using this technology in your classroom. You and your students can be technology pioneers. Allow your students to problem solve and seek new knowledge on their own, and then have them share with you. A great resource is Teaching with iPad **(tiny.cc/jdtg2y),** where you can learn more about how to teach with and use digital tablets in your classroom. This site from Apple gives you lots of information about what the iPad is capable of, connects you to examples of iPad lessons done by other teachers, and matching apps!

How Do I Determine What Works Best?

Perhaps the next place to look is the ISTE Standards for Students, which were developed by the International Society for Technology in Education (ISTE) and can be found on their website **(iste.org/standards).** These standards are a great framework to help you plan lessons and projects to support the technology standards in literacy, math, and critical thinking skills.

P21 developed a Framework for 21st Century Learning. This framework identifies key skills known as the 4C's: Critical Thinking, Collaboration, Communication, and Creativity. Table 7.1 takes those four skills and overlays them with digital resources that you can use in ELA. For instance, if you are a ninth-grade teacher and want to use Collaboration in your lesson, you might try any of the six digital resources suggested to plan your lesson: Popplet, GarageBand, Edmodo, Google Classroom, Google Docs, and Google Sites. These are suggestions, but there are many more apps and sites that might also fit well. You might notice that the 4C's mirror many of the ISTE Standards. This table is included to get you to think about how you can include the 4C's and technology in your daily lesson planning. All of

Digital resources for teaching ELA Standards.				Table 7.1
GRADE	CRITICAL THINKING	COLLABORATION	COMMUNICATION	CREATIVITY
6–12	DreamBox	Edmodo	Show Me	Microsoft Photos
	Feedly	Popplet	Skype	GarageBand
	Connected Learning	GarageBand	Edmodo	iMovie
	Newsmap	Google Classroom	Explain Everything	Keynote
	Reading/Science A-Z	Google Sites	GarageBand	Binumi
	Learning Network	Google Docs		
	NeoK12			
	WatchKnowLearn			

TABLE 7.1. Examples of Digital Resources for ELA that Fit into the 4C's.

the resources listed in Table 7.1 are included in the following chapters to provide concrete examples of how you might implement critical thinking, collaboration, communication and creativity.

Being an expert on all of the apps or programs listed in Table 7.1 is not necessary. Start with one you know, or find out which ones your students are familiar with and start there. Think about the target or lesson you want to teach. What is the goal? What technology device or app or program will support your teaching? Create an end product to show your students what you expect. Instead of step-by-step teaching of the technology, it is important to let the students explore and discover for themselves, as long as your end product and expectations have been met.

You can also teach yourself about many of the apps or programs available by searching for them online. YouTube has step-by-step how-to videos for many tech apps and programs. Have your students show what they know by creating samples for you. Save everything you, your colleagues, or your students create, and keep it all in a digital portfolio, so you can share the samples with your new students for years to come.

With an active learning environment and providing the tools your students need for digital age learning, watch the difference you will make as learning in your classroom skyrockets. All of this new technology is transforming today's classrooms. Social networking and mobile learning are just a few tech-related activities that students and teachers are embracing. The website for this book **(tinyurl.com/y9dfltpr)** contains further lists of resources for how to incorporate the technology you have (or want to have) and ways for your students to learn and interact with them. In the following chapters, we further explore the CCSS for grades 6–12 that incorporate technology, suggest specific applications and strategies, and provide lessons to help students successfully achieve those standards.

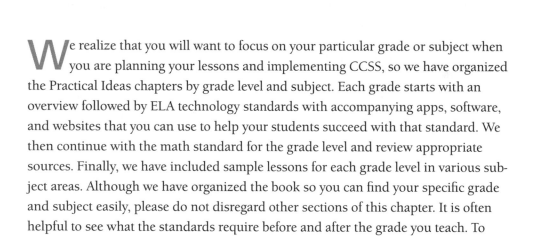

CHAPTER

8

Practical Ideas
for Sixth Grade

We realize that you will want to focus on your particular grade or subject when you are planning your lessons and implementing CCSS, so we have organized the Practical Ideas chapters by grade level and subject. Each grade starts with an overview followed by ELA technology standards with accompanying apps, software, and websites that you can use to help your students succeed with that standard. We then continue with the math standard for the grade level and review appropriate sources. Finally, we have included sample lessons for each grade level in various subject areas. Although we have organized the book so you can find your specific grade and subject easily, please do not disregard other sections of this chapter. It is often helpful to see what the standards require before and after the grade you teach. To see grades other than 6–12, look for the first book in this series, for grades K–5, as it provides information to help you differentiate for students at all levels of your class.

The CCSS have been set up to encourage cross-curricular work in ELA for Grades 6–12. Many of the same standards are used throughout the seven grade levels, making it imperative for all levels of teachers to work closely together to ensure that a spiral effect takes place. Many schools have block planning so teachers of the same grade level can plan together. However, when teachers from multiple grade levels need to plan together, you may need to get creative to find time that works for everyone. Discuss with your administrators how to schedule this time. These meetings will help ensure that the technology standards embedded in language arts, reading, and writing are addressed without overlapping across classes. Some suggestions are to meet during school or district professional planning days, during the summer (many districts pay for curriculum and unit writing during the summer), staff meetings, or better yet, during scheduled times your school builds in at the beginning of the year.

Math is also a subject area where the technological tools become more varied and complex as students advance. The math standards are meant to be embedded in, and a natural part of, the units your students study. Choosing the correct mathematical tools is an important part of your students' learning. There are wonderful new math resources available to help students become proficient in the standards, especially in the area of technology. We list some of our favorites later in this chapter.

We have pulled out the sixth-grade standards that include technology and listed them in this chapter so you have them at your fingertips. Sixth-graders are expected to use technology to enhance their literacy skills, such as comparing and contrasting with "live" video, and using digital texts and multimedia to help with reading comprehension. Writing is also important; they must use the internet to find sources of information, and then use publishing sources to publish their work in and out of the classroom. Sixth-graders are expected to have excellent typing skills, so you will need to make sure that your students are up-to-speed. An emphasis on finding needed information quickly and efficiently, as well as taking notes and documenting their sources and presenting their findings in a multimedia presentation, is expected. Using tools such as digital dictionaries and thesauruses, as well as read-along texts, is also emphasized. Technology should be used to practice math skills, and students will need to use digital mathematical tools, which are available through software programs, apps, or websites.

Reading Literature Resources

RL.6.7 • READING LITERATURE

Compare and contrast the experience of reading a story, drama, or poem to listening to or viewing an **audio, video**, or live version of the text, including contrasting what they "see" and "hear" when reading the text to what they perceive when they listen or watch.

Many media formats read text aloud to students. Audiobooks on digital devices or some ebooks are great sources. Program sites, such as Follett **(tiny.cc/cb2q3y),** TeachingBooks **(teachingbooks.net),** and TumbleBooks **(tumblebooks.com)** must be purchased but allow you to have access to multiple ebooks that include fiction and nonfiction. Video versions of literature are available at YouTube **(youtube.com)** and

SchoolTube **(schooltube.com)** apps and websites for free, or try the website Open Culture **(tinyurl.com/d8ww8ez).** All those sites have ads. You can also try Shoomp **(schools.shmoop.com),** another great resource. It's ad free, but there is a cost. You can also check out many ebooks at your local library or purchase them from book-sellers, such as Amazon or Barnes & Noble (especially if you have e-readers). There are also some free ebooks out there. The sites Project Gutenberg **(gutenberg.org),** FreeReadFeed **(freereadfeed.com),** and FreeBookSifter **(freebooksifter.com)** can help you find them. Be aware that there are adult titles on these sites, so choose carefully. Pay sites offer a much better selection.

Another good resource is ReadWriteThink **(readwritethink.org).** This free site allows students to make an online Venn diagram to compare and contrast what they see and hear when reading the text as opposed to what they perceive when they listen or watch.

Reading History Resources

RH.6–8.7 • READING HISTORY

Integrate visual information (e.g., in charts, graphs, photographs, videos, or maps) with other information in print and **digital texts**.

A multimedia story is some combination of text, still photographs, video clips, audio, graphics, and interactivity presented on a website in a nonlinear format in which the information in each medium is complementary, not redundant. A multi-media presentation integrates visual information with print and digital texts. **Table 8.1** shares some online resources that feature this type of presentation.

Table 8.1: Reading History Resources

	CNN cnn.com	The Cable News Network site is free but includes ads. It has trending news events and access to text, pictures, and video of current events.
	The Washington Post washingtonpost.com	This is the official site of the leading newspaper in the U.S. capital. There is access to current events in the nation and world. The site is free but does have ads.

WEBSITES

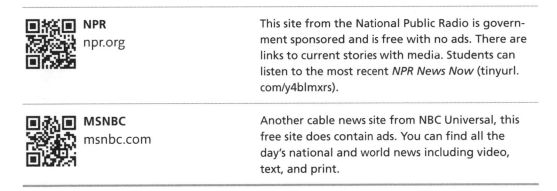

	NPR npr.org	This site from the National Public Radio is government sponsored and is free with no ads. There are links to current stories with media. Students can listen to the most recent *NPR News Now* (tinyurl.com/y4blmxrs).
	MSNBC msnbc.com	Another cable news site from NBC Universal, this free site does contain ads. You can find all the day's national and world news including video, text, and print.

Websites to Create Webpages

Your students can produce multimedia sites as well. Creating personal websites is a wonderful way to fulfill this standard. You can find many programs that allow you to create professional-looking webpages free. **Table 8.2** presents a few choices.

Table 8.2: Website Creation Tools

	Weebly weebly.com	This is an online website creator that is drag-and-drop easy and includes templates. The basics, which include five pages, are free. There is even an app available.
	Wix wix.com	This online website creator is also drag-and-drop easy and includes templates. The basics are free. An app version is available.
	Webs webs.com	This online website creator allows you to choose a template and then drag-and-drop elements on to webpages. Basic functionality is free, and an app is available.
	SiteBuilder sitebuilder.com	This is an online website creator that is drag-and-drop easy and includes templates. The website is free. With a domain name included, there is a cost.
	Shutterfly Share Sites tinyurl.com/5wjpu7	Manage parent communication, post important reminders, receive auto reminders for events and volunteer duties, share class photos and videos from daily activities and field trips—all free. It's private and secure. Free apps are also available.

WEBSITES

71

Writing Resources

W.6.2a • WRITING

Introduce a topic, organize ideas, concepts, and information, using strategies such as definition, classification, comparison/contrast, and cause/effect; include formatting (e.g., headings), graphics (e.g., charts, tables), and **multimedia** when useful to aiding comprehension.

WHST.6.2a • WRITING HISTORY, SCIENCE, AND TECHNICAL SUBJECTS

Introduce a topic clearly, previewing what is to follow; organize ideas, concepts, and information into broader categories as appropriate to achieving purpose; include formatting (e.g., headings), graphics (e.g., charts, tables), and **multimedia** when useful to aiding comprehension.

Mind-Mapping Apps, Software, and Websites

Mind-mapping programs are an effective way for students to organize their ideas, concepts, and information. Educators have used several wonderful mind-mapping software programs for many years. However, there are also free sites that do this. There are even templates, such as a Venn diagram that allows students to compare and contrast and show cause and effect. **Table 8.3** contains some digital tools you can use to teach note-taking and categorizing.

Table 8.3: Note-Taking and Categorizing Tools

Inspiration
inspiration.com

Webspiration Classroom
tinyurl.com/bmop3nh

This mind-mapping software program helps students organize their writing. It can be especially helpful for students who are learning to create paragraphs and organize big ideas into their smaller parts. The web-based version is Webspiration Classroom. This program has educational pricing.

SimpleMind
tinyurl.com/y7ualejm

This cross-platform mind-mapping app can have multiple mind-maps with unlimited page sizes. You can add photos, video, and images to make your mind-map stand out. Free version that can be upgraded for a price.

APPS & WEBSITES

▦	**Popplet** popplet.com	This is a wonderful online organizational tool for student writing. A free app called Popplet Lite is also available. It is easy to use, and students can import pictures and text to create web maps.
▦	**Bubbl.us** bubbl.us	This is a free (with limited use) mind-mapping website for Grades K–12. It can be shared by multiple students at a time and comes with an app. See the website for more options and to purchase a package.
▦	**MindMeister** tiny.cc/826i3y	This is a free, basic mind-mapping website for Grades 2–12. Upgrades are available and have a free trial period. See the website for details.
▦	**FreeMind** tinyurl.com/5qrd5	This is a free mind-mapping tool for Grades 2–12. Options for a basic or maximum install are available.

Charts and Graphs Software and Websites

Creating your own Venn diagram and having kids type in it from a word-processing document also works. Another option is to create an online Venn diagram using the free web-based program **ReadWriteThink (readwritethink.org).**

In this standard, you are also asked to include charts, tables, and multimedia when aiding comprehension. Using **Microsoft Excel (office.com), Apple Numbers (apple. com/numbers),** or **Google Sheets (google.com/sheets/about)** is a good way to teach students about charts and graphs. Making their own charts and graphs helps students learn how to interpret and present information. See **Table 8.4** for resources.

Table 8.4: Charting and Graphing Tools

	FASTT Math tinyurl.com/2rx2k8	This program really helps students visualize how charts and graphs compare, and it's extremely easy to use. The program includes ready-made activities in all subject areas, including rubrics and sample graphs. District purchasing and volume CDs are available. Contact a representative through the website for specific prices.

SOFTWARE & WEBSITES

Table 8.4: Charting and Graphing Tools

	Gliffy gliffy.com	Create professional-quality flowcharts, wireframes, diagrams, and more with this tool. It is free for limited use, and upgrades are available for a fee.
	Create A Graph tinyurl.com/yoedjn	Create bar, line, area, pie, and XY graphs with this free website. It is easy to use, and you can print, save, or email your completed graphs.
	Classtools classtools.net	Create graphs and charts, and use many other helpful classroom tools, such as a QR code generator or timeline, with this free website.

Reading Resources

RST.6–9.9 • READING SCIENCE AND TECHNICAL SUBJECTS

Compare and contrast the information gained from experiments, **simulations, video, or multimedia sources** with that gained from reading a text on the same topic.

Educational Video Websites

There are many places to see videos about educational topics. It's up to you to sift through them to find what you are looking for and locate reliable sources. **Table 8.5** includes some websites that we recommend.

Table 8.5: Educational Video Websites

	WatchKnowLearn watchknowlearn.org	The site has free educational videos that allow access to everything from frog dissection simulations to earthquake destruction. It organizes content by age range and provides reviews.
	NeoK12 neok12.com	There are many science experiments, simulations, and videos on all sorts of topics on this website, and they are guaranteed to be kid safe. As an added bonus, it is free.
	EarthCam earthcam.com	This interesting site allows you to view live video from many different places around the world (e.g., Times Square or Wrigley Field).

WEBSITES

[QR code]	**iTunes U** tinyurl.com/lbjbarh	As stated on their website, "Choose from more than 750,000 free lectures, videos, books, and other resources on thousands of subjects from Algebra to Zoology." Access it free through iTunes. A free app is also available.
[QR code]	**BrainPOP** brainpop.com	This website has been around for a long time. It offers educational videos on multiple educational topics in a fun, cartoon format. Price varies based on the subscription you choose.
[QR code]	**Open Culture** tinyurl.com/d8ww8ez	This free website is a one-stop shop for audio-books, ebooks, and movies. There are even courses for teachers! They do not create the media. They just compile it so we can find it easier.

Using these various sources, it will be easy for students to compare and contrast the information they gather from videos, simulations, webpages, or textbooks. Gathering information has never been so engaging!

Publishing Resources

W 6.6 • WRITING

Use technology, including the internet, to produce and publish writing as well as to interact and collaborate with others; demonstrate sufficient command of keyboarding skills to type a minimum of three pages in a single sitting.

WHST.6–6.8.6 • WRITING HISTORY, SCIENCE, AND TECHNICAL SUBJECTS

Use technology, including the internet, to produce and publish writing and present the relationships between information and ideas clearly and efficiently

Producing and publishing writing digitally is another standard sixth-graders are expected to meet. There are many websites that allow you to publish student writing. Using blogging websites such as **Edmodo (edmodo.com), Edublogs (edublogs. org),** and **Google Blogger (blogger.com)** lets you share student writing in a safe, protected environment. Blogging is also a good way for students to interact and collaborate with others. These sites allow teachers to set themselves up as administrators and add students to various groups. All student writing is kept secure in these groups when set up properly.

You can give assignments asking for short answers where everyone can respond, or you can ask students to write longer assignments on their own. They can then work on assignments and submit privately to you or post them on the site to share.

Publishing Websites

There are also sites that ask students to submit their work for possible publication. **Table 8.6** lists a few options.

Table 8.6: Publishing Tools

	Scholastic Publishing tinyurl.com/plwnn6f	This free website allows teachers to submit student writing for publication.
	PBS Kids Writer's Contest wtvp.org/writers-contest	This free site asks for student writing and serves as a nice incentive to get students to do their best.
	Lulu lulu.com	These sites allow you to create real books and publish them online. Parents can purchase the books as keepsakes. The site is free to use, but a fee is required to publish.
	Lulu Junior lulujr.com	
	TikaTok tikatok.com	This is another site that allows students to write, create, and publish stories as ebooks or hardcover books. Classroom pricing is available on the website. TikaTok StorySpark is the app version, also available for purchase.
	CAST UDL Book Builder bookbuilder.cast.org	This free site lets you publish your ebook and see what others have published.

WEBSITES

Penzu
penzu.com

This writing website can be accessed with their app, and it's all free! Created for journaling and diaries, it is very customizable and secure. It even allows you to set up reminders.

 Flipsnack
flipsnackedu.com

This publishing tool is great for brochures, catalogs, and visual presentations. It is cross-platform and includes links, buttons, pictures, and has templates. Your work can be privately or publicly published on their website, embedded in a blog, emailed, or sent through social media. The limited version is free but can be upgraded for a price.

 Poetry Idea Engine
tiny.cc/0afs3y

The Scholastic site allows students to use templates to make different forms of poetry—another great way technology gets kids writing. Better still, it is free!

 **Shmoop**
schools.shmoop.com

This site helps students build great videos for presentations and review. There are many templates included, and it uses the student's face and voice in the videos that range from ELA to math, science, social studies, test prep and more. It can be costly for individual teachers, but school pricing is well worth it.

Animation Apps and Websites

Table 8.7 shares some apps that allow students to create shorter versions of their stories in an animated way.

Table 8.7: Animation Tools

 iFunFace
ifunface.com

Students can create a read-aloud to show how the main idea and details flow by using a photo and audio recording to create an animation. It helps students visualize how to support details that branch off from the main ideas and how they flow together. The app is free but can be upgraded for a price.

APPS & WEBSITES

Table 8.7: Animation Tools

	Blabberize blabberize.com	Students can speak the text and use photos to illustrate in an animated format. Free.
	Voki voki.com	Students speak the text and use photos to illustrate in an animated format. It is free, but there are ads.
	Fotobabble fotobabble.com	Students speak the text and use photos to illustrate. Free.

Keyboarding Software and Websites

By sixth grade, students are expected to type three pages in one sitting. Paying for a good typing program is worth the expense. Quality programs track student progress and levels of proficiency, teach necessary skills, and allow students access from home. If you can't buy a program, there are many free sites that offer instruction and games. **Table 8.8** shares some of the resources available.

Table 8.8: Typing and Keyboarding Tools

	Mavis Beacon Keyboarding Kidz tinyurl.com/254v9on	Set words-per-minute goals and discover what keys you need to practice and what keys you know well. Play games to practice what you've learned and to improve your speed and accuracy to become a typing pro. Check the website for pricing.
	Type to Learn ttl4.sunburst.com	This typing program for Grades K–12 emphasizes both accuracy and words-per-minute speed, and it provides each student with individualized remediation and goals for success. Consult the website for various pricing options and to request a quote.
	TypingInstructorWeb typinginstructor.com	This is the top-rated typing website for students. It has multiple courses, feedback, progress tracking, and practice. Look for educational pricing.

WEBSITES

	Dance Mat Typing bbc.co.uk/guides/z3c6tfr	This free website by BBC schools teaches typing in an easy format.
	Typing.com typing.com	This site has ads, but it does track student progress with typing skills and allow reports. Free.
	TypeRacer play.typeracer.com	This is a free website that allows you to race opponents by typing words in paragraph form. This is great for experienced typists to bone up on accuracy and typing speed. There are ads.

Some districts send students to computer labs to practice keyboarding. Other schools fit it in where they can in the classroom, and still others have students practice and learn at home. The best way is to combine all three approaches. Students benefit from formal keyboarding instruction, even at the sixth grade level, but they need to practice both in the classroom and at home. When students work at computers in your classroom, remind them to practice good technique, such as sitting up straight, keeping hands in home row, holding wrists slightly curved, and moving fingers instead of the hands.

Information Gathering Resources

RI.6.7 • READING INFORMATION

Integrate information presented in different **media or formats** (e.g., visually, quantitatively) as well as in words to develop a coherent understanding of a topic or issue.

W.6.8 • Writing

Gather relevant information from multiple print and **digital sources**; assess the credibility of each source; and quote or paraphrase the data and conclusions of others while avoiding plagiarism and providing basic bibliographic information for sources.

By the time students are in sixth grade, they should be able to search the internet independently to gather information on a given topic. Your class will need guidance, of course, so lessons on internet searching are critical, as well as lessons on media literacy. Media literacy is especially crucial because students need to be able to critique a website before using it—anyone can put up a webpage. As stated by the **W.6.8** standard, students will also need to be able to take notes from these sites, assess the credibility of each source, and quote or paraphrase the data and conclusions of others. They must do this while avoiding plagiarism, and they must provide a list of bibliographic sources. We discuss these techniques in the following paragraphs.

Although students are net-savvy these days, even sixth-graders still need assistance with the basics of searching. Various search engines work differently, and each will return different information. Therefore, your students need to know how to use multiple engines.

Smart searching will help students avoid wasting time. Teaching them to analyze search results will help them find better information and think more critically about information they find on the internet. Following are some basic guidelines.

GUIDELINES FOR SMART SEARCHING

- Choose your search terms carefully. Be precise about what you are looking for, but use phrases and not full sentences.

- Adding more words can narrow a search. Use Boolean searches to narrow your topic with quotation marks. There's a big difference between the term "gopher" and "habitats of gophers in North America."

- Use synonyms! If students can't find what they're looking for, have them try keywords that mean the same thing or are related.

- Type "site:". Typing the word *site:*(with the colon) after your keyword and before a URL will tell many search engines to search within a specific website.

- Add a minus sign. Adding a minus sign (a hyphen) immediately before any word, with no space in between, indicates that you don't want that word to appear in your search results. For example, "Saturn-cars" will give you information about the planet, not the automobile.

Note-Taking Resources

WHST.6–8.8 • WRITING HISTORY, SCIENCE, AND TECHNICAL SUBJECTS

Gather relevant information from multiple print and **digital sources**, using search terms effectively; assess the credibility and accuracy of each source; and quote or paraphrase the data and conclusions of others while avoiding plagiarism and following a standard format for citation.

Tried-and-true methods for paraphrasing and summarizing information from books can still be used to gather information and take notes on websites. Teaching students to use data sheets, note cards, and Know, What, Learn (KWL) techniques still works. However, technology can make this easier. The **Kentucky Virtual Library (kyvl.org)** is an excellent source for some of these techniques. **Evernote (evernote. com)** allows students to take notes and to import a worksheet, document, or picture (including a snapshot of a webpage) and annotate it using tools common to interactive whiteboard software. It lets them highlight words, cut and paste, and add sticky notes. The sticky notes are especially useful to summarize or paraphrase students' notes. Evernote also allows students to use voice recognition and send their annotated sheet to someone else (including the teacher).

Another way to take notes is to use an "add-on" to your internet browser. The free add-on **Diigo (diigo.com)** is made for note-taking on documents, PDFs, and screenshots. Students can also save sites and documents as resources to take notes on later with annotations and highlighting.

Modeling is essential when teaching students how to glean information from a website. An interactive whiteboard is a perfect tool for modeling lessons. Don't have an interactive whiteboard? Use **Miro (realtimeboard.com).** It's a free website that allows you to turn an ordinary whiteboard into an interactive, virtual one. All you need is a computer and a projector! Using the many tools an interactive whiteboard and its software have to offer will really help teach your students how to navigate information posted on the internet. Using note-taking tools (such as the ones shared below or previously in **Table 8.3**) when gathering information will help your students organize their research.

Evernote
evernote.com

This free app allows you to import a worksheet, document, or picture, including a snapshot of a webpage, and then annotate it using tools common to interactive whiteboard software. You can highlight words, cut and paste, and add sticky notes. It also allows you to use voice recognition. You can then send your annotated sheet to someone else.

 Simplenote
simplenote.com

This great note-taking app is simple to use and has the ability to share notes with others, search notes, track changes, and use it over multiple platforms. All notes are backed up online and synchronized. Best of all, it's free.

Of course, students can also use word-processing programs, such as **Microsoft Office (office.com), Apple Pages (apple.com/pages),** or **Google Docs (google.com/docs/about).** Some teachers make digital templates, with spaces to summarize or paraphrase, to help students find specific information and organize their notes.

Table 8.9: Bibliographic Sources Websites

 EasyBib
easybib.com

This is a free website and app for ages five to twelve that students can use to generate citations in MLA, APA, and Chicago formats. Just copy and paste or scan a book's barcode.

 Citation Machine
citationmachine.net

This is another free website students can use to generate citations in MLA, APA, Turabian, and Chicago formats. Just copy and paste, and the website does the rest.

StyleWizard
stylewizard.com

This free website generates citations in MLA or APA formats easily. It also has a validity checker and offers career guidance.

Bibliographic Sources Websites

Sixth-graders will also need to provide basic bibliographic information for sources. Making your own template and having the students fill it in using a word-processing program works. However, there are websites that are designed to do this. **Table 8.9** shares some tools we recommend.

Speaking and Listening Resources

SL.6.2 • SPEAKING AND LISTENING

Interpret information presented in **diverse media and formats** (e.g., visually, quantitatively, and orally) and explain how it contributes to a topic, text, or issue under study.

SL.6.5 • SPEAKING AND LISTENING

Include **multimedia components (e.g., graphics, images, music, sound)** and visual displays in presentations to clarify information.

Microsoft Powerpoint is often the presentation program of choice, but it can be expensive. There is now a free educational version called **Microsoft Office 365 (tinyurl.com/zsfogge)** that includes PowerPoint. While this is still a great program, other presentation tools are just as useful. Apple offers **Keynote (apple.com/keynote)** as part of its software package. Its features are very similar to PowerPoint's, but it does require a purchase. Another program that has emerged is **Google Slides (google.com/slides/about).** There are other resources that help with presentations, such as **Microsoft Paint 3D (tinyurl.com/zsfogge)** and **Google Drawings (tiny.cc/5gfs3y).** Although Office 365 is free to schools, Google Drive products such as Slides and Drawings are free and web-based. Google Slides makes it very easy to share a project that multiple users can work on at once, which makes it an especially good program to use when interacting and collaborating remotely. Students can also add audio recordings to their slides, as well as visual displays such as pictures and short video clips. Consider having your students use some of the digital tools from **Table 8.10** to develop speaking and listening skills.

WEBSITES

Table 8.10: Speaking and Listening Resources

iMovie apple.com/ios/imovie	This app, which is also available as a program, has many uses in the classroom to create full edited videos or short one-minute trailers. The trailers can be useful for recounting and presenting ideas to others. See Apple for pricing.
Animoto animoto.com	This website allows you to turn your photos and music into stunning video slideshows. Educational use is free for unlimited videos of twenty minutes.
Microsoft Photos tinyurl.com/y7wcwxma	This is Microsoft's newest version of a movie-editing program. It comes standard with any Windows computer.
Prezi prezi.com	You can sign up for a free educational account, and your students can create and share presentations online. Prezi has mind-mapping, zoom, and motion, and it can import files. Presentations can be downloaded. A Prezi viewer app is available.
Clips apple.com/clips	This free app is for creating and sharing videos. Students can create selfie videos with green-screen effects, emojis, stickers, and filters. They can also turn speech into captions and have animated titles.
Kizoa kizoa.com	This web-based program makes and edits movies, slideshows, collages, and photos. There are templates available, along with stock video clips, photos, and music to make your presentations look and sound great. Students can also upload their own files to edit. This program is free for basic use, but you can upgrade for a price.
Wideo wideo.co	Wideo allows you to easily make animation videos. Educational pricing is available.

	Explain Everything explaineverything.com	This app uses text, video, pictures, and voice to help students present a variety of possible creations. The company offers educational pricing.
	Movavi movavi.com	Make movies using your photos and videos or create slideshows, video blogs, or screen-capture tutorials. It's easy to enhance, edit, and tell your story, and it's a lot of fun! Check the website for educational pricing.
	SchoolTube schooltube.com	This is educators' best free source for a video-sharing community where students can watch or post videos.
	YouTube youtube.com	There are many short, free videos that your students can listen to, including folktales, science, and people reading popular books that are in your classroom. Your students can listen and then ask and answer questions. There is also a free app.

Language Resources

L.6.4c • LANGUAGE

Consult reference materials (e.g., dictionaries, glossaries, thesauruses), both print and **digital**, to find the pronunciation of a word or determine or clarify its precise meaning or its part of speech.

Digital Dictionary and Thesaurus Websites

Although digital dictionaries and thesauruses are not updated as often as digital encyclopedias, they are still very convenient to use and are kept current. **Table 8.11** shares some of the available resources. Bookmark these sites or add them to your website for easy access. The more students use them, the more comfortable they will become. Offer lessons and activities to learn and practice the necessary skills with an online dictionary.

Table 8.11: Dictionary and Thesaurus Tools

WEBSITES

	Merriam-Webster merriam-webster.com	This is a free digital dictionary for all ages. It is the most commonly used digital dictionary, and it includes a thesaurus.
	Wordsmyth wordsmyth.net	This site shows three levels of a student dictionary. When looking up a word, you also see links to a thesaurus and rhyming dictionary for that word. You can sign up for an ad-free version that will not cost your school.
	Word Central wordcentral.com	This student online dictionary includes an audio pronunciation of the word as well as the definition. There are many teacher resources.
	Thesaurus.com thesaurus.com	This is a fine thesaurus site with many extra features. It does have some ads, but it is available free online and as an app.
	Wordle wordle.net	This is a free site for generating "word clouds" from text that you provide. The clouds give greater prominence to words that appear more frequently in the source text. You can tweak your clouds with different fonts, layouts, and color schemes.
	Tagxedo tagxedo.com	This free site turns the words of famous speeches, news articles, slogans, and themes into visually stunning word clouds.
	The Trading Cards tinyurl.com/8lqftek	This app or website is a good way to document vocabulary words by adding definitions, a picture, and recordings of voices for pronunciation. You can also use Trading Cards by doing an activity with an online thesaurus. Simply give students a word on a trading card and ask them to make as many trading cards as they can of synonyms and antonyms of that word. Students can print these out and trade them with others or make them into digital books. The Explain Everything app is also easy to use to import a picture, record your voice, and make a digital presentation.

Math Resources

MP5 • MATH

Use appropriate **tools** strategically.

There are two main sets of standards for the Common Core math standards: processes and practices. First, you have the math targets, written similarly to ELA (Ratios and Proportional Relationships, The Number System, Expressions and Equations, Geometry, and Statistics and Probability). While you work with sixth-grade students on mathematical processes, such as Expressions & Equations or Geometry, you need to teach your students how to apply the SMP (which include problem solving and precision) to those processes. One practice, the only one that includes technology, is mathematical practice 5: "Use appropriate tools strategically." Following is the explanation CCSS provides for **MP5**.

Mathematically proficient students consider the available tools when solving a mathematical problem. These tools might include pencil and paper, concrete models, a ruler, a protractor, a calculator, **a spreadsheet, a computer algebra system, a statistical package, or dynamic geometry software**. Proficient students are sufficiently familiar with tools appropriate for their grade or course to make sound decisions about when each of these tools might be helpful, recognizing both the insight to be gained and their limitations. For example, mathematically proficient high school students analyze graphs of functions and solutions generated using a **graphing calculator**. They detect possible errors by strategically using estimation and other mathematical knowledge. When making mathematical models, they know that technology can enable them to visualize the results of varying assumptions, explore consequences, and compare predictions with data. Mathematically proficient students at various grade levels are able to identify relevant external mathematical resources, such as **digital content located on a website**, and use them to pose or solve problems. They are able to use **technological tools** to explore and deepen their understanding of concepts.

Because this description does not give examples for all grades, we have provided lists of appropriate apps, websites, software, and lessons that will help translate this standard for sixth grade.

Currently, this is the only sixth-grade math standard that involves technology. Because using any kind of technology to have students practice math can grab their attention, help long-term learning, and make math fun, technology is a math tool students should use as much as possible. Many math programs, websites, and apps allow students to explore and deepen their understanding of math concepts. The best of them have students learning in creative ways and are not merely electronic worksheets. They automatically adapt to the students' skill levels and tell you where students are in their learning and what they need to advance. **Table 8.12** lists many good math resources. Some are free and some are not. The free resources (many with ads) are often less interesting to students and not as well organized. They don't give you the feedback you need. However, you must make the decision about what is best for your circumstances and budget.

Table 8.12: Math Resources

WEBSITES	**ScootPad** scootpad.com	This web-based math site is totally customizable for individual students. It adapts to the student and keeps the teacher in the loop with multiple reports. It is completely aligned to the CCSS. Pricing is available on the website.
	DreamBox Learning dreambox.com	Individualized, adaptive game-based math resource that keeps kids coming back for more. Available online or through an app. Check the website for pricing information.
	Study Island studyisland.com	This is a web-based program where students work on engaging, interactive lessons and activities at their own pace to learn aligned Common Core math standards. Teachers can also choose to guide students and assign specific areas to work through. This program must be purchased. Pricing information is available on the website.

IXL Math
ixl.com/math

This site features adaptive, individualized math through gameplay, including data and graphing problems. It gives students immediate feedback and covers many skills, despite its emphasis on drills. Levels range from prekindergarten to Grade 8. There is a limited free version.

 National Library of Virtual Manipulatives
tinyurl.com/b4qe7

This website has every imaginable math-related manipulation you might want, from geoboards to Pascal's Triangle and from pattern blocks to the Pythagorean Theorem. It is all free, but it uses Java.

 XtraMath
xtramath.org

A free site for practicing math facts. It tracks student progress, it's easy to pick what you want students to work on, and it's easy for kids to use independently. There is a specific sixth-grade level. You can purchase an extended version.

 Khan Academy
khanacademy.org

This free website has every math application you can think of, and it has short video tutorials on how to solve problems. The site includes feedback and many resources.

 AdaptedMind
tinyurl.com/997geeg

This free website provides good practice for all sorts of sixth-grade mathematical problems.

 Get the Math
tiny.cc/u3ar3y

This website relates algebra to the real world. Students can learn how math is an integral part of everyday life through combining theory and application. There are videos, exercises, and other ways that students can engage with algebra in its real-world setting. Free.

Table 8.12: Math Resources

WEBSITES	**WebQuest** webquest.org	These are good tools to use for presentations. The WebQuest site allows students to follow an already-created, project-based lesson where information is found solely on the internet. Students can create their own WebQuest if a website-building program or a website such as Sitebuilder (sitebuilder.com) is available. WebQuest.org is the original and most popular site, but if you search the internet, you will find more sites that you can use.
	Mathplanet mathplanet.com	This website is completely free and offers pre-algebra, algebra, geometry, and also ACT and SAT coursework. Think of this as a great resource of extra practice and instruction; it has examples and instructional videos on each concept.
APPS	**Math Blaster HyperBlast** mathblaster.com	The classic game many teachers used when they were students, now updated. Pricing available on the website.
	Geoboard tinyurl.com/kzyxjv7	This app is the digital recreation of a geoboard. It is simple to use, and the geometry activities are open-ended and endless. The app is free.
	Swipea Tangram Puzzles for Kids tinyurl.com/nsnoazj	This is a digital version of tangrams where students can manipulate, flip, and rotate shapes to create different pictures. The app is free; a full upgrade is available for a fee.
	Explain Everything explaineverything.com	This app uses text, video, pictures, and voice to help students present a variety of possible creations. The company offers educational pricing.

As stated in the standard, "Mathematically proficient students consider the available tools when solving a mathematical problem. These tools might include a calculator, a spreadsheet, a computer algebra system, a statistical package, or dynamic geometry software. Proficient students are sufficiently familiar with tools appropriate for their grade or course to make sound decisions about when each of these tools might be helpful, recognizing both the insight to be gained and their limitations."

Many sites offer math tools, such as a graphing calculator. **SoftSchool** has an elementary-level graphing calculator. **IXL Math** allows you to create your own graph paper, which you can then use with an interactive whiteboard, if you have one. Use **Miro** if you do not have an interactive whiteboard. Some good programs and sites to use when graphing include **Gliffy, Create A Graph**, and **Classtools**.

In sixth grade, students are also expected to use a protractor to measure angles. They can use the app **Smart Protractor** found on Google Play at **tiny.cc/9m207y** or **Protractor** on Apple's App Store at **tiny.cc/qp207y**. These can be used just like a regular protractor and function as a converter as well. **Softpedia (softpedia.com)** allows you to download a protractor to use online. The site is free, but it has ads. Using your interactive whiteboard protractor also works well.

Literacy Lessons

Cross-curriculum planning is encouraged with the CCSS by using ELA standards in history, science, and technical subjects. However, we encourage you to go further and include the arts, math, and physical education teachers in your planning. How will you ever get through everything if you teach standard by standard? The key to planning with the CCSS is to teach multiple standards in one lesson, when you can. We hope the following list of sample lessons for sixth grade will inspire you to become an effective technology lesson planner.

Word Clouds

This lesson asks students to create a Wordle or a word cloud. You can use a concept or novel that students are studying to provide a list of words. This could be spelling words, vocabulary words, site words, nouns and verbs, characters, plot, and so on. Students should be encouraged to use resource materials to find as many creative words as they can, which would then satisfy **L.6.4c.** In addition, students should feel free to explore the different formatting tools to make their word clouds stand out. Finished projects can be displayed around the classroom, scanned and uploaded to a website, or made into a book. This is fun with a purpose because students use technology to produce and publish writing. They also interact and collaborate with each other, which satisfies **W.6.6.** And, if you are using this as an activity for stories or plays, it satisfies **SL.6.5** by adding visual displays to emphasize or enhance certain facts or details. Students are developing a coherent understanding of the topic or issue and presenting it in a different media format, so **RI.6.7** is also satisfied.

ISTE STUDENT STANDARDS

Students will use these ISTE Standards in this lesson.

- **Empowered Learner 1.d.** by understanding fundamental concepts of technology operations, demonstrating the ability to choose, use, and troubleshoot current technologies.

- **Digital Citizen** by acting and modeling technology ways that are safe, legal, and ethical.

- **Knowledge Constructors** by employing research, evaluating, and building knowledge using digital resources.

- **Creative Communicators** with their presentations choosing the appropriate platform and publishing and presenting customized content.

Movie Trailers

For this next lesson, you will need to do a little prep before you begin. Start with an internet search for student iMovie Trailer examples. There are some good examples on YouTube. Of course, you will want to preview these iMovie Trailers before showing them to your students. Begin the lesson with a discussion on the last movie trailers students have seen. Ask them to identify what makes a good trailer: one that captures the interest of the audience, does not reveal the ending, has music that reflects the mood of the movie, and so on. After viewing several examples, lead students through a discussion about what made those trailers interesting.

Next, have a discussion about these important elements and how they can be included in a movie trailer:

- Readable text

- Clear recordings

- Interesting, clear images

- Timing of images

- Concise language

- Music that reflects the mood of the book

- Narration that is louder than the background music

- Enough details to be interesting but not enough to give away the ending

- Ends with a question or scene that makes the audience want to read the book

Choose a book you are reading in class, or have students use a self-selected book they are reading independently, because movie trailers make an excellent alternative to book reports. Let the students know your expectations for the completed project. For example:

- Introduce the book: Include the title, the author's name, and the genre.

- Tell about the book: Introduce the main characters and action. Don't try to tell every detail.

- Tell about your favorite part of the book or make a connection: Persuade the audience to read the book and leave the audience wanting to know more. For example, explain what the main character has to overcome, but don't tell if he or she is successful.

- Give a recommendation: Provide closure for the book trailer. This also helps match the perfect reader and the book.

- Short and sweet is best.

Using your favorite way to make trailers (iMovie, Animoto, Wideo, Shmoop, etc.), students begin working on the trailers for their book. If students work together collaboratively, **W.6.6** will be satisfied, using technology, including the internet, to produce and publish writing. In the beginning, you may find your students need to plan and organize for their trailer. Apple's iMovie for Mac site has more than twenty-nine free templates to help students work through their trailers. Students may need adult supervision and help when the time comes to scan, upload, or download pictures for their trailer. Certainly students can provide their own illustrations and graphics, either done by hand or digitally using any graphic art program (such as Microsoft Photos or Google Drawings). If their book has pictures, students can scan and use those for their trailers. Or, students can also search the internet to find pictures to use.

Once all trailers are complete, establish a class internet site and post them for everyone to see. You may even wish to publish the address to the class website for parents and members of the community to view. Or, trailers can be posted at SchoolTube.

In addition to **W.6.6,** other standards satisfied include **SL.6.5,** as students are using technology to clarify information in their presentations. **SL.6.2** and **RI.6.7** are also satisfied because students are interpreting information using a diverse media format, all to develop a coherent understanding of a topic (their novel or book).

ISTE STUDENT STANDARDS

Students will use these ISTE Standards in this lesson.

- **Empowered Learner** by understanding fundamental concepts of technology operations, demonstrating the ability to choose, use, and troubleshoot current technologies.

- **Digital Citizen** by acting and modeling technology ways that are safe, legal, and ethical.

- **Knowledge Constructor** by employing research, evaluating and building knowledge using digital resources.

- **Creative Communicator** by choosing the appropriate platform for their presentations, and publishing and presenting customized content.

Student Blogs

Blogs give students an authentic reason to think through their writing because they know their audience can respond to them. In this lesson, students read blogs written by students their own age and learn to shape a well-thought-out response that addresses and answers the questions posed in the blog. It is important to note that this lesson can be adapted in several ways and can be used in any grade, 6–12. Doing this, students learn to communicate digitally by writing and posting clear, concise, and well-written blog entries to accomplish their purposes (i.e., learning, enjoyment, persuasion, or the exchange of information). By writing blog entries, students also learn to adjust their use of written language to communicate effectively with a variety of audiences and for different purposes. This allows students to actually apply their knowledge of language structure and conventions by writing knowledgeable, reflective, creative, and critical blog posts. Students also learn to demonstrate the benefits and uses of blogging by reading, writing, and discussing successful and unsuccessful blogs. After reading, discussing, and deciding what makes a good blog entry or comment, students create their own response to a teacher-created blog entry to discuss the sequel possibilities of a favorite book. To learn more about blogging, see our series on blogging **(tinyurl.com/ybk4exvr).**

Start this lesson by first assessing what students know about blogs. You can introduce them to various blogs, especially those written by students. Tell them the word *blog* is actually short for *weblog*. Using your Smart Board or Miro **(realtimeboard. com),** show students a variety of blogs written by students. There are many to be found by searching "elementary student's classroom blogs". We found Kathleen Morris' post **(tinyurl.com/y9eoaehj)** to be particularly helpful, as it offers blogs by many different age groups. Next, have a discussion about the pros of having a classroom blog in which everyone participates. In your discussion, ask students what kind of blog entries they enjoy reading, as well as what they think makes a good blog entry and why. Discuss whether it is important to pay attention to grammar, even though the blog entries may be short. Also talk about using adjectives, as well as other descriptive words, to create a picture in their readers' minds.

You may wish to have students explore blogs on their own or in small groups. They can explore **tinyurl.com/y9eoaehj** or **The Literacy Shed Blog (literacyshedblog.com),** which are blogs by teachers and educators. Or they can check out **The Studential (tinyurl.com/y7vtcqld),** which are blogs for students by students. It is a good idea to have set sites that you have previewed and bookmarked, instead of allowing students to search freely.

Have students use **Simplenote (simplenote.com), Evernote (evernote.com),** or **Penzu (penzu.com)** to take online notes about what they find on the blogs they read. Have students discuss what types of things they think are important to share on their classroom blog. What things were interesting about the blogs they read? Is there anything they read that was not interesting and should not be included in the classroom blog?

Using your Smart Board or **Miro (realtimeboard.com),** show students Read-WriteThink's **Literature Response Blog Rubric (tinyurl.com/y83k7f6g).** This is a good sample of how students will be evaluated for their blog writing. Review each category, explaining what everything means. You may even want to give each student a digital copy to keep on their tablets, so they can continually refer to it.

You may wish to begin writing the classroom blog together, using book reviews for the first few blogs. For example, read the book *Tuesday* by David Weisner. Also watch the **YouTube** animated version **(tinyurl.com/mspaxlc).** The author of *Tuesday* includes few words but has lots of pictures. Discuss how long they think it took the author to get his pictures just right. Compare this to blog writing. To create a blog people want to read, they will need to take time to get it right.

Next, ask students to write a book review for the book *Tuesday*. You may want to read several examples of book reviews. Students can work in small groups to complete this task. Their book-review blog entry might include their favorite part of the book, what they wish the author would have included, what they would change, and why they recommend others read the book. Encourage students to use expressive words. As students finish, have them share their sample book-review blogs. Discuss elements of each sample blog that should be included in the class blog. Remind students that blogs need to be reviewed several times before hitting the button to post online. Once blogs are posted, they are out there for everyone to see. Once the final copy has been decided, post on your classroom's website. Now is also a good time to talk to your students about internet safety. They should never post their last name on the blog, nor their pictures, addresses, or phone numbers.

Before you allow students to post their blogs online, you may want to have several more practice sessions using book reviews, as outlined in the *Tuesday* book review lesson. Next, you could ask students to begin writing their ideas for a blog. They can conference with other students and yourself before going live. Encourage students to use online dictionaries and thesauruses to find stronger and more colorful words to use.

You will also have to spend some time showing students where their blogs are going (e.g., on your website), how to post, and so on. Also, you need to talk to the students about blog content. Should all students write book reviews? What other content can be included on your blog website? Photographs, news stories, videos, charts, graphs, and so on, can be uploaded and blogged about. Students can also include narrative, persuasive, or informational (history, science, or technical) writing in their blog.

It is important to remember that students progress at different levels. Some students may need to work in groups to create a blog. Other students may be ready for their own blog page very quickly. Allow them to create their own blog pages from your class website, as soon as they devise a plan and conference with you. Definitely check each blog before they go live.

Students love seeing their work online. Many also love to see that they make a difference or can create change. Giving students a real-world reason to blog is very desirable. Talk with your principal about ideas and ways your students can blog about a school-related issue (after-school activities, school dances, sports teams, vending machines in the cafeteria, etc.). If their persuasive blogs work and result in change, it clearly demonstrates to them the power of online words.

Your students may also love seeing others respond to their blog ideas and writing. Talk with colleagues, parents, other classes, and your principal about reading the blogs on your website and responding to the students' entries. Then help students to respond to the comments with substantial comments of their own.

By comparing and contrasting the book *Tuesday* to the video, students satisfy **RL.6.7.** Encourage them to compare and contrast what they "see" and "hear" when reading the text to what they perceive when they watch and listen. **RH.6-8.7, WHST.6-8.2a, W.6.2a,** as well as **RST.6-8.9** are also satisfied when students blog about other topics, information, and visual information. **W.6.6** and **WHST.6-8.6** are definitely satisfied when students write and publish their blogs on the internet. Students will need to gather their information prior to posting their blogs and take notes, thus satisfying **RI.6.7** and **W.6.8. SL.6.2** and **W.6.5** are also satisfied when sharing blogs and consulting with classmates and/or the teacher. **L.6.4c** is also satisfied in this lesson, as students are using dictionaries and thesauruses to help with their writing.

ISTE STUDENT STANDARDS

Students will use these ISTE Standards in this lesson.

- **Empowered Learner** by understanding fundamental concepts of technology operations, demonstrating the ability to choose, use, and troubleshoot current technologies.

- **Digital Citizen** by acting and modeling technology ways that are safe, legal, and ethical.

- **Knowledge Constructor** by employing research, evaluating and building knowledge using digital resources.

- **Creative Communicator** by selecting a platform and publishing and presenting content on their blogs.

Science and Social Studies Lessons

The following sample lessons address CCSS ELA standards and teach lessons based on national standards in social studies and science.

Around the World

Sixth-graders across the country study people, places, and societies from around the world. A history teacher, in conjunction with a technology teacher/coach, gave this lesson. Students worked on the project in both classes. In this exercise, students describe the influence of individuals and groups on historical and contemporary events within a specific country or region. They identify the location and geographic characteristics of their chosen society because geography also influences the locations and characteristics of societies. Identifying different ways of organizing economic and government systems for that society is a goal for students. Citizenship should also be discussed. For example, what does it mean to be a member of a society, an educational institution, or a religious institution? Students should identify and include major physical and human geographic figures such as landforms, bodies of water, and major cities.

Students use research they gather from multiple print and digital sources **(W.6.8),** (making sure to quote sources accurately as well as citing each one) to put together a photo story presentation on a foreign country they have been assigned or chosen. Each photo must cite the website from which the picture was obtained. Each slide needs a narration of key facts. Give students a choice of ways they can display their research (Microsoft PowerPoint, Keynote, iMovie Trailer, Prezi, Clips, etc.). Following are key elements to include in a presentation:

- Name of the country

- Map of the country

- Flag of the country

- One or more major landforms

- One or more famous landmarks

- Type of government

- Type of economic system

- One or more major export

- Official language(s) of country

- Religions of country

- Major holidays celebrated

- Special foods from the country

- Famous person from that country

Since students may be working on this project in several locations, you may want to encourage them to create a folder on Google Drive to store photos of their country. Students can use Google Docs to write their scripts and record websites as they go along. Another idea is to have students save everything to a zip drive (USB), which they can easily bring back and forth to classes. Final projects will be presented to the class. You may wish to have students digitally take notes during each presentation.

In addition to **W.6.8,** many other standards are satisfied with this lesson. **WHST.6-8.2a, WHST.6-8.6, SL.6.5,** and **RI.6.7,** as well as **SL.6.2,** are satisfied when students introduce, organize, interpret, and illustrate their information and ideas. **RH.6-8.7** and **W.6.2** are satisfied, as students put together a presentation using information they gained, clearly and efficiently, to aid comprehension. **W.6.6** and **L.6.4c** are also satisfied, as students collaborate to publish a presentation for which they use multiple digital sources.

ISTE STUDENT STANDARDS

Students will use these ISTE Standards in this lesson.

- **Empowered Learner** by understanding fundamental concepts of technology operations, demonstrating the ability to choose, use, and troubleshoot current technologies.

- **Digital Citizen** by acting and modeling technology ways that are safe, legal, and ethical.

- **Knowledge Constructors** by employing research, evaluating and building knowledge using digital resources.

- **Creative Communicators** with their presentations choosing the appropriate platform and publishing and presenting customized content.

Many changes occurred in technology during the twelve years my kids spent in their kindergarten through high school years. They started by using the internet in their early years to research lessons in many of their classes, to having school-provided iPads to use for assignments and to replace textbooks. The skills and standards required taught life lessons not just in what was learned but also in organization and time management. Best of all, the learning was done in a fun and meaningful way, which is what every parent wants for their child. **—Melissa Kallis, parent**

Diseases

Science teachers we know used this lesson to teach about disease. One objective teachers had was to tie-in reading and writing with science. Teachers first developed a list of diseases in various categories. For example:

- **Communicable Diseases**
    - influenza
    - measles
    - hepatitis
    - mononucleosis
    - meningitis
    - Ebola
    - tuberculosis
- **Noncommunicable Diseases**
    - diabetes
    - heart disease
    - cancer
    - sickle cell anemia
    - hypertension
    - osteoporosis
    - Alzheimer's

Next, teachers found articles, text, movies, and so on, about as many of the diseases as they could. Time was spent reading and discussing diseases, causes, and cures. Students were then allowed to choose a disease to research. Teachers had specific information that needed to be included in each presentation. For example:

1. What causes this disease?

2. What are the symptoms for this disease? (How do people know if they have the disease?)

3. How is the disease spread among humans (if it is)?

4. How can the disease be prevented? If it can't be prevented, explain why not.

5. After a person has the disease, what is the treatment? If there is no treatment available, explain the current research and what is being done to find a treatment or cure.

6. List three important facts about the disease not already mentioned.

7. Cite your sources.

Students spend time researching their diseases using a variety of print and digital sources **(W.6.8).** Give students a choice of ways they can display their research (Microsoft PowerPoint, Keynote, iMovie Trailer, Prezi, Kizoa, etc.). Once all projects are complete and have been presented to the class, establish a class wiki and post them for everyone to see. You may even wish to publish the address to the class website for parents and members of the community to view. Or, projects can be posted at SchoolTube.

In addition to **W.6.8,** many other standards are satisfied with this lesson. **WHST.6-8.2a, WHST.6-8.6, SL.6.5,** and **RI.6.7,** as well as **SL.6.2,** are satisfied when students introduce, organize, interpret, and illustrate their information and ideas. **RH.6-8.7** and **W.6.2** will also be satisfied, as students will need to put together presentations using information they gained, clearly and efficiently, to aid comprehension. **W.6.6** and **L.6.4c** are also satisfied, as students collaborate to publish a presentation where they used multiple digital sources.

ISTE STUDENT STANDARDS

Students will use these ISTE Standards in this lesson.

- **Empowered Learner** by understanding fundamental concepts of technology operations, demonstrating the ability to choose, use, and troubleshoot current technologies.

- **Digital Citizen** by acting and modeling technology ways that are safe, legal, and ethical.

- **Knowledge Constructor** by employing research, evaluating and building knowledge using digital resources.

- **Innovative Designer** students use a variety of technologies within a process to identify and solve problems by creating new, useful, or imaginative solutions.

- **Creative Communicator** students use their presentations choosing the appropriate platform and publishing and presenting customized content.

Math Lessons

The following lesson samples help students meet the technology benchmarks found in standard **MP5.**

Mathematical Reasoning

In sixth grade, students need to be able to explain their mathematical reasoning to others, as part of the **MP5** standard. Explain Everything is one resource they can use to convey their understanding. Students make their own math videos using this app to explain a concept. An example of this is showing fractions. Students can use a tablet (or other device) and take a picture of something that has equal parts (examples: tiles, cement blocks, door frames, windows). Students are encouraged to find examples of equivalent as well as mixed fractions. Next, they use Explain Everything to show how they would represent a fraction (such as 4 ¾) by drawing and shading 4 whole parts first and then shading in 3 out of the 4 next equal parts. Students are encouraged to upload their fraction pictures to help illustrate their fraction examples. The pencil feature on Explain Everything is useful to draw lines (dividing fractions into pieces) directly on the uploaded picture. Different colors for shading can be chosen as well. Add another by shading in 2 out of 3 and adding these fractions together. They can then record their voice explaining their fraction pictures. In addition to math standard **MP5,** many other standards are satisfied with this lesson. **WHST.6-8.2a, WHST.6-8.6, SL.6.5,** and **RI.6.7,** as well as **SL.6.2,** are satisfied when students introduce, organize, interpret, and illustrate their fraction problem using Explain Everything.

ISTE STUDENT STANDARDS

Students will use these ISTE Standards in this lesson.

- **Empowered Learner** by understanding fundamental concepts of technology operations, demonstrating the ability to choose, use, and troubleshoot current technologies.

- **Digital Citizen** by acting and modeling technology ways that are safe, legal, and ethical.

- **Knowledge Constructor** by employing research, evaluating and building knowledge using digital resources.

- **Innovative Designer** students use a variety of technologies within a process to identify and solve problems by creating new, useful, or imaginative solutions.

- **Computational Thinker** students develop and use strategies for understanding and solving problems in ways that use technology to develop and test solutions.

- **Creative Communicator** students use their presentations choosing the appropriate platform and publishing and presenting customized content.

Math Explorations

A local sixth-grade class had great fun with the following math exploration, which they adapted from a WebQuest developed at George Mason University. Students work in pairs to plan a three-day trip to New York City with limited time and a limited budget. They need to decide how they will get there, where they will stay, and what they will see and do. Each team must put together a proposal, including cost, which they will share with the class. They also need to put together a presentation that convinces others that their proposal is the best. Resources and websites for this lesson can be found on our website **(tinyurl.com/y9dfltpr).**

First, students use resources you provide to choose the best way to travel to New York City. They might go by air, train, or bus.

Next students decide where they will stay while in New York City. You may want to suggest to students that, because New York is a very large city, they should look for a place to stay in Manhattan, near Times Square. You may also want to mention that there are websites that offer packages for airfare and hotel accommodations (included on our website).

It is important to remind students that they do not need to make an account at any of these travel websites when searching for fares. They can search without logging in.

Next, teams decide what they will see and do while in New York. They need to be reminded that with travel, they have only two days for sightseeing.

Finally, students decide a budget for their trip. Students may need some background knowledge on how to make a budget. Others may decide their budget after they do their research. You may wish to have a template for students to record their budget, or give them guidelines on how to set up a budget. This budget item analysis sheet would be shared with the class. Give students a choice of ways they can display their research (Microsoft PowerPoint, Keynote, iMovie Trailer, Prezi, etc.). Students then put together a presentation outlining their choices, keeping in mind they need to convince the class their trip is economical and the best!

In addition to math standard **MP5,** many other standards are satisfied with this lesson. **WHST.6-8.2a, WHST.6-8.6, SL.6.5,** and **RI.6.7,** as well as **SL.6.2,** are satisfied when students introduce, organize, interpret, and illustrate their information and ideas. **RH.6-8.7** and **W.6.2** are satisfied, as students will need to put together a presentation using information they gained, clearly and efficiently, to aid comprehension. **W.6.6** and **L.6.4c** are also satisfied, as students are working together to publish their presentation, where they used multiple digital sources. Students also need to cite their sources in their presentation, which satisfies **W.6.8.**

ISTE STUDENT STANDARDS

Students will use these ISTE Standards in this lesson.

- **Empowered Learner** by understanding fundamental concepts of technology operations, demonstrating the ability to choose, use, and troubleshoot current technologies.

- **Digital Citizen** by acting and modeling technology ways that are safe, legal, and ethical.

- **Knowledge Constructor** by employing research, evaluating and building knowledge using digital resources.

- **Innovative Designer** students use a variety of technologies within a process to identify and solve problems by creating new, useful, or imaginative solutions.

- **Computational Thinker** students develop and use strategies for understanding and solving problems in ways that use technology to develop and test solutions.

- **Creative Communicator** students use their presentations choosing the appropriate platform and publishing and presenting customized content.

- **Global Collaborator** students use collaborative technologies to work with peers to examine solutions to a problem from multiple viewpoints.

Stock Market Simulation

This lesson plan may be used by any grade level, but it is great for teaching and applying math at the sixth-grade level. Students will not need any prior stock market or investing knowledge. The time involved will vary—from one week to an entire school year—depending on how much time you wish to spend on this material. We recommend continuing this exercise throughout the entire school year because this will keep students interested in current events while they learn important skills.

Unlike typical stock market simulations that make it a contest among students, the goal here is to learn and understand basic investing principles, the basics of how the economy works, money-management skills, applied math skills, and of course, reading comprehension and writing skills.

Next, setup your classroom for the activity. Students may work in groups or individually. Feel free to adjust and improvise as appropriate. Each group (or individual) begins with the same set amount of money (e.g., $1000, $5000, $10,000). Each group must invest in five stocks if you are using the higher dollar amounts, or you may set the number to three stocks for each group if they are using a lower amount of money. Make sure to have your students include a 3% commission to be paid for every stock transaction (buying or selling a stock).

When choosing stocks, students should pick companies with products or services with which they are familiar. Students should include companies that their families or friends work for, or are familiar with, to help make the learning process more interesting and understandable. In addition, some basic "fundamental analysis" should be performed. Ask students what companies they are familiar with and write the answers on the board. Students may choose from those companies or other companies in which they are interested. You might require additional fundamental analysis, such as PE analysis or making sure they create diversified portfolios, for students who need differentiation. In addition, students should write their reasoning and analysis in their digital journals.

You can also pick some of the stocks chosen by the students to create an example portfolio. Choose three-to-five stocks and list their names and stock tickers on the board (use a newspaper or computer to get the stock information). List the closing price as well. Ask the students how much of each stock they should purchase. Total the amounts and see how close it comes to their budget.

Each group (or individual) should keep a journal of their activities and thoughts, and a transaction history of all buys and sells using Google Docs or some other collaborative word processor. This would satisfy **W.6.6**, using technology to produce and publish writing and linking to and citing sources. In addition, the group is responsible for keeping track of the current portfolio's market value. Excellent resources can be found online for tracking stocks, and you might consider asking an investment advisor to come and speak to the class.

Continuing this activity throughout the end of school year is the best choice, because it will help reinforce longer-term investment skills. In addition, this will keep students interested in current economic events while reinforcing fundamental skills.

On a predetermined day, perhaps once a week (monthly if the project is ongoing), students will report on their portfolio's value and what they learned during the activity (or previous month). They should analyze stock price and portfolio performance, news items related to the stock, and economic items related to the portfolio and the stock market. Is there any correlation between the news and the stock or portfolio? Students can record this in the journal and create weekly performance sheets.

At the end of the project, students should sell their stocks and report their final value, including commission. They should report what they learned about the stock market, how the economy works, and what they learned about money management using Prezi, iMovie, or other presentation apps or software. **SL.6.2** and **SL.6.5** are satisfied as students share their work using technology. In addition to **MP5,** standards **W.6.2a, W.6.6, W.6.8, WHST.6-8.6,** and **WHST.6-8.2a** are addressed if word processing and note-taking through apps are used, as students not only need to use their math skills but also write a stock market report with analysis of the credibility of the source and draw conclusions about their investments.

ISTE STUDENT STANDARDS

Students will use these ISTE Standards in this lesson.

- **Empowered Learner** by understanding fundamental concepts of technology operations, demonstrating the ability to choose, use, and troubleshoot current technologies.

- **Digital Citizen** by acting and modeling technology ways that are safe, legal, and ethical.

- **Knowledge Constructor** by employing research, evaluating and building knowledge using digital resources.

- **Innovative Designer** students use a variety of technologies within a process to identify and solve problems by creating new, useful, or imaginative solutions.

- **Computational Thinker** students develop and use strategies for understanding and solving problems in ways that use technology to develop and test solutions.

- **Creative Communicator** students use their presentations choosing the appropriate platform and publishing and presenting customized content.

- **Global Collaborator** students use collaborative technologies to work with peers to examine solutions to a problem from multiple viewpoints.

The use of technology to teach math standards has provided so many more options for my students. The most palpable difference is the ease with which lessons can be differentiated. Videos, online games and tools, as well as real-world problem solving can all be accessed using websites and applications. All students can be learning the same standard in the way that is most appropriate for their current level of mastery and learning style. This ultimately paves the way for their future learning and strengthens their proficiency with technology. **—Bridgette Calamari, teacher**

A Final Note

As students progress through the grades, they establish their baseline of proficiency in technology. This will definitely enhance their experiences with technology in high school, as well as satisfy the CCSS performance standards at the 6–8 levels. We hope you find the resources and lesson ideas presented in this chapter useful and that they are easy to adapt to your class.

You will find more resources on our website **(tinyurl.com/y9dfltpr),** which may be helpful as you look to differentiate your instruction. Visit our site for updated information about this book. To learn more about meeting technology standards found within the CCSS for other grades, look for our additional title in this series.

Practical Ideas for Seventh Grade

We realize that you will want to focus on your particular grade or subject when you are planning your lessons and implementing the standards, so we have organized the Practical Ideas chapters by grade level and subject. Each grade starts with an overview followed by ELA technology standards with accompanying apps, software, and websites that you can use to help your students succeed with that standard. We then continue with the math standard for the grade level and review appropriate resources. Finally, we have included sample lessons for each grade level in various subject areas. Although we have organized the book so you can find your specific grade and subject easily, please do not disregard other sections of this chapter. It is often helpful to see what the standards require before and after the grade you teach. To see grades other than 6–12, look for our other title in this collection, as it provides information to help you differentiate for students at all levels of your class.

The CCSS have been set up to encourage cross-curricular work in ELA for Grades 6–12. Many of the same standards are used throughout the seven grade levels, making it imperative for all levels of teachers to work closely together to ensure that a spiral effect takes place. Many schools have block planning so teachers of the same grade level can plan together. However, when teachers from multiple grade levels need to plan together, you may need to get creative to find time that works for everyone. Discuss with your administrators how to schedule this time. These meetings will help ensure that the technology standards embedded in language arts, reading, and writing are addressed without overlapping across classes. Some suggestions are to meet during school or district professional planning days, during the summer (many districts pay for curriculum and unit writing during the summer), during staff meetings, or better yet, during scheduled times your school builds into the schedule at the beginning of the year.

Math is also a subject area where technological tools become more varied and complex as students advance. The math standards are meant to be embedded in, and a natural part of, the units your students study. Choosing the correct math tools is an important part of your students' learning. There are wonderful new math resources available to help students become proficient in the standards, especially in the area of technology. We list some of our favorites later in this chapter.

We have pulled out the seventh-grade standards that include technology and listed them in this chapter so you have them at your fingertips. Seventh-graders are expected to use technology to enhance their literacy skills, such as comparing and contrasting a literary work to its audio, filmed, staged, or multimedia version. They will be required to use digital texts and multimedia to help with reading comprehension, and to be able to organize information. Writing is also important; they must use the internet to find sources of information, and then use publishing resources to share their work in and out of the classroom. An emphasis on finding needed information quickly and efficiently, as well as taking notes, documenting, linking as well as citing sources, and presenting their findings in a multimedia presentation, is expected. Using tools such as digital dictionaries and thesauruses, as well as read-along texts, is also emphasized. Technology should be used to practice math skills, and students will need to use digital mathematical tools, which are available through software programs, apps, or websites.

Literacy Resources

RL.7.7 • READING LITERATURE

Compare and contrast a written story, drama, or poem to its **audio, filmed**, staged, or **multimedia** version, analyzing the effects of techniques unique to each medium (e.g., lighting, sound, color, or camera focus and angles in a film).

RI.7.7 • READING INFORMATIONAL TEXT

Compare and contrast a text to an **audio, video, or multimedia** version of the text, analyzing each medium's portrayal of the subject (e.g., how the delivery of a speech affects the impact of the words).

RH.6–8.7 • READING HISTORY

Integrate visual information (e.g., in charts, graphs, photographs, **videos**, or maps) with other information in print and **digital texts.**

There are free ebooks available. **Project Gutenberg (gutenberg.org), FreeReadFeed (freereadfeed.com)** or **FreeBookSifter (freebooksifter.com)** are possibilities. There are adult titles on these sites too. Choose carefully. Of course, pay sites offer a much better selection. You can also check out ebooks from your local library or purchase them from booksellers such as Barnes & Noble. **Table 9.1** shares a few places to find audiobooks.

After reading a familiar story or text, then listening to the audio version, students can create Venn diagrams with programs such as **ReadWriteThink (readwritethink. org).** It's a free site that allows you to make online Venn diagrams to compare and contrast the effects of techniques in audiobooks, such as sound and audio visual, and then analyze each medium's portrayal of the subject (e.g., how the delivery of a speech affects the impact of the words).

As **RL7.7** above states, seventh-grade students will need to compare and contrast a video or multimedia version to a text. Therefore, videos and multimedia on famous books can be used to satisfy this standard. **Table 9.1** shares some websites that you can use.

Table 9.1: Literacy Resources

	FreeClassicAudioBooks freeclassicaudiobooks.com	This site houses many classic titles for free download. There are ads.
	Follett tiny.cc/cb2q3y	This is one of a group of online providers that allows access to multiple ebooks, which includes both fiction and nonfiction. Various pricing.
	TeachingBooks teachingbooks.net	This is among a group of online providers (must be purchased) that allows access to multiple ebooks, which includes both fiction and nonfiction
	NeoK12 neok12.com	This is a great website with short stories on video.
	Netflix netflix.com	Film adaptations of Jane Austen's books, Shakespeare's plays, and titles such as Because of Winn-Dixie can be found at sites such as this, or at your local library.
	Open Culture tinyurl.com/d8ww8ez	This free website is one-stop shop for audiobooks, ebooks, and movies. There are even courses for teachers! They do not create the media. They just compile it so we can find it easier.
	CNN cnn.com	The Cable News Network site is free but includes ads. It has trending news events and access to text, pictures, and video of current events.
	The Washington Post washingtonpost.com	This is the official site of the leading newspaper in the U.S. capital. There is access to current events in the nation and world. The site is free, but it does have ads.

Table 9.1: Literacy Resources

	NPR npr.org	This site from the National Public Radio is government sponsored and is free with no ads. There are links to current stories with media. Students can listen to the most recent NPR News Now (tinyurl.com/y4blmxrs).
	MSNBC msnbc.com	Another cable news site from NBC Universal, this free site does contain ads. You can find all the day's national and world news including video, photos, and text.

MULTIMEDIA PRESENTATIONS

What is a multimedia version of a written story? A multimedia story is some combination of text, still photographs, video clips, audio, graphics, and interactivity presented on a website in a nonlinear format. The information in each medium is complementary, not redundant.

Your students can produce multimedia sites as well. Creating personal websites is a wonderful way to fulfill this standard. You can find many programs that allow you to create professional-looking webpages free. **Table 8.2** in the previous chapter shares several wesbite creation tools you might try with your students.

Informational Text Resources

RST.6–8.9 • READING, SCIENCE, AND TECHNICAL SUBJECTS

Compare and contrast the information gained from experiments, **simulations, video**, or **multimedia** sources with that gained from reading a text on the same topic.

Educational Video Websites

As evidenced by the resources in **Table 9.2**, there are so many places where you can go to get videos on a variety of educational topics. Using these various sources, it will be easy for students to compare and contrast the information they gather from videos, simulations, webpages, or textbooks. Gathering information has never been so engaging! Anyone and everyone puts up videos, so it's up to you to sift through them to find information from reliable sources.

Table 9.2: Educational Video Websites

YouTube youtube.com	There are many short, free videos that your students can watch, including folktales, science, and people reading popular books that are in your classroom. Your students can watch or listen and then ask and answer questions. There is also a free app.
WatchKnowLearn watchknowlearn.org	The site has free educational videos that allow access to everything from frog dissection simulations to earthquake destruction. It organizes content by age range and provides reviews.
NeoK12 neok12.com	There are many science experiments, simulations, and videos on all sorts of topics on this website, and they are guaranteed to be kid safe. As an added bonus, it is free.
EarthCam earthcam.com	This interesting site allows you to view live video from many different places around the world (e.g., Times Square or Wrigley Field).
iTunes U tinyurl.com/lbjbarh	As stated on their website, "Choose from more than 750,000 free lectures, videos, books, and other resources on thousands of subjects from Algebra to Zoology." Access it free through iTunes. A free app is also available.
BrainPOP brainpop.com	This website has been around for a long time. It offers educational videos on multiple topics in a fun, cartoon format. Price varies based on the subscription you choose.
Open Culture tinyurl.com/d8ww8ez	This free website is a one-stop shop for audiobooks, ebooks, and movies. There are even courses for teachers! They do not create the media. They just compile it so we can find it easier.

Research Resources

W.7.2a • READING INFORMATIONAL TEXT

Introduce a topic clearly, previewing what is to follow; organize ideas, concepts, and information, using strategies such as definition, classification, comparison/contrast, and cause/effect; include formatting (e.g., headings), graphics (e.g., charts, tables), and **multimedia** when useful to aiding comprehension.

WHST.6–8.2a • WRITING HISTORY, SCIENCE, AND TECHNICAL SUBJECTS

Introduce a topic clearly, previewing what is to follow; organize ideas, concepts, and information, using strategies such as definition, classification, comparison/contrast, and cause/effect; include formatting (e.g., headings), graphics (e.g., charts, tables), and **multimedia** when useful to aiding comprehension.

Mind-mapping programs are an effective way for students to organize their ideas, concepts and information. Educators have used several wonderful mind-mapping software programs for many years. However, there are also free sites that do this. There are even templates, such as a Venn diagram that allows students to compare and contrast and show cause and effect. **Table 8.3** in the previous chapter shares some tools you can use to teach note-taking and categorizing.

Of course, creating your own Venn diagram and having students type in it from a word-processing program also works. You can create an online Venn diagram using the free web-based program **ReadWriteThink (readwritethink.org).**

In this standard, you are also asked to include charts, tables, and multimedia when aiding comprehension. Using programs like **Microsoft Excel (office.com), Apple Numbers (apple.com/numbers),** or **Google Sheets (google.com/sheets/about)** is a good way to teach charts and graphs. Additional charting and graphing tools are shared in **Table 8.4** in the previous chapter.

Writing Resources

W.7.6 • WRITING

Using technology, including the internet, to produce and publish writing and link to and cite sources as well as to interact and collaborate with others, including linking to and citing sources.

WHST.6–8.6 • WRITING HISTORY, SCIENCE, AND TECHNICAL SUBJECTS

Use technology, including the Internet, to produce and publish writing and present the relationships between information and ideas clearly and efficiently

Producing and publishing writing digitally is another standard seventh-graders are expected to meet. There are many websites that allow you to publish student writing. Using blogging websites such as **Edmodo (edmodo.com), Edublogs (edublogs.org),** and **Google Blogger (blogger.com)** lets you share student writing in a safe, protected environment and is a great way to interact and collaborate with others. These sites allow teachers to set themselves up as administrators and add students to various groups. All student writing is kept secure in these groups when set up properly.

You can give assignments asking for short answers where everyone can respond, or you can ask students to write longer assignments on their own. They can then work on assignments and submit privately to you or post them on the site to share. This is also a good way to interact and collaborate with others, either in school or at home. **Google Docs (google.com/docs/about)** is great for promoting collaboration, as it allows students to work on a document or presentation simultaneously at school or at home.

Many options exist thanks to resources that allow students to create and share their work. There are also sites that ask students to submit their work for possible publication. Other resources allow students to create shorter versions of their stories in an animated way. **Table 9.3** shares some of the possible websites and apps to use when teaching this standard.

Table 9.3: Publishing Resources

	Scholastic Publishing tinyurl.com/plwnn6f	This free website allows teachers to submit student writing for publication.
	PBS Kids Writer's Contest wtvp.org/writers-contest	This free site asks for student writing and serves as a nice incentive to get students to do their best.
	CAST UDL Book Builder **bookbuilder.cast.org)**	This free site lets you publish your ebook and see what others have published.
	Lulu Lulu.com **Lulu Junior** lulujr.com	These sites allow you to create real books and publish them online. Parents can purchase the books as keepsakes. The site is free to use, but a fee is required to publish.
	Poetry Idea Engine tiny.cc/0afs3y	This Scholastic site allows students to use templates to make different forms of poetry—another great way technology gets kids writing. Better still, it is free!
	Flipsnack flipsnackedu.com	This publishing tool is great for brochures, catalogs, and visual presentations. It is cross-platform and includes links, buttons, pictures, and has templates. Your work can be privately or publicly published on their website, embedded in a blog, emailed, or sent through social media. The limited version is free but can be upgraded for a price.

Seventh-graders will also need to cite their sources. Of course, making your own template and having the students fill it in using a word-processing program works, but there are some websites, such as **EasyBib (easybib.com), Citation Machine (citationmachine.net)**, and **StyleWizard (stylewizard.com)** that can be used as well. For more on these resources, see **Table 8.9** in the previous chapter.

Note-Taking Resources

W.7.8 | WRITING

and

WHST.6–8.8 • WRITING HISTORY, SCIENCE, AND TECHNICAL SUBJECTS

Gather relevant information from multiple print and **digital sources**, using search terms effectively; assess the credibility and accuracy of each source; and quote or paraphrase the data and conclusions of others while avoiding plagiarism and following a standard format for citation.

By the time students are in seventh grade, they should be able to search the internet independently to gather information on a given topic. Your class may need some reminders on effective searching, so lessons on internet searching are critical, as well as lessons on media literacy. Media literacy is especially crucial because students need to be able to critique a website before using it—anyone can put up a webpage. They will also need to be able to assess the credibility and accuracy of each source and quote or paraphrase the data and conclusions of others while avoiding plagiarism. We discuss these techniques in the following paragraphs.

Although students are net savvy these days, even seventh-graders still need assistance with the basics of searching. Various search engines work differently, and each will return different information. Therefore, your students need to know how to use multiple engines.

Smart searching will help students avoid wasting time. Teaching them to analyze search results will help them find better information and think more critically about any information they find on the internet. Following are some basic guidelines for students.

- Choose your search terms carefully. Be precise about what you are looking for, but use phrases and not full sentences.

- Adding more words can narrow a search. Use Boolean searches to narrow your topic with quotation marks. There's a big difference between "gopher" and "habitats of gophers in North America."

- Use synonyms! If students can't find what they're looking for, have them try keywords that mean the same thing or are related.

- Type "site:". Typing the word *site:* (with the colon) after your keyword and before a URL will tell many search engines to search within a specific website.

- Add a minus sign. Adding a minus sign (a hyphen) immediately before any word, with no space in between, indicates that you don't want that word to appear in your search results. For example, "Saturn-cars" will give you information about the planet, not the automobile.

Tried-and-true methods for paraphrasing and summarizing information from books can still be used to gather information and take notes on websites. Teaching students to use data sheets, note cards, and Know, What, Learn (KWL) techniques still works. However, technology can make this easier. The **Kentucky Virtual Library (kyvl.org)** is an excellent source for some of these techniques. **Evernote (evernote. com)** allows students to take notes and to import a worksheet, document, or picture (including a snapshot of a webpage) and annotate it using tools common to interactive whiteboard software. It lets them highlight words, cut and paste, and add sticky notes. The sticky notes are especially useful to summarize or paraphrase students' notes. Evernote also allows them to use voice recognition and send their annotated sheet to someone else (including the teacher).

Another way to take notes is using an "add-on" to your internet browser. The free add-on **Diigo (diigo.com)** is made for notetaking on documents, PDFs, and screenshots. Students can also save sites and documents as resources to take notes on later with annotations and highlighting.

Modeling is essential when teaching students how to glean information from a website. An interactive whiteboard is a perfect tool for modeling lessons. Don't have an interactive whiteboard? Use **Miro (realtimeboard.com).** It's a free website that allows you to turn an ordinary whiteboard into an interactive, virtual one. All you need is a computer and a projector! Using the many tools an interactive whiteboard and software have to offer will really help teach your students how to navigate information posted on the internet.

Seventh-graders will also need to provide basic bibliographic information and cite their sources. Of course, making your own template and having the students fill it in using a word-processing program works. However, there are some websites that can be used, such as EasyBib, Citation Machine, and StyleWizard.

Speaking and Listening Resources

SL.7.2 • SPEAKING AND LISTENING

Analyze the main ideas and supporting details presented in **diverse media and formats** (e.g., visually, quantitatively, and orally) and explain how the ideas clarify a topic, text, or issue under study.

SL.7.5 • SPEAKING AND LISTENING

Include **multimedia components and visual displays** in presentations to clarify claims and finding and emphasize salient points

Microsoft Powerpoint has been the presentation program of choice, but it can be expensive. There is now a free educational version called **Microsoft 365 (office.com)** that includes PowerPoint. While this is still a great program, other presentation tools are just as useful. Apple offers **Keynote (apple.com/keynote)** as part of its software package. Its features are very similar to PowerPoint's, but it does require a purchase. Another program that has emerged is **Google Slides (google.com/slides/about).** There are other resources that help with presentations, such as **Microsoft Paint 3D (tinyurl.com/zsfogge)** and **Google Drawings (tiny.cc/5gfs3y).** Although Office 365 is free to schools, Google Drive products such as Google Slides and Drawings are free and web-based. Google Slides makes it very easy to share a project that multiple users can work on at once, which it an especially good program to use when interacting and collaborating remotely. Students can also add audio recordings to their slides, as well as visual displays such as pictures and short video clips. Consider having your students use digital tools such as those listed below or in **Table 8.10** in the previous chapter.

Table 9.4: Speaking and Listening Resources

APPS & WEBSITES		
	Powtoon powtoon.com	This video-creating website is easy to use with ready-made templates and great content, such as music, objects, and photos. It is free for short (three minutes or less) videos, but you can upgrade for a price.
	Moovly moovly.com	This is a wonderful video-creation website for projects, portfolios, and presentations. It comes with access to the editor, unlimited videos, sounds, music, photos, and illustrations. You can even batch upload your own media. It is free for educators and their students.
	Adobe Spark tinyurl.com/yamq84lg	This free app from Adobe gives students and teachers a great way to make video presentations. Create a movie and narrate in your own voice. The app provides themes, photos, animations, and templates to organize the videos.
	Shmoop schools.shmoop.com	This site helps students build great videos for presentations and review. There are many templates included, and it uses the student's face and voice in the videos that range from ELA to math, science, social studies, test prep, and more. It can be costly for individual teachers, but school pricing is well worth it.

Language Resources

L.7.4c • LANGUAGE

Consult general and specialized reference materials (e.g., dictionaries, glossaries, thesauruses), both print and **digital**, to find the pronunciation of a word or determine or clarify its precise meaning or its part of speech.

Digital Dictionary and Thesaurus Websites

Although digital dictionaries and thesauruses are not updated as often as digital encyclopedias, they are still very convenient to use and are kept current. Bookmark sites such as **EasyBib (easybib.com)** and **Citation Machine (citationmachine.net)** or add them to your website for easy access. For more resources, see **Table 8.9** in the previous chapter. The more students use them, the more comfortable they will become. Offer lessons and activities to learn and practice the necessary skills with an online dictionary.

Math Resources

MP5 • MATH

Use appropriate **tools** strategically.

There are two main sets of standards for the Common Core math standards: processes and practices. First, you have the math targets, written similarly to ELA (Ratios and Proportional Relationships, The Number System, Expressions and Equations, Geometry, and Statistics and Probability). While you work with seventh-grade students on mathematical processes, such as Expressions and Equations or Geometry, you need to teach your students how to apply the SMPs (which include problem solving and precision) to those processes. One practice, the only one that includes technology, is mathematical practice 5: "Use appropriate tools strategically." Following is the explanation CCSS provides for **MP5.**

> Mathematically proficient students consider the available tools when solving a mathematical problem. These tools might include pencil and paper, concrete models, a ruler, a protractor, a calculator, **a spreadsheet, a computer algebra system, a statistical package, or dynamic geometry**

software. Proficient students are sufficiently familiar with tools appropriate for their grade or course to make sound decisions about when each of these tools might be helpful, recognizing both the insight to be gained and their limitations. For example, mathematically proficient high school students analyze graphs of functions and solutions generated using a **graphing calculator**. They detect possible errors by strategically using estimation and other mathematical knowledge. When making mathematical models, they know that technology can enable them to visualize the results of varying assumptions, explore consequences, and compare predictions with data. Mathematically proficient students at various grade levels are able to identify relevant external mathematical resources, such as **digital content located on a website**, and use them to pose or solve problems. They are able to use **technological tools** to explore and deepen their understanding of concepts.

Because this description does not give examples for all grades, we have listed appropriate apps, websites, software, and lessons that will help translate this standard for seventh grade.

Currently, this is the only seventh-grade math standard that involves technology. Because using any kind of technology to have students practice math can grab their attention, help long-term learning, and make math fun, technology is a math tool students should use as much as possible. Many math programs, websites, and apps allow students to explore and deepen their understanding of math concepts. The best of them have students learning in creative ways and are not merely electronic worksheets. They automatically adapt to the students' skill levels, and tell you where students are in their learning and what they need to advance. We list many good math resources here. Some are free. Some are not. The free resources (many with ads) are often less interesting and not as well organized. They don't give you the feedback you need. It is up to you to decide what is best for your circumstances and budget.

Table 9.5 includes some resources we recommend that you can use to enhance the seventh-grade math standards. Additional resources can be found in **Table 8.12** in the previous chapter.

Table 9.5: Math Resources

	AdaptedMind tinyurl.com/997geeg	This free website provides good practice for all sorts of seventh-grade mathematical problems.
	Coolmath Games coolmathgames.com	There are several sites that offer free games covering all math topics at each grade level. However, these sites have ads, are not able to track students' success rates, and are not generally self-adaptive to the students' skill levels.
	SoftSchools softschools. com	
	Sheppard Software tinyurl.com/ccrxoa	
	AAA Math aaamath.com	
	PBS Kids Cyberchase pbskids.org/cyberchase	
	National Library of Virtual Manipulatives tinyurl.com/b4qe7	This website has every imaginable math-related manipulation you might want, from geoboards to Pascal's Triangle and from pattern blocks to the Pythagorean Theorem. It is all free, but it uses Java.

	Explain Everything explaineverything.com	This app uses text, video, pictures, and voice to help students present a variety of possible creations. In seventh grade, students need to be able to explain their mathematical reasoning to others, and this app is particularly great for this standard. Students can make their own math videos, using this app to explain a concept. They can then record their voices to explain what they did.

As stated in the standard, "Mathematically proficient students consider the available tools when solving a mathematical problem. These tools might include a calculator, a spreadsheet, a computer algebra system, a statistical package, or dynamic geometry software. Proficient students are sufficiently familiar with tools appropriate for their grade or course to make sound decisions about when each of these tools might be helpful, recognizing both the insight to be gained and their limitations."

Many sites offer mathematical tools, such as a graphing calculator, or you can use software that comes with your interactive whiteboard—these have all sorts of mathematical tools, such as protractors, rulers, and grids. SoftSchools has an elementary-level graphing calculator, and IXL Math allows you to create your own graph paper, which you can then use with an interactive whiteboard, if you have one. Use Miro if you do not have an interactive whiteboard. Some good programs and sites to use when graphing include Gliffy, Create A Graph, and Classtools.

In seventh grade, students are also expected to use a protractor to measure angles. They can use the app Smart Protractor found on Google Play or Apple's App Store. It can be used just like a regular protractor and is a converter as well. **Softpedia (softpedia.com)** allows you to download a protractor to use online. The site is free, but it has ads. Using your interactive whiteboard protractor also works well.

Literacy Lessons

Cross-curriculum planning is encouraged with the CCSS by using ELA standards in history, science, and technical subjects. However, we encourage you to go further and include the arts, math, and physical education teachers in your planning. How will you ever get through everything if you teach standard by standard? The key to planning with the CCSS is to teach multiple standards in one lesson, when you can. We hope the following list of sample lessons for seventh grade will inspire you to become an effective technology lesson planner.

Project-Based Learning

At a local middle school, the ELA teacher, technology coach, and librarian collaborated on a project-based learning experience, connecting a literature unit (*Under the Persimmon Tree* by Suzanne Fisher Staples) with technology. Students created websites or documentary movies based on the essential question: How does conflict impact people and places? In class, the ELA teacher led students through the reading of the book, having them annotate places of conflict using Evernote. The librarian instructed students in research skills, including using print materials, evaluating online resources, selecting and searching databases, note-taking, organizing research, and citing sources. The technology coach helped students scan or find illustrations for their projects and also worked on webpage design, as well as how to make documentary movies. All teachers collaboratively coached students throughout the project, concentrating on how to write and answer essential questions. Students were introduced to several web-based tools that they could use during the research process (Evernote, Diigo, etc.) as well as tools for creating websites (Weebly, Wix, Webs, SiteBuilder, and even Shutterfly) and documentaries (iMovie, Animoto, Microsoft Photos, YouTube, etc.). You can have students share their creations with the class. Websites and documentary movies can be made available for parents to view. This project-based learning experience incorporates a multitude of standards. **RH.6-8.7** is satisfied, as students integrate visual information. **WHST.6-8.2a, W.7.2a, W.7.6,** and **WHST.6-8.6** are also met when students introduce and work their way through the essential question and produce and publish writing, as well as present their ideas clearly and efficiently. Standards **RI.7.7** and **W.7.8** are satisfied when students gather, integrate, and present their information in original ways. Using diverse media and formats (including music, graphics, voiceovers, etc.) to present and clarify information is definitely a part of this project, so **SL.7.2** and **SL.7.5** are fulfilled. Also satisfied is **L.7.4c,** using reference materials to help with writing.

ISTE STUDENT STANDARDS

Students will use these ISTE Standards in this lesson.

- **Empowered Learner** by understanding fundamental concepts of technology operations, demonstrating the ability to choose, use, and troubleshoot current technologies.

- **Digital Citizen** by acting and modeling technology ways that are safe, legal, and ethical.

- **Knowledge Constructor** by employing research, evaluating and building knowledge using digital resources.

- **Creative Communicator** with their presentations choosing the appropriate platform and publishing and presenting customized content.

Technology Collaboration

Another lesson from the files of our middle-school friends is a collaboration between the librarian and technology teacher. Picture students wandering the stacks of the library with handheld devices, smartphones, tablets, or any device with a QR reader, excitedly engaged, trying to find that special title they heard others discussing. That book with the code on the back that takes them to a book trailer . . . made by their best friend! This appealing project begins with pairs of students reflecting, planning, and creating a trailer for a book they recommend others read. Using iMovie to create the trailer, students get at the heart of the conflict and theme of the book in about a minute. A template for each theme helps students plan their words and images before creating their trailers. Next, completed projects are uploaded to the teacher's YouTube channel (the teacher, tech coach, or librarian helps with this step). Finished trailers are also shared with the librarian, who can create, print, and affix QR codes to the backs of titles. Books are returned to the stacks with their special codes. The rest is word of mouth! Students share their own projects while promoting books to read with the entire school. This creative and unique way to promote literacy and technology standards includes **RH.6-8.7,** as students must integrate visual information in their iMovie trailers. **WHST.6-8.2a, W.7.2a, W.7.6,** and **WHST.6-8.6** are also satisfied, as students reflect, plan, create, and publish their trailers, clearly and efficiently. **RI.7.7** and **W.7.8** are also met, as students are gathering, integrating, and presenting their information in original ways (iMovie trailers through QR codes). This project has students definitely using diverse media and formats (including music, graphics, voiceovers, etc.) to present and clarify information. Therefore, **SL.7.2** and **SL.7.5** are satisfied. Last, students are using reference materials to help with writing, so **L.7.4c** is also satisfied.

ISTE STUDENT STANDARDS

Students will use these ISTE Standards in this lesson.

- **Empowered Learner** by understanding fundamental concepts of technology operations, demonstrating the ability to choose, use, and troubleshoot current technologies.

- **Digital Citizen** by acting and modeling technology ways that are safe, legal, and ethical.

- **Knowledge Constructor** by employing research, evaluating and building knowledge using digital resources.

- **Creative Communicator** with their presentations choosing the appropriate platform and publishing and presenting customized content.

A Night at the Museum

The following lesson asks students to create a digital documentary about a person's life, which will motivate them to tell a compelling biographical story while, at the same time, practicing informational and expository writing. It is important to note that this lesson can be adapted in several ways and can be used in any grade, 6–12. The filmmaker Ken Burns has made digital biographies very popular; start this lesson with a discussion about why this is the case. YouTube has many snippets of Ken Burns' stories **(tinyurl.com/y89evjfb).** You may wish to show several to your class.

Also introduce your students to biographies by having them read several. There is a myriad of good biographies available. For example: Jerry Spinelli's *Knots in My Yo-Yo String: The Autobiography of a Kid* or *Jack London: A Biography* by Daniel Dyer. As they read biographies, help students understand how the reader gains insight into the subject's background and how personal experiences affect the tone and voice of the book.

Have students use **Simplenote (simplenote.com), Evernote (evernote.com),** or **Penzu (penzu.com)** to take online notes about the biographies they read and/or watch. This will be particularly helpful with your class discussions on factors that make good biographies. Remind them that a great biography is also a great story, and while a biography needs to include facts, a simple listing of them is not compelling for the reader or viewer. Have students brainstorm questions while they take notes.

- What makes a biography great?

- Did the person's background influence what he/she believed in or how the person acted?

- What personal qualities helped or hindered this person?

- Was this person admirable or simply famous?

Let your students know they will be researching a person, writing a biography, and transforming the biography into a digital documentary. You do not want any duplicates, so encourage students to come up with a variety of subjects. You may even want to encourage students to look within their family tree. For example, do they have a relative who fought in the Civil War? Perhaps a relative wrote a song? A book? Is there someone in the school or community who has an interesting story to tell? Brainstorm a list of people with your students. You might focus on presidents, people from your state, inventors, or authors. Let students know that they will be sharing their digital documentaries with family, friends, and peers. The culmination of this activity will be A Night at the Museum, where students will dress as their subject, present their documentaries, and answer questions by viewers.

There are many websites where your students can research their biographical subject, including:

- **Library of Congress (tinyurl.com/2knoku)**

- **Internet Archive (archive.org)**

- **Biography (biography.com)**

- **Time (time.com)**

- **Feedly (feedly.com)**

When students' research is complete, work through your biography writing process. Depending on your student's writing ability, you may want to give them an outline for what information should be included in each paragraph of the biography. There are many online outlines and templates from which to choose **(tinyurl.com/yaynd7lw).** You may wish to share with your students and have them complete this template on their tablets, prior to beginning their rough drafts.

When the first draft is complete, students work in small groups to edit and revise before moving on to final drafts. Before students begin their video work, you may wish to have them conference with you or present their biographies to the class and then make changes.

There are many presentation tools your students can choose from to make their documentaries. **Animoto (animoto.com)** or **iMovie (apple.com/ios/imovie)** are some of the more popular choices. Encourage your students to try some of the new presentation tools available: **Powtoon (powtoon.com), Moovly (moovly.com), Shmoop (schools.shmoop.com),** or **Adobe Spark (spark.adobe.com).** These are just a few examples. There are many presentation tools available. Some are free, while others do have a cost.

Once the biographical documentaries are finished, your students will need to think about their Night at the Museum presentation. They will need to dress up to resemble their biographical subjects. You may wish to have a dress rehearsal in your classroom, prior to presentation night. Encourage students to ask questions of the presenters, so they can practice this skill. Next, set up an evening for "A Night at the Museum" presentations. Encourage parents, siblings, other classmates, and community members to attend.

By comparing and contrasting a biographical book to a corresponding biographical video (e.g., read a biography on Jackie Robinson and watch Ken Burns' documentary), students satisfy **RL.7.7.** Encourage them to compare and contrast what they "see" and "hear" when reading the text to what they perceive when they watch and listen. **RI.7.7, RH.6-8.7, WHST.6-8.2a, W.7.2a,** as well as **RST.6-8.9** are also satisfied when students research and write about their subject. **W.7.6** and **WHST.6-8.6** are satisfied when students write, video their presentations, and present to others. You may even wish to publish their projects on your website, so those who cannot attend A Night at the Museum can view students' work. Students will need to gather their information prior to writing and creating videos. Taking notes is also a very important part of the writing process, thus satisfying **W.7.8.** and **WHST.6.8.8. SL.7.2** and **W.7.5** are satisfied by sharing their documentaries and listening and answering questions by teachers, classmates, parents, and so on. **L.7.4c** is satisfied in this lesson, especially when students are encouraged to use dictionaries, glossaries, and thesauruses.

ISTE STUDENT STANDARDS

Students will use these ISTE Standards in this lesson.

- **Empowered Learner** by understanding fundamental concepts of technology operations, demonstrating the ability to choose, use, and troubleshoot current technologies.

- **Digital Citizen** by acting and modeling technology ways that are safe, legal, and ethical.

- **Knowledge Constructor** by employing research, evaluating, and building knowledge using digital resources.

- **Creative Communicator** with their presentations choosing the appropriate platform and publishing and presenting customized content.

Social Studies/Science Lessons

The following sample lessons address CCSS ELA standards and teach lessons based on national standards in social studies and science.

Human Body

Students at this level across the country study the human body. After teaching all of the body systems, our colleagues were looking not only for a unique way for students to show what they learned about a specific human body system, but also an interesting way for them to present to the class. In this lesson, after all teaching and learning is complete, students pick which of the eleven systems they wish to present to the class. Using the app Explain Everything, students draw, appropriately color, and label the entire system. Using their notes, as well as any additional research they find, students record a narration of how their system works. Next, students present their systems to the class by projecting the tablet onto the interactive whiteboard with the Explain Everything app. Each student listens carefully to each presentation and asks questions at the end. Students presenting must be able to answer the questions quickly and efficiently. Researching and reading about the human body satisfies standard **RI.7.7. Standards W.7.2, W.7.6,** and **W.7.8** also are addressed with this activity. In addition, the presentation part of this activity satisfies **SL.7.2** and **SL.7.5.**

ISTE STUDENT STANDARDS

Students will use these ISTE Standards in this lesson.

- **Empowered Learner** by understanding fundamental concepts of technology operations, demonstrating the ability to choose, use, and troubleshoot current technologies.

- **Digital Citizen** by acting and modeling technology ways that are safe, legal, and ethical.

- **Knowledge Constructor** by employing research, evaluating and building knowledge using digital resources.

- **Creative Communicator** with their presentations choosing the appropriate platform and publishing and presenting customized content.

Antiques Roadshow

Yet another lesson from our middle school friends involves the seventh-grade social studies unit on medieval China and Japan during the time when traveling minstrels entertained with their stories. This project was designed so students become modern-day storytellers and animators of historical tales. Students start out reading *Beowulf, Adam of the Road, Sign of the Chrysanthemum,* or any other book of your choosing that covers the time period. Every year, this school traditionally has an author visit. (Coincidentally, the visit was scheduled before this project began. The author stressed to the students how important it is to keep your audience in mind at all times, as well as to research and really know your topic.) Using primary sources, students research the culture of medieval China or Japan through an ancient art piece. Based on that research, students write an "Antiques Roadshow" script, using Microsoft Office, Google, or any word-processing program of your choosing. Next, students create a replica of the art (Microsoft Photos, Google Drawings, or any other drawing tool will work). Finally, students are required to video their "Antiques Roadshow" performance (iMovie, Animoto, Movavi, YouTube, etc.). Blabberize, iFunFace, Voki, or Fotobabble are also sites students can use for avatars or animation. Remind students that their presentations need to be in costumes and scenery that is correct for the time period. You may want to give students a graphic organizer to keep them on track, outlining goals and objectives. Have students share their creations with the class. Finished projects can also be made available for parents to view. This project-based learning experience incorporates many standards. **RH.6-8.7** is satisfied, as students integrate visual information. **WHST.6- 8.2a, W.7.2a, W.7.6,** and **WHST.6-8.6** are also met when students introduce, produce, and publish writing, as well as work together to present their ideas clearly and efficiently. **RI.7.7** and **W.7.8** are also satisfied when students gather, integrate, and present their information in original ways. Using diverse media and formats (including music, graphics, voiceovers, etc.) to present and clarify information is definitely a part of this project, so **SL.7.2** and **SL.7.5** are fulfilled. Standard **L.7.4c,** using reference materials to help with writing, is also satisfied.

ISTE STUDENT STANDARDS

Students will use these ISTE Standards in this lesson.

- **Empowered Learner** by understanding fundamental concepts of technology operations, demonstrating the ability to choose, use, and troubleshoot current technologies.

- **Digital Citizen** by acting and modeling technology ways that are safe, legal, and ethical.

- **Knowledge Constructor** by employing research, evaluating and building knowledge using digital resources.

- **Creative Communicator** with their presentations choosing the appropriate platform and publishing and presenting customized content.

Technology has been extremely important to my success in school. We have our own Chromebooks to do research, write papers, and take tests/ quizzes on Google Classroom. Also, we have Smart Boards to write on, select answers, and solve equations. Overall, technology has made me a better student. Almost everything at school revolves around technology, and I am very grateful for it. **—Jacob Szabo, student**

Math Lessons

The following two sample lessons satisfy the math practice standard **MP5.**

Los Angeles Trip

A local seventh-grade class in our former district had great fun with this math WebQuest, which they adapted from a Kansas middle school WebQuest. Make your own, or do a Google Search for math WebQuests to see what is out there! Students plan a five-day trip to Los Angeles, calculating costs and the things that they will do.

After students complete this activity, they will have a good idea of all of the different entertainment and sites to see in Los Angeles, as well as the costs of such experiences. Upon completion, students will share their itinerary with the class, explaining how they decided what to do, and what not to do. Students will work with a partner, thus satisfying **W.7.6.**

Partners decide which section of websites to take, deciding what part (or all) to include in the vacation. For the theater section, students need to include show times that work in the vacation schedule and ticket prices of each show for the number of people who will attend. Also, students researching the theater section of the vacation will need to read about each show and write a two-to-three-sentence summary describing what it is about. This review of each show should be included in the final presentation.

Another partner decides what sights to see, and when. Students with this job review each website to find times of tours and other pertinent information, and decide what time works best. They keep track of the ticket prices for each person who will be attending. They write a two-or-three-sentence summary of each place, which must be included in the final presentation to the class.

Partners decide where to eat. Students can assume that their hotel will provide a free breakfast, but they must plan to eat out for other meals. When considering restaurants, students should compare pricing and decide when to visit each restaurant. Also, students must identify a typical price for dinner at the restaurants, including dessert. If students are going to a show after dinner, special attention must be given to the timing of the meal.

Finally, students will need to decide on the most important part of the trip: where to stay. Partners should research hotels in the Los Angeles area and find the one that best meets the needs of their group. They should be reminded not to choose the first one, but instead compare pricing and keep track of how much the hotel will cost per night. Remind students not to sign up or provide any information on any site. Most sites offer free searches.

For suggested links to theaters, sights to see, restaurants, and lodging in Los Angeles, as well as other resources for this activity, see our website **(tinyurl.com/y9dfltpr).**

When students finish their research, they share their findings with their partner and discuss their best options. Partners should decide together which places and activities they will visit based on the information they found, and they should have a rationale for their choices. Narrow options if necessary. Allow students time to adjust their schedules, change plans, and perhaps even do more research. Once selections have been made and times of events scheduled, partners will need to put the itinerary and presentation together using Prezi, PowerPoint, or another presentation app. Finally, students present their findings to the class, as well as field any questions and/or suggestions from their classmates and defend their choices. Presentations can also be made available to parents using some of the sites mentioned earlier. The rubric found in our website **(tinyurl.com/y9dfltpr)** is a helpful way to evaluate the quality of your students' work. Our website also has additional resources for this activity.

This project-based learning experience incorporates a myriad of standards. **MP.5** and **RH.6-8.7** are satisfied as students integrate visual information into their presentations (graphics and even music). **WHST.6-8.2a, W.7.2a, W.7.6,** and **WHST.6-8.6** are also addressed when students introduce, produce, and publish writing, as well as work together to present their ideas clearly and efficiently. Standards **RI.7.7** and **W.7.8** are also satisfied when students gather, integrate, and present their information in original ways. Using diverse media and formats (including music, graphics, voiceovers, etc.) to present and clarify information is definitely a part of this project, so **SL.7.2** and **SL.7.5** are fulfilled. And **L.7.4c** is also satisfied when students use reference materials to help with writing.

ISTE STUDENT STANDARDS

Students will use these ISTE Standards in this lesson.

- **Empowered Learner** by understanding fundamental concepts of technology operations, demonstrating the ability to choose, use, and troubleshoot current technologies.

- **Digital Citizen** by acting and modeling technology ways that are safe, legal, and ethical.

- **Knowledge Constructor** by employing research, evaluating and building knowledge using digital resources.

- **Innovative Designer** students use a variety of technologies within a process to identify and solve problems by creating new, useful, or imaginative solutions.

- **Creative Communicator** students use their presentations choosing the appropriate platform and publishing and presenting customized content.

- **Global Collaborator** students use collaborative technologies to work with peers to examine solutions to a problem from multiple viewpoints.

Math Review

This math lesson, again from the files of one of our middle school friends, is used as a review at the end of a semester, but you can use it to review at the end of any unit. On the whiteboard, the teacher and students make a list of all the concepts and skills studied throughout the semester. In pairs or groups of three (depending how many total), students pick a topic they want to "be an expert" on. Teams pick the technology method they prefer to present their topic (see our suggestions earlier in **SL.7.2** and **SL.7.5,** or ask students to brainstorm with you): by making a presentation (Prezi), movie (iMovie), creating Trading Cards, or using Explain Everything. When teams finish their presentations, have them project the presentations and "teach" the class. Since this could potentially occur before a final assessment, have students take notes for studying, using Evernote, Diigo, or Explain Everything (which can be written and voice recorded), and so on. Teams present and project (RealtimeBoard) to the class, making sure they save time for answering any questions, as they are "the experts" on the math topic. These review presentations can then be uploaded to YouTube or shared in any other way with absent students and/ or parents! They can be used to review later, or they could be great for "flipping the classroom" use. In addition to **MP5,** standard **RH.6-8.7** is satisfied, as students should be encouraged to include visual information into their presentations (graphics and even music). Students are introducing, producing, and publishing writing, as well as working together to present their ideas clearly and efficiently, so **WHST.6-8.2a, W.7.2a, W.7.6,** and **WHST.6-8.6** are also met. **RI.7.7** and **W.7.8** are also satisfied when students gather, integrate, and present their information in an original way. Using diverse media and formats (including music, graphics, voiceovers, etc.) to present and clarify information is definitely a part of this project, so **SL.7.2** and **SL.7.5** are also fulfilled.

ISTE STUDENT STANDARDS

Students will use these ISTE Standards in this lesson.

- **Empowered Learner** by understanding fundamental concepts of technology operations, demonstrating the ability to choose, use, and troubleshoot current technologies.

- **Digital Citizen** by acting and modeling technology ways that are safe, legal, and ethical.

- **Knowledge Constructor** by employing research, evaluating and building knowledge using digital resources.

- **Innovative Designer** students use a variety of technologies within a process to identify and solve problems by creating new, useful, or imaginative solutions.

- **Computational Thinker** students develop and use strategies for understanding and solving problems in ways that use technology to develop and test solutions.

- **Creative Communicator** students use their presentations choosing the appropriate platform and publishing and presenting customized content.

- **Global Collaborator** students use collaborative technologies to work with peers to examine solutions to a problem from multiple viewpoints.

My Own Home

Students will be able to create hand-drawn and digital forms of homes they design themselves using area and perimeter formulas. This is perfect for the seventh-grade geometry unit because not only does it satisfy **MP5,** it also demonstrates students' knowledge of drawing to scale, drawing freehand, and drawing digitally as called for in the math standards. It also allows students to show knowledge of area and perimeter and solve real-world problems involving area, surface area, and volume of two- and three-dimensional objects.

First have students brainstorm, with a partner, when they will use area and perimeter in the real world. Have a brief, whole-class discussion and introduce architecture (if not mentioned by a student). Show examples of blueprints to the students. You can search on line and find an unlimited number of blueprints (Google "house plans" select subtopic images). Allow five-to-ten minutes for students to examine and discuss what they see, think, and wonder about the blueprints. Draw students' attention toward the area and perimeter of the blueprint.

Next, have students (as individuals, pairs, or teams) use Evernote or Diigo for note-taking and to find additional resources and ideas. They need to keep these organized for a final presentation. They may need to use an online dictionary (Merriam-Webster, Word Central, or Wordsmyth), for the vocabulary with which they are unfamiliar. This satisfies **L7.4c**.

Students should make a list of what they want in their homes. You can require certain rooms (kitchen, bathroom, bedroom) and features (garage, patio, closets). They should hand-draw what they might want in a one-story home of their own. Put some limits on the house, such as a maximum square footage for the house or lot.

Students create their own blueprints using 1 cm grid paper **(tinyurl.com/zqempyd),** with 1 centimeter = 1 foot. Students must record the area and perimeter of each room in a spreadsheet such as Google Sheets, Excel, or Numbers. Once they are finished with the house, they must find its total area and perimeter. Students can be challenged or required to add round rooms and diagonal walls, creating quadrilaterals, polygons, and any other geometric figures you want to stress.

Then students create a digital form of their homes using **homestyler.com, floorplan-creator.net,** or another house-planning website of your choice. Once on the website, they should click on the floor planner. Students can drag-and-drop rooms onto the plan to create the floor plan. Both websites allow you to experiment with windows, doors, furniture, and appliances to create a realistic version of a house. All of the directions are clearly stated on the websites, making the programs very practical and user-friendly.

Have students use their hand-drawing to replicate their dream home digitally. To increase difficulty, you can ask students to reproduce the scale drawing at a different scale, satisfying another math standard **[AU: add specific standard here?]**in seventh-grade geometry. Students must manipulate the rooms to create the same area and perimeter as their hand-drawing. Although this is not a standard, this provides a creative opportunity for students to learn a new form of technology and have an experience as an architect.

When students have completed their homes, they will need to create a digital report or slideshow using an application such as PowerPoint, Keynote, or Google Slides, that includes their drawings, data, and cites resources they used (including the blueprint website), a written summary of the home's features, and how they came to choose those features. They also should share their report with another team or individual, allowing time for their audience to look more deeply at the other person or teams plans. The other team/individual can check their math data for accuracy.

SL.7.2 and **SL.7.5** are satisfied as students are sharing their work using technology. In addition to **MP5,** standards **W.7.2a, W.7.6, W.7.8, WHST.6-8.6,** and **WHST.6-8.2a** are covered if word processing and note-taking through apps are used, as students not only need to use their math, but also to write coherent reports.

ISTE STUDENT STANDARDS

Students will use these ISTE Standards in this lesson.

- **Empowered Learner** by understanding fundamental concepts of technology operations, demonstrating the ability to choose, use, and troubleshoot current technologies.

- **Digital Citizen** by acting and modeling technology ways that are safe, legal, and ethical.

- **Knowledge Constructor** by employing research, evaluating and building knowledge using digital resources.

- **Innovative Designer** students use a variety of technologies within a process to identify and solve problems by creating new, useful, or imaginative solutions.

- **Computational Thinker** students develop and use strategies for understanding and solving problems in ways that use technology to develop and test solutions.

- **Creative Communicator** students use their presentations choosing the appropriate platform and publishing and presenting customized content.

- **Global Collaborator** students use collaborative technologies to work with peers to examine solutions to a problem from multiple viewpoints.

A Final Note

As students progress through the grades, they establish their baseline of proficiency in technology. This will definitely enhance their experiences with technology in high school, as well as satisfy the CCSS performance standards at the 6–8 levels. We hope you find the resources and lesson ideas presented in this chapter useful and that they are easy to adapt to your class.

You will find more resources on our website **(tinyurl.com/y9dfltpr),** which may be helpful as you look to differentiate your instruction. Visit our website for updated information about this book. To learn more about meeting technology standards found within the CCSS for other grades, look for our additional title in this series.

CHAPTER 10

Practical Ideas for Eighth Grade

We realize that you will want to focus on your particular grade or subject when you are planning your lessons and implementing the standards, so we have organized the Practical Ideas chapters by grade level and subject. Each grade starts with an overview followed by ELA technology standards with accompanying apps, software, and websites that you can use to help your students succeed with that standard. We then continue with the math standard for the grade level and review appropriate resources. Finally, we have included sample lessons for each grade level in various subject areas. Although we have organized the book so you can find your specific grade and subject easily, please do not disregard other sections of this chapter. It is often helpful to see what the standards require before and after the grade you teach. To see grades other than 6–12, look for our other title in this series, as it could provide information to help you differentiate for students at all levels of your class.

The CCSS have been set up to encourage cross-curricular work in ELA for Grades 6–12. Many of the same standards are used throughout the seven grade levels, making it imperative for all levels of teachers to work closely together to make sure that a spiral effect takes place. Many schools have block planning so teachers of the same grade level can plan together. However, when teachers from multiple grade levels need to plan together, you may need to get creative to find time that works for everyone. Discuss with your administrators how to schedule this time. These meetings will help ensure that the technology standards embedded in language arts, reading, and writing are addressed without overlapping across classes. Some suggestions are to meet during school or district professional planning days, during the summer (many districts pay for curriculum and unit writing during the summer), during staff meetings, or better yet, during scheduled times your school builds into the schedule at the beginning of the year.

Math is also a subject area where technological tools become more varied and complex as students advance. The math standards are meant to be embedded in, and a natural part of, the units your students study. Choosing the correct math tools is an important part of your students' learning. There are wonderful new math resources available to help students become proficient in the standards, especially in the area of technology. We list some of our favorites later in this chapter.

We have pulled out the eighth-grade standards that include technology and listed them in this chapter so you have them at your fingertips. Eighth-graders are expected to use technology to enhance their literacy skills, such as analyzing the extent to which a filmed or live production of a story or drama stays faithful to, or departs from, the text or script. They will be required to use digital texts and multimedia to help with reading comprehension, and be able to organize information. Writing is also important; they must use the internet to find sources of information, and then use publishing resources to share their work in and out of the classroom. An emphasis on finding needed information quickly and efficiently, evaluating these sources, taking notes, documenting, linking and citing sources, and presenting their findings in a multimedia presentation, is expected. Using tools such as digital dictionaries and thesauruses, as well as read-along texts, is also emphasized. Technology should be used to practice math skills, and students will need to use digital mathematical tools, which are available through software programs, apps, or websites.

Reading Literature Resources

RL.8.7 • READING LITERATURE

Analyze the extent to which a **filmed** or live production of a story or drama stays faithful to or departs from the text or script, evaluating the choices made by the director or actors.

This is a fun and creative standard! Many classic stories have been turned into movies or live productions. Shakespeare is, of course, the most popular. Most of his plays are still performed around the world and have been turned into countless film productions. Jane Austen is another classic author whose books have been turned into films. *Little Women* by Louisa May Alcott has been made into several films. The list goes on: *Black Beauty* (directed by Caroline Thompson), *Robinson Crusoe* (directed Rodney Hardy and George Miller), *The Lord of the Rings* (directed by Peter Jackson), *The Chronicles of Narnia* (directed by Andrew Adamson), Disney classics *Where the Red Fern Grows* (directed by Lyman Dayton and Sam Pillsbury) and *Old Yeller* (directed by Robert Stevenson), *The Great Gatsby* (directed by Jack Clayton), *Of Mice and Men* (directed by Gary Sinise), *Jane Eyre* (directed by Franco Zeffirelli), *The Scarlet Letter* (directed by Roland Joffé), and *12 Years a Slave* (directed by Steve McQueen). You can find these books-turned-movies simply by using a search engine. Many of these movies can be found at your local library, downloaded from a movie site such as Netflix, or purchased at places such as Amazon. You can use prerecorded "live" productions if going to the theater is not an option. The standard requires that these films are compared to their original stories or dramas and that students evaluate the choices made by the directors or actors. This can be done the old-fashioned way by using paper and pencil or a word processor. Or, your students can get creative and make their own videos of these comparisons using practically any electronic device, and even do some acting of their favorite parts to be made into a short clip using movie-making software that we recommend below.

Informational Text Resources

RI.8.7 • READING INFORMATIONAL TEXT

Evaluate the advantages and disadvantages of using **different mediums** (e.g., print or **digital text, video, multimedia**) to present a particular topic or idea.

This standard begins in kindergarten with comparing illustrations and text and is developed through the grades using all types of media to compare, support, and analyze a story's meaning. So, the standard is essentially to get meaning from more than the text; it can come from the accompanying media, even the format of the story.

Traditionally Microsoft PowerPoint has been the presentation program of choice, but it can be expensive. There is now a free educational version called **Microsoft 365 (office.com)** that includes PowerPoint. While this is still a great program, other presentation tools are just as useful. Apple offers **Keynote (apple.com/keynote)** as part of its software package. Its features are very similar to PowerPoint's, but it does require a purchase. Another program that has emerged is **Google Slides (google.com/slides/about).** The best thing about it is, it is free and web-based. It is also very easy to share, and multiple users can work on it at once, which makes it an especially good program to use when interacting and collaborating with others. Students can add audio recordings to slides as well as visual displays, such as pictures and short video clips. Creating multimedia presentations and presenting them to the class allows students to analyze how visual and multimedia elements contribute to the meaning, tone, or beauty of a text. Tools and resources for teaching this standard can be found in the previous chapter in **Table 9.5** and **Table 9.6**. Following are a few additional presentation tools we recommend for this standard.

 BaiBoard (baiboard.com): This whiteboard app allows students to create, collaborate, and share—and it's free. The difference between this and other whiteboard apps is that multiple students can have real-time access to one project and collaborate.

 PBS LearningMedia (pbslearningmedia.org): This site is a great source for classroom-ready, free digital resources at all grades and in all subjects.

Reading History Resources

RH.6-8.7 • READING HISTORY

Integrate **visual information** (e.g., in charts, graphs, **photographs, videos**, or maps) with other information in print and **digital texts**.

A multimedia story is some combination of text, still photographs, video clips, audio, graphics, and interactivity presented on a website in a nonlinear format. The information in each medium is complementary, not redundant. They allow the integration of visual information and information in print and digital texts. Examples of these sites can be found in the previous chapter in **Table 9.1**.

Your students can produce multimedia sites as well. Creating personal websites is a wonderful way to fulfill this standard. You can find many programs that allow you to create professional-looking webpages free. **Table 9.1** in the previous chapter shares many resources.

Technical Reading Resources

RST.6-8.9 • READING HISTORY

Compare and contrast the information gained from experiments, **simulations, video,** or **multimedia sources** with that gained from reading a text on the same topic.

There are so many places where you can go to get videos on a variety of educational topics. A sampling is given in **Table 9.3** in the previous chapter. Anyone and everyone puts up videos, so it's up to you to sift through them to find information from reliable sources.

Writing Resources

W.8.2a • WRITING

Introduce a topic clearly, previewing what is to follow; organize ideas, concepts, and information into broader categories; include formatting (e.g., headings), graphics (e.g., charts, tables), and **multimedia when useful** to aiding comprehension.

W.8.6 • WRITING

Use technology, including the Internet, to produce and publish writing and present the relationships between information and ideas efficiently as well as to interact and collaborate with others.

WHST.6-8.2a • WRITING HISTORY, SCIENCE, AND TECHNICAL SUBJECTS

Introduce a topic clearly, previewing what is to follow; organize ideas, concepts, and information into broader categories as appropriate to achieving purpose;

include formatting (e.g., headings), graphics (e.g., charts, tables), and **multimedia when useful** to aiding comprehension.

WHST.6-8.6 • WRITING HISTORY, SCIENCE, AND TECHNICAL SUBJECTS

Use technology, including the Internet, to produce and publish writing and present the relationships between information and ideas clearly and efficiently.

WHST.6-8.8 • WRITING HISTORY, SCIENCE, AND TECHNICAL SUBJECTS

Gather relevant information from multiple print and **digital sources**, using search terms effectively; assess the credibility and accuracy of each source; and quote or paraphrase the data and conclusions of others while avoiding plagiarism and follow a standard format for citation.

By the time students are in eighth grade, they should be able to search the internet independently to gather information on a given topic. Your class may need some reminders on effective searching, so lessons on internet searching are critical, as well as lessons on media literacy. Media literacy is especially crucial because students need to be able to critique a website before using it—anyone can put up a webpage. They will also need to be able to assess the credibility and accuracy of each source and quote or paraphrase the data and conclusions of others while avoiding plagiarism. We discuss these techniques in the following paragraphs.

Although students are net-savvy these days, and have done a lot of searching in previous grades, eighth-graders still need assistance with the basics of searching. Various search engines work differently, and each will return different information. Therefore, your students need to know how to use multiple engines.

Smart searching will help students avoid wasting time. Teaching them to analyze search results will help them find better information and think more critically about any information they find on the internet. Following are some basic guidelines for students.

- Choose your search terms carefully. Be precise about what you are looking for, but use phrases and not full sentences.

- Adding more words can narrow a search. Use Boolean searches to narrow your topic with quotation marks. There's a big difference between "gopher" and "habitats of gophers in North America."

- Use synonyms! If students can't find what they're looking for, have them try keywords that mean the same thing or are related.

- Type "site:". Typing the word *site:* (with the colon) after your keyword and before a URL will tell many search engines to search within a specific website.

- Add a minus sign. Adding a minus sign (a hyphen) immediately before any word, with no space in between, indicates that you don't want that word to appear in your search results. For example, "Saturn-cars" will give you information about the planet, not the automobile.

Tried-and-true methods for paraphrasing and summarizing information from books can still be used to gather information and take notes on websites. Teaching students to use data sheets, note cards, and Know, What, Learn (KWL) techniques still works. However, technology can make this easier. The **Kentucky Virtual Library (kyvl.org)** is an excellent resource for some of these techniques. **Evernote (evernote.com)** allows students to take notes and to import a worksheet, document, or picture (including a snapshot of a webpage) and annotate it using tools common to interactive whiteboard software. It lets them highlight words, cut and paste, and add sticky notes. The sticky notes are especially useful to summarize or paraphrase students' notes. Evernote also allows them to use voice recognition and send their annotated sheet to someone else (including the teacher).

Another way to take notes is using the "add-on" to your internet browser. The free add-on **Diigo (diigo.com)** is made for note-taking on documents, PDFs, and screenshots. Students can also save sites and documents as resources to take notes on later with annotations and highlighting.

Modeling is essential when teaching students how to glean information from a website. An interactive whiteboard is a perfect tool for modeling lessons. Don't have an interactive whiteboard? Use **Miro (realtimeboard.com).** It's a free website that allows you to turn an ordinary whiteboard into an interactive, virtual one. All you need is a computer and a projector! Using the many tools an interactive whiteboard and software have to offer will really help teach your students how to navigate information posted on the internet.

Using mind-mapping tools when gathering information will help your students organize their research. Information gathering tools are shared in Table 9.3 in the previous chapter.

Of course, students can also use word-processing software programs, such as **Microsoft Office (office.com), Apple Pages (apple.com/pages),** or **Google Docs (google.com/docs/about).** Some teachers make digital templates, with spaces to summarize or paraphrase, to help students find specific information and organize their notes.

Eighth-graders will also need to provide basic bibliographic information for sources. Making your own template and having the students fill it in using a word-processing program works. However, there are websites that are designed to do this, such as **EasyBib (easybib.com), Citation Machine (citationmachine.net)**, and **StyleWizard (stylewizard.com).**

Producing and publishing writing digitally is another standard eighth-graders are expected to meet. There are many websites that allow you to publish student writing. Using blogging websites such as **Edmodo (edmodo.com), Edublogs (edublogs.org),** and **Google Blogger (blogger.com)** lets you share student writing in a safe, protected environment and is an excellent way for students to interact and collaborate with others. These sites allow teachers to set themselves up as administrators and add students to various groups. All student writing is kept secure in these groups when set up properly.

You can give assignments asking for short answers where everyone can respond, or you can ask students to write longer assignments on their own. They can then work on assignments and submit privately to you, or post them on the site to share.

Table 9.4 in the previous chapter shares publishing resources for students.

Animation allows students to create shorter versions of their stories in an animated way. For animation resources, see **Table 9.4** in the previous chapter. These are not conducive to stories in paragraph form. However, you can use your voice to speak the text and photos can be used to illustrate in an animated format.

Speaking and Listening Resources

SL.8.2 • SPEAKING AND LISTENING

Analyze the purpose of information presented in **diverse media and formats** (e.g., visually, quantitatively, orally) and evaluate the motives (e.g., social, commercial, political) behind its presentation

SL.8.5 • SPEAKING AND LISTENING

Integrate **multimedia and visual displays** into presentations to clarify information, strengthen claims and evidence, and add interest.

Microsoft powerpoint is often the presentation program of choice, but it can be expensive. There is now online free educational version called **Microsoft Office 365 (tinyurl.com/zsfogge)** that includes PowerPoint. While this is still a great program, other presentation tools are just as useful. Apple offers **Keynote (apple.com/keynote)** as part of its software package. Its features are very similar to PowerPoint's, but it does require a purchase. Another program that has emerged is **Google Slides (google.com/slides/about).** There are other resources that help with presentations, such as **Microsoft Paint 3D (tinyurl.com/zsfogge)** and **Google Drawings (tiny. cc/5gfs3y).** Although Office 365 is free to schools, Google Drive products such as Slides and Drawings are free and web-based. Google Slides makes it very easy to share a project that multiple users can work on at once, which makes it an especially good program to use when interacting and collaborating remotely. Students can also add audio recordings to their slides, as well as visual displays such as pictures and short video clips. Consider having your students use the following digital tools to develop their speaking and listening skills.

Movie and slideshow apps and websites are listed in Table 9.5 in the previous chapter. Another useful resource is **WebQuest (webquest.org):** Webquests are good tools to use for presentations. The WebQuest site allows students to follow an already-created, project-based lesson where information is found solely on the internet. Students can create their own WebQuest if a website-building program or a website such as **SiteBuilder (sitebuilder.com)** is available. WebQuest.org is the original and most popular site, but if you search the internet, you will find more sites that you can use.

Language Resources

L.8.4c • LANGUAGE

Consult general and specialized reference materials (e.g., dictionaries, glossaries, thesauruses), both print and **digital**, to find the pronunciation of a word or determine or clarify its precise meaning or its part of speech.

Digital Dictionary and Thesaurus Websites

Although digital dictionaries and thesauruses are not updated as often as digital encyclopedias, they are still very convenient to use and are kept current. Bookmark these sites or add them to your website for easy access. The more students use them, the more comfortable they will become. Offer lessons and activities to learn and practice the necessary skills with an online dictionary.

Table 10.1: Dictionary and Thesaurus Tools

Merriam-Webster merriam-webster.com	This is a free digital dictionary for all ages. It is the most commonly used digital dictionary, and it includes a thesaurus.
Wordsmyth wordsmyth.net	This site shows three levels of a student dictionary. When looking up a word, you also see links to a thesaurus and rhyming dictionary for that word. You can sign up for an ad-free version that will not cost your school.
Word Central wordcentral.com	This student online dictionary includes an audio pronunciation of the word as well as the definition. There are many teacher resources.
Thesaurus.com thesaurus.com	This is a fine thesaurus site with many extra features. It does have some ads, but it is available free online and as an app

WEBSITES

The **Trading Cards (tinyurl.com/8lqftek)** app or website is a good way to document vocabulary words by adding definitions, a picture, and recordings of voices for pronunciation. You can also use Trading Cards by doing an activity with an online thesaurus. Simply give students a word on a trading card and ask them to make as many trading cards as they can of synonyms and antonyms of that word. Students can print these out and trade them with others or make them into digital books. The Explain Everything **(explaineverything.com)** app is also easy to use to import a picture, record your voice, and make a digital presentation.

Math Resources

MP5 • MATH

Use appropriate **tools** strategically.

There are two main sets of standards for the Common Core math standards: processes and practices. First, you have the math targets, written similarly to ELA (Ratios and Proportional Relationships, The Number System, Expressions and Equations, Functions, Geometry, and Statistics and Probability). While you work with eighth-grade students on mathematical processes, such as Expressions and Equations or Geometry, you need to teach your students how to apply the SMPs (which include problem solving and precision) to those processes. One practice, the only one that includes technology, is mathematical practice 5: "Use appropriate tools strategically." Following is the explanation CCSS provides for **MP5.**

Mathematically proficient students consider the available tools when solving a mathematical problem. These tools might include pencil and paper, concrete models, a ruler, a protractor, a calculator, **a spreadsheet, a computer algebra system, a statistical package, or dynamic geometry software**. Proficient students are sufficiently familiar with tools appropriate for their grade or course to make sound decisions about when each of these tools might be helpful, recognizing both the insight to be gained and their limitations. For example, mathematically proficient high school students analyze graphs of functions and solutions generated using a **graphing calculator**. They detect possible errors by strategically using estimation and other mathematical knowledge. When making mathematical models, they know that technology can enable them to visualize the results of varying assumptions, explore consequences, and compare predictions with data. Mathematically proficient students at various grade levels are able to identify relevant external mathematical resources, such as **digital content located on a website**, and use them to pose or solve problems. They are able to use **technological tools** to explore and deepen their understanding of concepts.

Because this description does not give examples for all grades, we have listed appropriate apps, websites, software, and lessons that will help translate this standard for eighth grade.

Currently, this is the only eighth-grade math standard that involves technology. Because using any kind of technology to have students practice math can grab their attention, help long-term learning, and make math fun, technology is a math tool students should use as much as possible. Many math programs, websites, and apps allow students to explore and deepen their understanding of math concepts. The best of them have students learning in creative ways and are not merely electronic worksheets. They automatically adapt to the students' skill levels and tell you where students are in their learning and what they need to advance. We list many good math resources in **Table 10.2.** Some are free. Some are not. The free resources (many with ads) are often less interesting and not as well organized. They don't give you the feedback you need. It is up to you to decide what is best for your circumstances and budget.

Table 10.2: Math Resources

APPS & WEBSITES		
	Virtual Nerd virtualnerd.com	This is a free website with well-made videos on math subjects through Algebra 2 that you can use for instruction or to flip the classroom.
	Khan Academy khanacademy.org	This free website has every math application you can think of, and it has short video tutorials on how to solve problems. The site includes feedback and many resources.
	IXL Math ixl.com/math	This site features adaptive, individualized math through gameplay, including data and graphing problems. It gives students immediate feedback and covers many skills, despite its emphasis on drills. Levels range from prekindergarten to Grade 8. There is a limited free version.

National Library of Virtual Manipulatives
tinyurl.com/b4qe7

This website has every imaginable math-related manipulation you might want, from geoboards to Pascal's Triangle and from pattern blocks to the Pythagorean Theorem. It is all free, but it uses Java.

Microsoft Excel
office.com

Apple Numbers
apple.com/numbers

Google Sheets
google.com/sheets/about

Programs such as Microsoft Excel (office.com), Apple Numbers (apple.com/numbers), and Google Sheets (google.com/sheets/about) are good ways to teach students about charts and graphs and how to interpret and present information.

Gliffy
gliffy.com

Create professional-quality flowcharts, wireframes, diagrams, and more with this tool. It is free for limited use, and upgrades are available for a fee.

Create A Graph
tinyurl.com/yoedjn

Create bar, line, area, pie, and XY graphs with this free website. It is easy to use, and you can print, save, or email your completed graphs.

Classtools
classtools.net

Create graphs and charts (and use many other helpful classroom tools, such as a QR code generator or timeline) with this free website.

Edheads
edheads.org

Real-world medical and engineering scenarios will intrigue students on this free website. The site adeptly weaves content into authentic simulations. In-activity definitions and glossaries provide solid vocabulary support. There is no ability to monitor progress, and students can't fast forward/rewind within segments.

AlgebraTouch
regularberry.com

This intuitive app makes learning algebra easy. Teachers can track students' progress, and it is especially great for struggling students. There is a cost.

Table 10.2: Math Resources

	MathPickle mathpickle.com	This free website for Grades 5–12 is loaded with math challenges, puzzling games, videos for flipping the classroom, and great ideas. There is a lot here, and you might need to guide your students, unless they are very independent.
	GeoGebra geogebra.org	Although it will take some time for teachers and students to learn how to use the site, if they are willing to put in the time, GeoGebra offers endless math learning possibilities. The site is free and for Grades 7–12. There are free apps available for every OS.
	iCrosss tinyurl.com/phsouuf	This app helps students learn solid geometry in an easy and funny way. Spin and rotate shapes, and create cross-sections to boost spatial understanding of geometric solids. There is a cost.
	**Algodoo** algodoo.com	This free software is a virtual sandbox tool that helps students play with the concepts of physics to design, construct, and explore. There is a corresponding app for a price.
	Desmos desmos.com/calculator	This website is a next-generation graphing calculator where students can use a "slider" to change the function and see how it affects the graph. It is an elegant math tool that makes concepts more concrete, and it's free.
	Autodesk Digital STEAM Measurement tinyurl.com/na3sn9h	This app is free and shows students differing ways to measure quantity, dimension, time, temperature, capacity, weight, and mass in real-world situations. It is mostly interactive and teaches international units of measurement.
	GetTheMath thirteen.org/get-the-math	This is a free website through PBS that uses video games, music, fashion, sports, restaurants, and special effects to teach math concepts. It is targeted for teenagers and has some great challenges, videos, and resources. It includes resources for teachers.

Mathplanet
mathplanet.com

This website is completely free and offers pre-algebra, algebra, geometry, and also ACT and SAT coursework. Think of this as a great resource for extra practice and instruction; it has examples and instructional videos on each concept.

Study Island
studyisland.com

This is a web-based program where students work on engaging, interactive lessons and activities at their own pace to learn aligned Common Core math standards. Teachers can also choose to guide students and assign specific areas to work through. This program must be purchased. Pricing information is available on the website.

DreamBox Learning
dreambox.com

Individualized, adaptive, game-based math resource that keeps kids coming back for more. Available online or through an app. Check the website for pricing information.

The Radix Endeavor
radixendeavor.org

This is an online multiplayer game for STEM learning. Students play in the math or science strands. Teachers can enroll classes, but enrollment is not necessary for students to play this free role-playing math game created by MIT.

HippoCampus
hippocampus.org

The ways to use this free website vary greatly. It offers high school– and college-level math, but also English, social studies, science, and even religion. There are assessments, teacher resources such as rubrics, tips about teaching, and so on. You must dig to find some of the great resources, but they are well worth it.

Gooru
gooru.org

This is a free, K–12 website with a supportive app. The site is a place to share information and make resources globally available. It covers math, science, social studies, and language arts by providing videos, worksheets, assessments, and other resources for students, broken out by standard. Great for flipping the classroom.

Table 10.2: Math Resources

	Math Open Reference mathopenref.com	This free website provides a myriad of math resources for teachers to use with their students. The site does have ads.
	Knowre knowre.com	This online site allows students to practice math skills in a supportive and adaptive environment. Based on the CCSS standards and with plenty of teacher data, differentiation, and support. It is not free, but focuses on high school level math skills. Has instruction, practice and even an assessment modeled after PARCC.

Literacy Lessons

Cross-curriculum planning is encouraged with the CCSS by using ELA standards in history, science, and technical subjects. However, we encourage you to go further and include the arts, math, and physical education teachers in your planning. How will you ever get through everything if you teach standard by standard? The key to planning with the CCSS is to teach multiple standards in one lesson, when you can. We hope the following list of sample lessons for eighth grade will inspire you to become an effective technology lesson planner.

Vocabulary

From the files of our eighth-grade friends, this vocabulary lesson is done in conjunction with reading a novel or nonfiction text. As you know, vocabulary plays a vital role in reading comprehension. This lesson is a fun way to aid vocabulary development. Before you begin the book, develop a list of key vocabulary words for the first few chapters. Students consult digital and print reference materials to understand and learn what words mean, as well as use them in sentences. (See our list of suggested materials under **L.8.4c.**) This satisfies **L.8.4c**. Next, students pick a way to present their vocabulary words, definitions, and sentences (Prezi, Trading Cards, iMovie Trailer, Explain Everything, etc.). Teams present and project (Miro) to the class, making sure they save time for asking and answering any questions. They are "the experts" on these vocabulary words. The presentations can then be uploaded to YouTube or any program you use to share with absent students and/

or parents! The presentations can be used for review later or could be used for flipping the classroom. Our former eighth-grade colleagues repeated this process for the remainder of the book. Students were encouraged to try different technology methods each time. Some students may even ask to try new technology! **RH.6-8.7** is satisfied, as students should be encouraged to include visual information in their presentations (graphics and even music). Students are introducing, producing, and publishing writing, as well as working together to present their ideas clearly and efficiently, so **WHST.6-8.2a, W.8.2a, W.8.6,** and **WHST.6-8.6** are also met. **RI.8.7** and **W.8.8** are satisfied when students gather, integrate, and present their information in an original way. Using diverse media and formats (including music, graphics, voiceovers, etc.) to present and clarify information is definitely a part of this project, so **SL.8.2** and **SL.8.5** are also fulfilled.

ISTE STUDENT STANDARDS

Students will be using two ISTE Standards in this lesson.

- **Knowledge Constructors (ISTE 3)** by employing research, evaluating and building knowledge using digital resources.

- **Creative Communicators (ISTE 6)** through choosing the appropriate platform and publishing and presenting customized content.

Shakespeare

This lesson has students studying Shakespeare by reading one of his works and then watching a film or live production of the same play. However, this lesson can be taught with any film or live production to support a text. (See our text/video suggestions under **RL.8.7.**) Next, students take notes (using Evernote or the Kentucky Virtual Library) on where the video or live production stayed faithful to the text and where it departed from the original. Encourage students to look up any words, terms, or phrases with which they are unfamiliar. Using word-processing software of their choosing, students write an analysis of these differences and similarities, offering personal reflections on choices made by the actors and/or directors. In addition, students must evaluate the advantages and disadvantages of a medium different from the text to present their text's theme, thus satisfying standards **RI.8.7** and **L.8.4c.** Conversely, this document can serve as their "blueprint" for the technology phase of this lesson.

Next, students create a publication (complete with visual information) that compares and contrasts their text to the film or live production. Ideas on the website, video post, or blog should be well organized, including headings, appropriate graphics, charts, tables (if needed), and perhaps even short snippets of the film or live production to illustrate their points. This lesson also satisfies **RH.6-8.7, RST.6-8.9, W.8.2a, W.8.6, WHST.6-8.2a,** and **WHST.6-8.6.** Encourage students to gather any information, from multiple print and digital sources, that supports their analysis and position. Make sure they cite references accurately and correctly; this satisfies **WHST.6-8.8.** Before presentations are uploaded to YouTube, SiteBuilder, Edublogs, or any sharing method you prefer, students should present their findings to the class. Miro is great for this! When each presentation is complete, presenters field questions and/or constructive comments from the audience, defending and strengthening their positions or clarifying anything that needs further explanation. Doing so satisfies both speech standards (**SL.8.2** and **SL.8.5**). This lesson satisfies many standards and helps students further their technology knowledge by creating and maintaining blogs or websites.

ISTE STUDENT STANDARDS

Students will be using several ISTE Standards in this lesson.

- **Digital Citizen (ISTE 2)** by demonstrating rights of intellectual property when using digital resources.

- **Knowledge Constructor (ISTE 3)** by employing research, evaluating and building knowledge using digital resources.

- **Creative Communicator (ISTE 6)** by communicating complex ideas using a variety of media and publishing for an intended audience.

- **Global Collaborator (ISTE 7)** by connecting to other learners to broaden mutual understanding.

Disney, Oh My!

This lesson can be adapted in several ways, and it can be used in any Grade 6–12. Students analyze, compare, and contrast a Disney presentation of a mythology character (Hercules) or a fairytale character (Cinderella) to the original text. This allows students to become critical consumers of the media that surrounds them.

In this lesson, students will evaluate the changes made by Disney to the myth of "Hercules." Not only do students compare and contrast two different types of media, but they also sequence elements of plot through the creation of plot diagrams. Students will also analyze how audience and purpose drive media decisions, evaluate the advantages and disadvantages of using different mediums, as well as evaluate changes across media by writing summaries and critiques. This, in turn, satisfies **RL.8.7** and **RI.8.7.**

Explain to students that they will be learning about Hercules. You may want to do a quick assessment to determine how many have heard about Hercules, read a story about Hercules, or watched Disney's animated version, *Hercules*. You can find Disney's movie *Hercules* at the library, or on **YouTube (tinyurl.com/y8gevwhl).** Most of the critical differences between the film and book occur in the first twenty minutes of the film. If time permits, you can finish the movie or have students finish watching on their own. You may want to use Disney's plot summary for *Hercules* **(tinyurl.com/ychve7m4)** to start a discussion with your students. Using **Read-WriteThink's (tinyurl.com/y92qjsc)** interactive plot diagram (or any other interactive plot diagram you find), have students organize the aspects of the film.

Next, have students read an online text version of the Hercules myth. You can find online copies at **FreeClassicAudioBooks (freeclassicaudiobooks.com), Follet (tiny.cc/cb2q3y),** or **TeachingBooks (teachingbooks.net).** This is also a great teachable moment to discuss that myths are not real and how they adapt over time.

For the next part of this lesson, students need to review ReadWriteThink's **Compare & Contrast Guiding Questions (tinyurl.com/y7vysh8f).** Discuss what they should compare and contrast between the film version and text. As a class, or in small groups, complete ReadWriteThink's Venn diagram **(tinyurl.com/ny7f64g),** looking for similarities and differences.

Once the Venn diagrams have been completed, begin a class discussion on what students discovered. They should quickly point out differences such as the antagonist (Hera in myth; Hades in film), Pegasus's presence, noticeable changes to the 12 Labors, timing of when Hercules became partially mortal, and Hercules's relationships (widower in myth; in love with Meg in the film).

Have a discussion about the keywords *audience* and *purpose*. Students should realize that Disney's intended audience is young children and parents. The purpose of the film (to sell tickets and entertain people) drove the changes in the film. Ask students to discuss the intended audience for the original myth of Hercules. While Disney's film was meant to entertain young children, myths in Greek society were geared toward entertaining and teaching values to all ages, including adults.

Using your Smart Board, or **Miro (realtimeboard.com)** show students the difference between writing a summary and writing a critique. Highlight that just as Disney's film differed from the original myth, summaries differ from critiques. Use a current situation at your school that is familiar for your students (school lunches, homework policies, etc.), and model writing a critique with the students' help. Instruct the students to use the third person point of view, as this creates a more professional tone. Allow students to ask questions prior to beginning the assignment.

Have students use their favorite word-processing program, such as **Microsoft Word (products.office.com/en-us/word), Google Docs (google.com/docs/about),** or **Abi-Word (abisource.com),** to create two paragraphs. One should be a summary of the differences between the original myth and the animated film; the other should be a critique of the changes. Students should use third person throughout their writing. You will also want to encourage students to mention both a positive change and a negative change in their critiques to provide a balanced analysis. Next, students should be encouraged to present their summary critiques to the class, answering any questions posed by their peers. Students should then be allowed to make changes to their critiques before the final assignment.

Finally, students choose a presentation tool to make a short video of their summary critiques. There are many presentation tools from which to choose. **Animoto (animoto.com)** or **iMovie Trailer (apple.com/ios/imovie)** are some of the more popular choices. Encourage your students to try some of the new presentation tools available: **Powtoon (powtoon.com), Moovly (moovly.com), Shmoop (schools.shmoop.com),** or **Adobe Spark (tinyurl.com/yamq84lg).** These are only a few examples. There are many presentation tools available. Some are free, while some do have a cost.

When your students finish their presentations, have a sharing session. These presentations can also be saved to their digital portfolios or published on your website for others to see. This activity can also be used throughout the year. There are many film and text versions of myths or fair-use fairy tales.

RH.6-8.7 is satisfied when students create and interpret a plot summary graph. When information is compared and contrasted from film to text, **RST.6-8.9** is also satisfied. **W.8.2a**, **W.8.6** and **WHST.6-8.2a** are also satisfied when students research and write about their topics using technology. Standards **WHST.6-8.6** and **WHST.6-8.8** are definitely satisfied when students write, produce, and publish their writing, presenting their information clearly and efficiently. You may even wish to publish their writing on your website. **SL.8.2** and **SL.8.5** are also satisfied when students contribute to class discussions and present their plot diagrams, Venn diagrams, and critiques to the class. **L.8.4c** is also satisfied in this lesson, when students use dictionaries, glossaries, and thesauruses, not only to search for words to bolster their writing, but to clarify the precise meaning of a word.

ISTE STUDENT STANDARDS

Students will be using multiple ISTE Standards in this lesson.

- **Empowered Learner (ISTE 1)** through use of technology to seek feedback that informs and improves their learning.

- **Digital Citizen (ISTE 2)** by engaging in safe behavior when using digital technology.

- **Knowledge Constructor (ISTE 3)** by evaluating accuracy, perspective and credibility of media and digital resources.

- **Creative Communicator (ISTE 6)** by communicating effectively using a variety of media and publishing for an intended audience.

- **Global Collaborator (ISTE 7)** by connecting to other learners to broaden mutual understanding.

Social Studies/Science Lessons

The following sample lessons address ELA standards and teach lessons based on national standards in social studies and science.

Great Depression

A local eighth-grade class in our former district had great fun with this social studies WebQuest on the Great Depression, which they adapted from a WebQuest developed by a Kansas middle school. Do a Google search for "Great Depression WebQuests" or make your own using Google Sites or your favorite website design software, app, or online provider. Students work in teams to develop a plan to prevent the Great Depression. An intriguing idea is to make teams of four, with each member having a different role—the economist, the historian, the policy analyst, or the biographer. Team members need to make sure they fulfill their specific roles—not only will they have to share information with other team members, but the entire team will present their preventative solutions to the class. In class, have a discussion about the Great Depression, its causes, and so on. Utilize many different sources (texts, videos, movies, etc.) to facilitate this discussion. You will also need many websites covering a multitude of aspects of the Great Depression. See our suggestions listed on our website **(tinyurl.com/y9dfltpr).**

Teams "travel" back in time to 1928 and research what life was like at that time, leading up to the Great Depression. During their research, teams take notes (Evernote or the Kentucky Virtual Library) of any and all factors contributing to the Great Depression. Once students feel their research is complete and they have learned all they can about the causes of the Great Depression, teams develop plans to prevent it. We have outlined specific duties for each role below. See our website **(tinyurl.com/y9dfltpr)** for a list of resources for this lesson.

THE ECONOMIST

One facet of the Great Depression was the sudden drop in the stock market (the Great Crash). Your mission is to find out what events triggered the crash. Prepare a presentation (PowerPoint, Keynote, iMovie Trailer, Prezi, Clips, etc.) outlining what you think triggered the Great Crash, as well as your thoughts on how it could have been prevented. (Teachers may want to give the economists some guiding questions.)

For their research, economists will need a variety of sources—text, websites, videos, and so on. Students also need to be encouraged to look up in reference materials any words or terms they are unfamiliar with, as well as cite appropriately all of the sources they used (thus satisfying standard **L.8.4c**). These are only a few suggestions for economists to use for their research. You will want to provide more to guide them in their work.

THE HISTORIAN

As the historian, you will explain the extent and depth of business failures, unemployment, and poverty during the Depression. Prepare a presentation (PowerPoint, Keynote, iMovie Trailer, Prezi, Clips, etc.) outlining a history of events leading to the stock market crash and Great Depression, as well as your thoughts on how it could have been prevented. (Teachers may want to give the historians some guiding questions.)

To help historians with their research, they will need a variety of sources, text, websites, videos, and so on. Students also need to be encouraged to look up in reference materials any words or terms they are unfamiliar with, as well as cite appropriately all of the sources they used (thus satisfying standard **L.8.4c**). These are only a few suggestions for historians to use for their research. You will want to provide more to guide them in their work.

THE POLICY ANALYST

The mission of the policy analyst is to learn about the New Deal and how it impacted the Depression and the role of the government in the economy. Prepare a presentation (PowerPoint, Keynote, iMovie Trailer, Kizoa, Prezi, etc.) outlining a history of events leading to the stock market crash, the Great Depression, and the New Deal, as well as your thoughts on how it could have been prevented. Policy analysts may want to work closely with economists and historians. (Teachers may want to give the policy analysts some guiding questions.)

To help policy analysts with their research, they will need a variety of sources, text, websites, videos, and so on. Students also need to be encouraged to look up in reference materials any words or terms they are unfamiliar with, as well as cite appropriately all of the sources they used (thus satisfying standard **L.8.4c**). These are only a few suggestions for policy analysts to use for their research. You will want to provide more to guide them in their work.

THE BIOGRAPHER

The mission of the biographer is to find out how the following people influenced the time period before, during, and after the Great Depression.

- Will Rogers

- Eleanor Roosevelt

- Franklin Roosevelt

- Charles Lindberg

Prepare a presentation (PowerPoint, Keynote, iMovie Trailer, Kizoa, Flipsnack, Prezi, etc.) detailing each of the people listed and what role they played, as well as your thoughts on what each of them could have done to prevent the Great Depression. (Teachers may want to give the biographers some guiding questions.)

To help biographers with their research, they will need a variety of sources, text, websites, videos, and so on. Students also need to be encouraged to look up in reference materials any words or terms they are unfamiliar with, as well as cite appropriately all of the sources they used (thus satisfying standard **L.8.4c**). These are only a few suggestions for historians to use for their research. You will want to provide more to guide them in their work.

Students should present their findings to the class. (Miro would be great for this!) After each presentation is complete, presenters should field questions and/or constructive comments from the audience, defending, strengthening their positions, or clarifying anything that needs further explanation. Doing so satisfies both speech standards (**SL.8.2** and **SL.8.5**). Other standards this in-depth lesson covers include **RH.6-8.7, W.8.2a, W.8.6, WHST.6-8.6, WHST.6-8.8,** and **WHST.6-8.2a.,** as students are researching, writing, and organizing ideas, concepts, and information to produce a presentation on their thoughts of how the Great Depression could have been prevented. Students should be encouraged to use headings, charts, tables (when and where necessary), pictures, graphics, and/or music to enhance their presentations. They may wish to include short videos.

ISTE STUDENT STANDARDS

Students will be using a variety of ISTE Standards in this lesson.

- **Digital Citizen** by demonstrating respects for rights in using and sharing intellectual property.

- **Knowledge Constructor** by employing research, evaluating and building knowledge, developing ideas and pursuing solutions to real-world issues using digital resources.

- **Creative Communicator** by choosing the appropriate platforms and communicating effectively using a variety of media and customized publishing for an intended audience.

- **Global Collaborator** by working as a team member and connecting to other learners to broaden mutual understanding.

Engineering

Eighth-graders across the country are studying engineering, technology, and applications of science. This lesson is from the file of a middle school teacher and serves as an introduction to one of the science units. In this lesson, students explore the world of engineering (for some this will be an introduction to engineering) and what it means to have a career as an engineer. Start your lesson with a class discussion, learning about your students and their thoughts about what career they may pursue. Lead the conversation toward the career of engineering. You may wish to spark the conversation by asking questions such as: Have you ever heard of a career called engineering? What does an engineer do? What do you know about engineering? or Do you know someone who is an engineer? The conversation should lead into a discussion of different types of engineers. Using your whiteboard to make a list, have students brainstorm different kinds of engineers (mechanical, electrical, chemical, civil, etc.) You may need to bring in some outside sources to help spark this brainstorm session. Encourage students to use print and digital reference materials like Merriam-Webster, Word Central, Wordsmyth, or Thesaurus.com. See our detailed explanation under **L.8.4c,** which is also the standard students will be satisfying with this lesson. Adding a sketch or drawing of the vocabulary term or phrase is a great way for students to internalize the words. Next, you may want to preview engineering by showing students videos. There are many places to search. Please refer to our detailed explanation earlier, under **RST.6-8.9,** (fe.g.: YouTube, WatchKnowLearn, iTunes U, and BrainPOP). Students can use Evernote, The Kentucky Virtual Library, or Diigo for note taking. See our explanation above at standard **WHST.6-8.2a,** as you can even "share" worksheets and other items with your students. Students can also "share" their work with you. Explain Everything is another good site to use for note-taking, as students can write notes or vocabulary definitions and even draw or sketch pictures to go with their words. Once students are comfortable with the vocabulary, explain that the assignment will be to design a presentation about one of the engineering careers the class just brainstormed. Before they actually begin their presentations, students need to come up with a list of questions (about their specific engineering category) they wish to answer while researching. Encourage students to dig deeper than "How much money do they make?" Students may need to use resources before doing research, to ensure they are prepared with quality questions. There are some excellent websites and videos to consider for students. See our website **(tinyurl.com/y9dfltpr)** for more ideas.

Next, students design a presentation on their engineering career (PowerPoint, Keynote, iMovie Trailer, Clips, Prezi, etc.). Students present their projects (Miro would be great for this), using diverse media and formats (including music, graphics, voiceovers, etc.). After each presentation is complete, presenters should field questions and/or constructive comments from the audience, defending, strengthening their position, or clarifying anything that needs further explanation (thus fulfilling **SL.8.2** and **SL.8.5**). Students listening to the presentations may want to take notes, either for themselves or to share positive feedback with the presenters.

Other standards this lesson covers include **RH.6-8.7, W.8.2a, W.8.6, WHST.6-8.6, WHST.6-8.8, W.6.2a,** and **WHST.6-8.2a,** as students are researching, writing, and organizing ideas, concepts, and information to produce a presentation about their ideas on the career of engineering. Students should be encouraged to use headings, charts, and tables (when and where necessary), as well as pictures, graphics, and/or music to enhance their presentations. They may even wish to include short videos.

ISTE STUDENT STANDARDS

These are the ISTE Standards students are using in this lesson.

- **Knowledge Constructor** by employing research, evaluating and building knowledge using digital resources.

• **Creative Communicator** by communicating effectively using a variety of media and publishing for an intended audience.

Math Lessons

Mathematics Review

This math lesson, again from the files of one of our middle school friends, is similar to a lesson in seventh grade math. Teachers used this lesson as a review at the end of a semester, but you can use it to review at the end of any unit. Or you can use it as a preview before a lesson ("flipping the classroom.") Teams of students are "experts" on a math topic or skill and will make instructional videos similar to those found at Virtual Nerd or Khan Academy. You may wish to give a pretest in advance of starting a new unit, to determine your "experts" in each area. Or, on the whiteboard, you and your students make a list of all the concepts and skills studied throughout the semester. In pairs or groups of three (depending how many total), students pick a topic they want to "be an expert" on. Using iMovie, MovieMaker, or any other movie-making software, teams begin making their teaching videos. Teams should view several examples from Virtual Nerd or Khan Academy before beginning. Students may also need access to tablets and the whiteboard as they begin to film their lesson. At the appropriate time, have students project their movie and "teach" the class. "Learning" students take notes to use for studying using Evernote, Diigo, Explain Everything (which can be written and voice recorded), and so on. Teams present (Miro) to the class, making sure they save time for asking and answering any questions, as they are "the experts" on the math topic. These movies can then be uploaded to YouTube or your favorite posting site to share with absent students and/or parents. They can then be used to review later, or could be great for flipping the classroom. In addition to **MP5,** standard **RH.6-8.7** is satisfied, as students should be encouraged to include visual information in their presentations (graphics and even music). Students are introducing, producing, and publishing writing, as well as working together to present their ideas clearly and efficiently, so **WHST.6-8.2a, W.8.2a, W.8.6,** and **WHST.6-8.6** are also met. **RI.8.7** and **W.8.8** are also satisfied when students gather, integrate, and present their information, in an original way. Using diverse media and formats (including music, graphics, voiceovers, etc.) to present and clarify information is definitely a part of this project, so **SL.8.2** and **SL.8.5** are also fulfilled.

ISTE STUDENT STANDARDS

These are the ISTE Standards students are using in this lesson.

- **Empowered Learner** by leverage technology to reflect on the learning process and improve learning outcomes and demonstrating learning in a variety of ways.

- **Knowledge Constructor** by curating information using a variety of tools to create a collection of artifacts that demonstrate learning.

- **Computational Thinker** through data collection, breaking problems into component parts, and developing models to help understanding.

- **Creative Communicator** by communicating complex ideas effectively through creation of new resources using a variety of media and publishing for an intended audience.

Quadratic Equation

This next math lesson comes from the files of our former eighth-grade colleagues at the local middle school. Students are introduced to simple quadratic equations, graphing, and exploring parabolas. Because this is their first exposure to quadratic equations, you may need to do some vocabulary work and activating schema with the students before actually beginning your lessons. Providing students with a list of vocabulary words they will encounter when learning about quadratic equations might be helpful. Students can use Evernote, the Kentucky Virtual Library, or Diigo for note-taking. See our explanation above under **WHST.6-8.2a,** as you can even "share" worksheets and so on with your students. Students can also "share" their vocabulary work with you. Encourage students to use print and digital reference materials like Merriam-Webster, Word Central, Wordsmyth, or Thesaurus.com. See our detailed explanation under **L.8.4c,** which is also the standard this lesson addresses. Adding a sketch or drawing of the vocabulary term or phrase is a great way for students to internalize the words. It can easily be done on their tablets, using one of the note-taking sites previously mentioned. Next, you may want to preview quadratic equations by showing students videos. There are many places to search for videos on the subject. Please refer to our detailed explanation earlier, under **RST.6-8.9** (e.g.: YouTube, WatchKnowLearn, iTunes U, BrainPOP, and Khan Academy). As you begin instruction, you may want students to explore or to refresh their minds concerning lines of symmetry, as well as reflecting lines. You can also do this on tablets or computers as well. Microsoft Office's Excel, Apple's Numbers, or Google Sheets is a great way to teach charts and graphs. Making your own charts and graphs is also a good way to learn how to interpret and present information. Gliffy, Create A Graph, and Classtools are free sites you can use. You may also have your own sites to use for graphing. Students will need these graphing sites more as you get deeper into the lesson. By the way, you are addressing **W.8.2a** when using and applying online graph sites.

Ask students to team up. One student is in charge of using the graphing calculator, while the other sketches and writes. You may want to assign quadratic equations from a textbook, make up an activity sheet, or use an online an activity sheet on quadratic equations. Students perform all work (which will be submitted to you) on their tablets, making sure they both verify their answers and check to make sure their explanations are clear and complete. Halfway through the assignment, students can switch roles. Encourage students to consult other teams for ideas and suggestions before asking you, the teacher) as this will satisfy standard **W.8.6** (interacting and working collaboratively with others). Before class ends, bring students together as a whole group. Put a problem on the board and ask students to answer your questions about the problem. This is the student's "exit slip," as well as your way to check their understanding. Repeat several times so everyone has a chance to show their comprehension. You may also try this using Explain Everything, or another of the apps we mentioned previously, and have all students submit answers to you electronically. Finally, for homework, have students finish the assignment given in class, or hand out another assignment to be done and handed in electronically the next day.

In addition to the standards mentioned earlier that are satisfied by this lesson, if you have students present their quadratic equation work to the class (maybe going over homework and sharing in class the second day), **SL.8.2** and **SL.8.5** will be satisfied. In addition to **MP5, W. 8.2a, WHST.6-8.6,** and **WHST.6-8.2a** are also satisfied, as students need to write and use their learned math vocabulary terms correctly and efficiently, as well as write and present their ideas and explanations clearly and succinctly. Finally, **RH.6-8.7** is also satisfied, as teams are using visual information (graphs) to illustrate their written explanations.

ISTE STUDENT STANDARDS

Students will be using multiple ISTE Standards in this lesson.

- **Empowered Learner** by reflecting on the learning process to improve learning outcomes.

- **Knowledge Constructor** by curating information using a variety of tools to create a collection of artifacts that demonstrate learning.

- **Computational Thinker** by formulating problem definitions suited to technology solutions and through data collection, breaking problems into component parts, and developing models to help understanding.

- **Creative Communicator** by choose appropriate platforms for successfully communicating.

- **Global Collaborator** by connecting to other learners to broaden mutual understanding and contributing to a team project.

Pythagorean WebQuest

Several eighth-grade classes had great fun with this math WebQuest, which we adapted from several middle school WebQuests we found online. Make your own, or do a Google Search for Pythagorean WebQuests to see what is out there! Students need to complete several tasks that involve learning about Pythagoras, the theorem, solving applied problems, and creating their own word problems.

After students complete this activity, they will have a good foundation for the Pythagorean theorem and its applications. Upon completion, students will share their solutions with classmates and explain how they solved the problems. Students will work with partners on this WebQuest.

Partners complete the first two tasks together; they can split up the last tasks, which are applied math. They need to show all of their work, which will be included in the final sharing using an app such as Explain Everything.

TASK ONE: LEARNING ABOUT PYTHAGORAS

Follow these links to read more about Pythagoras. Each student should record four different interesting facts about his life and his work in mathematics, so the partners will have eight facts written in their Google Docs, Microsoft Word, or Apple

Pages document. If they need to check any vocabulary they should look online at Word Central, Merriam-Webster, or another online dictionary.

- **The Story of Mathematics (tinyurl.com/ydaeugf9)**

- **Phoenicia (phoenicia.org/pythagoras.html)**

- **The Life of Pythagoras (tinyurl.com/y93vb7ht)**

TASK TWO: TYPES OF TRIANGLES

Follow these links to learn more about the triangles, explore how to find area and perimeter, and experiment with the Pythagorean theorem. Students and their partners should explore these activities separately and then discuss their findings. They should keep track of their findings in Google Docs or a similar program. If they have trouble, they can select the Help tab on the site.

- **Triangle Explorer (tinyurl.com/7rbd68)**

- **Squaring the Triangle (tinyurl.com/yr96s9)**

- **Pythagorean Explorer (tinyurl.com/2rshqc)**

TASK THREE: APPLYING THE MATH

Follow the links to have students apply their new knowledge about the Pythagorean theorem. Make sure they each take a different task (or two). They need to write down their solution and show all work in the app they use. They will be sharing how they solved these problems.

- **Using the Pythagorean Theorem (tinyurl.com/yccdqtye)**

- **National Library of Virtual Manipulatives (NLVM) (tinyurl.com/qdodzqy)**

TASK FOUR: CREATE YOUR OWN PYTHAGOREAN REAL-WORLD PROBLEM

Follow these links to have students see real-world examples of using the theorem: **(tinyurl.com/y9769t6l)** and **(tinyurl.com/yb65uenz)**. After they see examples of word problems, they will create one or two of their own real-world problems, including illustrations using the Pythagorean theorem on Google Drawings or Microsoft Paint 3D, or create a video or animation in Animoto, Prezi, Powtoon, or Moovly. Have students determine which might be better to use.

When students finish their Webquests, they will share their findings about Pythagoras, the math data from tasks two and three, and the real-world, illustrated word problems with their partners. Then they will share their word problems with another pair/group of students. Finally, gather all of their problems to share with their classmates and defend their solutions, if necessary. Post them on the class website or blog for other classes to solve.

This project-based learning experience incorporates a myriad of standards. Of course, **MP.5** is covered as students use technology to solve math problems. Also, **RH.6-8.7** is satisfied, as students integrate visual information into their sharing. **WHST.6-8.2a, W.8.2a, W.8.6,** and **WHST.6-8.6** are also met when students produce and publish writing, as well as work together to present their ideas clearly and efficiently. Standard **RI.8.7** is also satisfied when students decide which medium is best to present their information to classmates. Integrating multimedia and visual displays into the presentation meets standard **SL.8.5,** while **L.8.4c,** using digital reference materials to help with writing, is also satisfied when they use the online dictionaries.

ISTE STUDENT STANDARDS

Students will be using most of the ISTE Standards in this lesson.

- **Empowered Learner** by leverage technology to reflect on the learning process and improve learning outcomes and using technology to seek feedback that improves practice and learning in a variety of ways.

- **Knowledge Constructor** by curating information using a variety of tools to create a collection of artifacts that demonstrate learning and build knowledge with real-world issues.

- **Innovative Designer** by using a design process for testing theories and solving authentic problems, including selection and use of the most appropriate digital tools.

- **Computational Thinker** by formulating problem definitions suited to technology solutions and through data collection, breaking problems into component parts, and developing models to help facilitate problem solving.

- **Creative Communicator** by creating original work and communicating complex ideas using effective digital tools.

- **Global Collaborator** by connecting to other learners to broaden mutual understanding and contributing to a team project.

A Final Note

As students progress through the grades, they establish their baseline of proficiency in technology. This will definitely enhance their experiences with technology in high school, as well as satisfy the CCSS performance standards at the 6–8 levels. We hope you find the resources and lesson ideas presented in this chapter useful and that they are easy to adapt to your class.

You will find more resources online at our website **(tinyurl.com/y9dfltpr),** which may be helpful to you as you look to differentiate your instruction. Visit our website for updated information about this book. To learn more about applying technology found within the standards for other grades, look for our additional title.

11 Practical Ideas for Grades 9–10

We realize that you will want to focus on your particular grade or subject when you are planning your lessons and implementing the standards, so we have organized the Practical Ideas chapters by grade level and subject. Each grade starts with an overview followed by ELA technology standards with accompanying apps, software, and websites that you can use to help your students succeed with that standard. We then continue with the math standard for the grade level and review appropriate resources. Finally, we have included sample lessons for each grade level in various subject areas. Although we have organized the book so you can find your specific grade and subject easily, please do not disregard other sections of this chapter. It is often helpful to see what the standards require before and after the grade you teach. To see grades other than 6–12, look for our other title in this series, as it could provide information to help you differentiate for students at all levels of your class.

The CCSS have been set up to encourage cross-curricular work in ELA for Grades 6–12. It standardizes the writing process through all classes in freshman through senior years by bringing the same writing standard into history, science, and technical subjects. The CCSS in high school are divided in two ranges: Grades 9–10 and Grades 11–12. As a high school teacher, you understand the difficulty of working with colleagues in other departments. There are systemic roadblocks that make communication with other departments difficult in most high schools. But, co-designing lessons between the language arts teachers and the history, science, and technical teachers will be a significant step in helping to create a strong foundation for your students before they enter college.

It is also important to work with your administrators to ensure that you have time to plan. Planning can take place during a school- or districtwide professional development day or during staff meetings. Of course, the best option is to build collaboration time into the regular schedule.

Math is also a subject area where technological tools become more varied and complex as students advance. The math standards are meant to be embedded in, and a natural part of, the units your students study. Choosing the correct math tools is an important part of your students' learning. There are wonderful new math resources available to help students become proficient in the standards, especially in the area of technology. We list some of our favorites later in this chapter.

Resources for Reading Literature

RL.9-10.7 • READING LITERATURE

Analyze the representation of a subject or a key scene in two different **artistic mediums,** including what is emphasized or absent in each treatment (e.g., Auden's *Musée des Beaux Arts* and Breughel's *Landscape with the Fall of Icarus*).

This standard begins in kindergarten with comparing illustrations and text and is developed through the grades to use all types of media to compare, support, and analyze a story's meaning. So, the standard is essentially to get meaning from more than the text; it can come from the accompanying media, even the format of the writing or media. It would be a perfect time to team up with art teachers to create a cross-curricular unit of study.

This standard can lead to many creative projects. Students can focus on a poem, drama, play, artwork, or narrative, and it can be in a digital medium (movie, audio file, photograph, etc.). In fact, a digital medium is one of the easiest forms to use when contrasting two forms of the same subject, because there are so many resources available.

Of course programs such as **Microsoft Office (office.com), Apple Pages (apple.com/pages),** or **Google Docs (google.com/docs/about),** can be used to create text and organize media. Google Docs has a real-time collaboration component that is very useful for group projects.

Your school district may subscribe to **Gale Literature Resource Center** or other Gale products **(tinyurl.com/o47ydvs).** These are fine sources for thousands of frequently studied works. Your public library may have digital resources that are free to your school district. **Table 11.1** shares some excellent media resources.

Table 11.1: Reading Literature Resources

WEBSITES

	YouTube youtube.com	There are many free videos that your students can view, including literature, reviews of art, and endless other topics that might fit your curriculum. There is also a free app.
	iTunes U tinyurl.com/lbjbarh	As stated on the Apple website, "Choose from more than 750,000 free lectures, videos, books, and other resources on thousands of subjects from Algebra to Zoology." Access it free through iTunes. A free iTunesU app is also available.
	SchoolTube schooltube.com	This is educators' best free source for a video-sharing community where students can watch or post videos.
	Netflix netflix.com	Find films based on classic literature, more current literature, and Shakespeare at this site. A subscription is required.
	Open Culture tinyurl.com/d8ww8ez	This free website is a one-stop shop for audiobooks, ebooks, and movies. There are even courses for teachers! They do not create the media. They just compile it so we can find it easier.
	NeoK12 neok12.com	There are many science experiments, simulations, and videos on all sorts of topics on this website, and they are guaranteed to be kid safe. As an added bonus, it is free.
	PBS LearningMedia pbslearningmedia.org	This site is a great source for classroom-ready, free digital resources at all grades and in all subjects. This includes Masterpiece Theatre with accompanying lessons.

	National Gallery of Art	This is the website for the United States' national art
	nga.gov	museum in Washington. There are many resources, including more than 45,000 digitized images from the national collection. All access is free.
	New York Art Resources Consortium	Containing artwork from three major New York art museums, this free website has many images of art
	nyarc.org	and art resources.
	Louvre	This famous French art museum has many great
	louvre.fr	works available free online. They are accompanied by explanations of the works, and some provide close-up details. A great resource.

Resources for Reading Informational Text

RI.9-10.7 • READING INFORMATION

Analyze various accounts of a subject told in different mediums (e.g., a person's life story in both print and **multimedia**), determining which details are emphasized in each account.

Of course, biographies are a natural for addressing this standard. Although it is not required in the standard **RI.9-10.7** can be a great jumping-off point if you are a history, science, or technical teacher (i.e., art, music, home economics, or government) to take a subject your students are learning about and analyze it through text. Documentaries, digital images of primary documents, opinion blogs, and more allow students to gain differing perspectives and a more complete idea of the issues they are studying. Your class should also be able to gain meaning from charts, maps, graphs, and data presented in any text (i.e., any textbook, PDF, website, pamphlet, brochure, etc.). If you are a writing teacher and can't coordinate with other departments, consider using what your students are learning in other subject areas, and use those subject areas to read and analyze informational text in your classroom.

Table 11.2 shares some software options we recommend for high school reading.

Table 11.2: Reading Informational Text Resources

	Have Fun with History havefunwithhistory.com	This free website offers many short videos about historical events. There are ads.
	Library of Congress tinyurl.com/2knoku	This free site, as part of the Library of Congress' website, offers easily searchable access to thousands of digital resources from the history of the United States.
	Internet Archive archive.org	This free site has more than twelve million books, films, audio files, photos, songs, and documents. They come from libraries worldwide, TV stations, radio stations, and many other for-profit and non-profit groups. Books include plays by Shakespeare and American classics.
	Biography biography.com	There are good resources on this site for biographies, including text, photos, and video of various subjects. Some of the subject matter may be graphic. The site does have ads.
	Time time.com	Time magazine's website has short biographies of Time's top 100 most influential people, organized by year. Many have video clips of the subjects. A great resource for current biographies. Free.

Resources for Reading Historical and Technical Texts

RH.9–10.7 • READING HISTORY, SCIENCE, AND TECHNICAL SUBJECTS

Integrate quantitative or technical analysis (e.g., charts, research data) with qualitative analysis in print or **digital text**.

RST.9–10.7 • REDING HISTORY, SCIENCE, AND TECHNICAL SUBJECTS

Translate quantitative or technical information expressed in words in a text into **visual form** (e.g., a table or chart) and translate information expressed **visually** or mathematically (e.g., in an equation) into words.

RST.9–10.9 • READING HISTORY, SCIENCE, AND TECHNICAL SUBJECTS

Compare and contrast findings presented in a text to those from **other sources** (including their own experiments), noting when the findings support or contradict previous explanations or accounts.

RH.9-10.7 and **RST.9-10.7** are similar in that they focus more on quantitative and technical information your students would deal with in reading historical and technical texts. Thus, you must keep in mind informational graphics, such as maps, photographs, diagrams, charts, and other media in history, science, and technical subjects, and how they augment the provided information or help to explain or solve a social or scientific problem or event.

RST.9-10.9 also involves comprehension of technical information; the difference is in the comparison and contrasting of what is read to other sources. So your students are being asked to look at test results, surveys, and studies and come to a conclusion about what they have read on the subject.

Translating words into visuals vice versa has become easier with technology. In this standard, you are also asked to include charts, tables, and multimedia when aiding comprehension. Programs such as **Microsoft Excel (office.com), Apple Numbers (apple.com/numbers),** or **Google Sheets (google.com/sheets/about)** are great ways to create charts, graphs, and tables. Making their own charts and graphs helps students learn to interpret and present information.

Table 11.3 lists some additional useful apps, programs, and websites to help students become proficient in this standard. Using these resources, students will become more adept at manipulating, comparing, and interpreting statistical results.

Table 11.3: Reading Historical and Technical Text Resources

	ChartGizmo chartgizmo.com	With your free account from ChartGizmo, you can create dynamic charts from static or collected data and place them on your website in minutes.
	Gliffy gliffy.com	Create professional-quality flowcharts, wireframes, diagrams, and more with this tool. It is free for limited use, and upgrades are available for a fee.
	Create A Graph tinyurl.com/yoedjn	Create bar, line, area, pie, and XY graphs with this free website. It is easy to use, and you can print, save, or email your completed graphs.
	Classtools classtools.net	Create graphs and charts (and use many other helpful classroom tools, such as a QR code generator or timeline) with this free website.
	Feedly feedly.com	Organize any information on the web with this free app and website. It is a great resource for STEM to follow current events, scientific breakthroughs, and so on. Find and follow any source of information.
	Gooru gooru.org	This is a free, K–12 website with a supportive app. The site is a place to share information and make resources globally available. It covers math, science, social studies, and language arts by providing videos, worksheets, assessments, and other resources for students, broken out by standard. Great for flipping the classroom.

Notability
gingerlabs.com

This note-taking app allows your students to draw, using handwriting, typing, and importing text and other media. It allows markup of PDFs, too. It includes a word processor for essays, outlines, and forms. There is a cost.

iAnnotate
iAnnotate.com

Similar to Notability, this app is primarily for note-taking and markup of PDFs, PPT, and Docs. It is a bit easier to import other formats than it is on Notability. See the website for pricing.

Evernote
evernote.com

This free app allows you to import a worksheet, document, or picture, including a snapshot of a webpage, and then annotate it using tools common to interactive whiteboard software. You can highlight words, cut and paste, and add sticky notes. It also allows you to use voice recognition. You can then send your annotated sheet to someone else.

Penzu
penzu.com

This writing website can be accessed with their app, and it's all free! Created for journaling and diaries, it is very customizable and secure. It even allows you to set up reminders.

Simplenote
simplenote.com

This great note-taking app is simple to use and has the ability to share notes with others, search notes, track changes, and use it over multiple platforms. All notes are backed up online and synchronized. Best of all, it's free.

Explain Everything
explaineverything.com

This app uses text, video, pictures, and voice to help students present a variety of possible creations. They can use graphs and illustrate an experiment with a chart or include historical documents and maps with their presentations to recount and explain the information. The company offers educational pricing.

Writing Resources

W.9-10.2.A • WRITING

WHST.9–10.2.A • WRITING HISTORY, SCIENCE, AND TECHNICAL SUBJECTS

Introduce a topic; organize complex ideas, concepts, and information to make important connections and distinctions; include formatting (e.g., headings), **graphics** (e.g., figures, tables), and **multimedia** when useful to aiding comprehension.

W.9-10.6 • WRITING

WHST.9–10.6 • WRITING HISTORY, SCIENCE, AND TECHNICAL SUBJECTS

Use **technology**, including the Internet, to produce, publish, and update individual or shared writing products, taking advantage of **technology's capacity** to link to other information and to display information flexibly and dynamically.

W.9-10.8 • WRITING

WHST.9-10.8 • WRITING HISTORY, SCIENCE, AND TECHNICAL SUBJECTS

Gather relevant information from multiple authoritative print and **digital sources**, using advanced searches effectively; assess the usefulness of each source in answering the research question; integrate information into the text selectively to maintain the flow of ideas, avoiding plagiarism and following a standard format for citation.

Writing Standard 2 is the "how to write a paper" standard. Your students have been experiencing informative or explanatory writing since kindergarten. But, as they reach this level, they need to become college and career ready. They have to step up their game. Outlining programs are wonderful ways for students to organize their ideas, concepts, and information. Several fine software programs have been used for mind-mapping and outlining for many years. However, there are also free sites available. There are even templates, such as a Venn diagram, that allow students to compare and contrast and show cause and effect.

Writing Standard 6 is one of the few anchor standards that is solely technology driven. Students from kindergarten to Grade 12 are required to use technology to collaborate with others when writing. In eighth grade, students produce and publish, but ninth grade will be the first time they will be required to "update" their writing and to "display information flexibly and dynamically." Updating their writing requires students to revise, react, and, in the case of argument, to rethink their positions when more information about the topic is discovered. A flexible and dynamic display of information is easily accomplished if students are already using well-constructed programs, apps, and websites.

Writing Standard 8 starts in Grade 3 and continues through Grade 12. This writing standard focuses on gathering information, analyzing it, avoiding plagiarism, and using multiple sources (digital as well as text) when writing informative or explanatory works. The standard does change slightly between the Grade 8 standard and the corresponding standard for Grades 9–10. First, they add the term *advanced* when searching effectively online. Next, instead of the "proper use of quoting and paraphrasing," as in eighth grade, the standard changes to integration of information "into the text selectively to maintain the flow of ideas." Students will need to demonstrate that they know advanced search techniques. You will also need to have your students become proficient at maintaining the flow of their writing while using others' written or spoken words or ideas.

Google Tools for Writing

- **Google Drive (google.com/drive):** offers many useful tools free, including the following.

  - **Google Docs:** This word-processing program makes collaboration easy, especially from home. Students are able to add pictures and short video clips, tables, and charts. These can be used to enhance the development of the main ideas or theme of their writing or presentations.

  - **Google Slides:** This is a simpler version of Microsoft's PowerPoint, and it's free. Students can use this for sharing projects, summarizing their work, and peer-to-peer teaching.

  - **Google Sites:** Use this tool to create websites to display your students' research or to create WebQuests. Great for presenting ideas, interactive learning, and can be updated easily when data or events change.

○ **Google Spreadsheet:** This tool can be used in many subject areas to share charts, graphs, and other data for analysis of topics or issues.

○ **Google Blogger:** This free blogging site has numerous features. Students can see other classes and can be cross-grouped with similar sections of the same course by ability or with mixed ability as needed.

○ **Google Form:** Great for checking student understanding instantly, getting any kind of feedback on issues being studied, and for peer-to-peer teaching.

○ **Google Drawing:** This provides your students a place to create art, illustrations, graphics, diagrams, and so on, to enhance presentations and meaning in their language, history, science, technical, and mathematical work.

○ **Add-ons:** Google has created many add-ons that can be attached to Docs, Spreadsheets, Blogger, Forms, and so forth, to add targeted functionality. One example is Doctopus. This add-on allows teachers to instantly distribute documents to their classes, which then show up in each student's folder. These documents can be used as a starting point in assignments, discussions, or practice.

Table 11.4 features some well-designed products that will help your students become more proficient in the writing standards for these grades.

Table 11.4: Writing Resources

<table>
<tr><td rowspan="2">SOFTWARE & WEBSITES</td><td> **iThoughts**
toketaware.com</td><td>Students can use this mind-mapping app to organize their writing and presentation ideas. It has good import and export capabilities (PDF, PowerPoint, and other formats). This app can also be used as an interactive whiteboard. See the website for current pricing.</td></tr>
<tr><td> **SimpleMind**
tinyurl.com/y7ualejm</td><td>This cross-platform mind-mapping app can have multiple mind-maps with unlimited page sizes. You can add photos, video, and images to make your mind-map stand out. Free version that can be upgraded for a price.</td></tr>
</table>

Inspiration Maps
inspiration.com/inspmaps

This app helps students organize, plan, and build thinking skills as well as create and analyze charts and other data by producing a mind-map that can include text, video, photos, audio, and so on. Volume discounts are available. The web-based version is called Webspiration Classroom (tinyurl.com/bmop3nh) and is subscription based.

Bubbl.us
bubbl.us

This is a free (with limited use) mind-mapping website for Grades K–12. It can be shared by multiple students at a time and comes with an app. See the website for more options and to purchase a package.

MindMeister
tiny.cc/826i3y

This is a free, basic, mind-mapping website for Grades 2–12. Upgrades are available and have a free trial period. See the website for details.

FreeMind
tinyurl.com/5qrd5

This is a free mind-mapping tool for Grades 2–12. Options for a basic or maximum install are available.

Edmodo
edmodo.com

A free website where teachers can create a safe, password-protected learning community, including blogs and document-sharing. This is a great way to get students to write daily. A free app is available.

EasyBib
easybib.com

Students can use this free website and app to generate citations in MLA, APA, and Chicago formats. Just copy and paste or scan the book's barcode.

Citation Machine
citationmachine.net

This is another free website students can use to generate citations in MLA, APA, Turabian, and Chicago formats. Just copy, paste, and the website does the rest.

Purdue Online Writing Lab
tinyurl.com/n8r94uf

This free website was developed for college students but is available to all. It has resources for any kind of writing, grammar, spelling, and mechanics.

Table 11.4: Writing Resources

	Gooru gooru.org	This is a free, K–12 website with a supportive app. The site is a place to share information and make resources globally available. It covers math, science, social studies, and language arts by providing videos, worksheets, assessments, and other resources for students, broken out by standard. Great for flipping the classroom.
	CAST UDL Book Builder bookbuilder.cast.org	Use this nonprofit website to create, share, publish, and read digital books that engage and support diverse learners according to their individual needs, interests, and skills. The site is free.
	Lulu lulu.com	This site allows you to create real books and publish them online. Parents and students can purchase the books. The site is free to use, but a fee is required to publish.
	Wix wix.com	This online website creator is drag-and-drop easy and includes templates. The basics are free. An app version is available.
	Webs webs.com	This online website creator allows you to choose a template and then drag-and-drop elements onto webpages. Basic functionality is free, and an app is available.
	SiteBuilder sitebuilder.com	This is an online website creator that is drag-and-drop easy and includes templates. The website is free. With a domain name included, there is a cost.
	Weebly weebly.com	This is an online website creator that is drag-and-drop easy and includes templates. The basics, which include five pages, are free. There is even an app available.

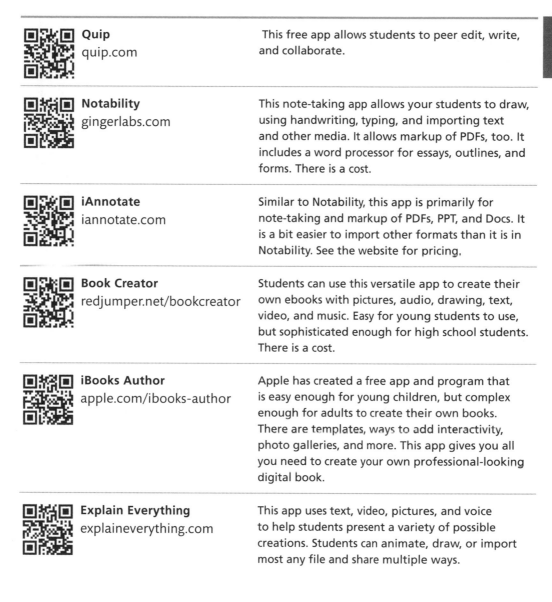

Quip
quip.com

This free app allows students to peer edit, write, and collaborate.

Notability
gingerlabs.com

This note-taking app allows your students to draw, using handwriting, typing, and importing text and other media. It allows markup of PDFs, too. It includes a word processor for essays, outlines, and forms. There is a cost.

iAnnotate
iannotate.com

Similar to Notability, this app is primarily for note-taking and markup of PDFs, PPT, and Docs. It is a bit easier to import other formats than it is in Notability. See the website for pricing.

Book Creator
redjumper.net/bookcreator

Students can use this versatile app to create their own ebooks with pictures, audio, drawing, text, video, and music. Easy for young students to use, but sophisticated enough for high school students. There is a cost.

iBooks Author
apple.com/ibooks-author

Apple has created a free app and program that is easy enough for young children, but complex enough for adults to create their own books. There are templates, ways to add interactivity, photo galleries, and more. This app gives you all you need to create your own professional-looking digital book.

Explain Everything
explaineverything.com

This app uses text, video, pictures, and voice to help students present a variety of possible creations. Students can animate, draw, or import most any file and share multiple ways.

Speaking and Listening Resources

SL.9-10.2 • SPEAKING AND LISTENING

Integrate multiple sources of information presented in **diverse media or formats** (e.g., visually, quantitatively, orally) evaluating the credibility and accuracy of each source.

SL.9–10.5 • SPEAKING AND LISTENING

Make strategic use of **digital media (e.g., textual, graphical, audio, visual, and interactive elements)** in presentations to enhance understanding of findings, reasoning, and evidence and to add interest.S

Speaking and Listening Standard 2 expects the use of technology from kindergarten through Grade 12. In today's world, we listen to all kinds of diverse media and constantly need to analyze and make decisions about its content. We also use multiple kinds of technology to speak to others. The idea behind Speaking and Listening Standard 2 changes slightly between middle school and ninth and tenth grades from one of analyzing and evaluating sources and the motives behind them to integrating sources and evaluating their credibility. These are nuances that can be achieved through rubrics and even the simple use of student reactions to the credibility of the texts they read.

Speaking and Listening Standard 5 begins with using pictures when speaking in kindergarten. This standard builds through the grades, making strategic use of digital media for presentations by high school. Learning to use media to help in presentations is critical for college and career readiness. Your ninth- and tenth-grade students need to make strategic use of digital media to enhance understanding for them and their audience. This highlights using technology effectively, not just using it because it is something "awesome."

Microsoft PowerPoint has been the presentation program of choice, but it can be expensive. There is now a free educational version called **Microsoft 365 (tinyurl. com/zsfogge)** that includes PowerPoint. While this is still a great program, other presentation tools are just as useful. Apple offers **Keynote (apple.com/keynote)** as part of its computer software package. Its features are very similar to PowerPoint's, but it does require a purchase. Another program that has emerged is **Google Slides**

(google.com/slides/about). There are other resources that help with presentations, such as **Microsoft Paint3D (tinyurl.com/zsfogge)** and **Google Drawings (tiny.cc/5gfs3y).** Although Office 365 is free to schools, Google Drive products such as Slides and Drawings are free and web-based. Google Slides makes it very easy to share a project that multiple users can work on at once, which makes it an especially good program to use when interacting and collaborating remotely. Students can also add audio recordings to their slides, as well as visual displays, such as pictures and short video clips. Consider having your students use the digital tools in **Table 11.5**.

Table 11.5: Speaking and Listening Resources

Explain Everything explaineverything.com	This app uses text, video, pictures, and voice to present a variety of possible creations. Whether it is writing or presenting, this app can do almost everything well. The company offers educational pricing.
Doceri doceri.com	This app combines an interactive whiteboard, screen-casting, and desktop control in one resource. Create a lesson or presentation, insert images, save and edit your project, and record a screen-cast video. Pricing for the app varies. There is a desktop app for both Mac and Windows with educational pricing.
iMovie and iMovie Trailer apple.com/ios/imovie	This app, which is also available as a program, has many uses in the classroom. Students can use it to create presentations, movies, documentaries, and motion slideshows. Students can also create short trailers that focus on important points about issues and events studied.
TouchCast touchcast.com	This free app video creator lets you embed linkable websites, pictures, photos, and more into your video. It is also available on PC. There is some concern about privacy. TouchCast does have the EduCast channel, which is geared to education, with teacher tutorials and other resources.

APPS

Table 11.5: Speaking and Listening Resources

	HP Reveal hpreveal.com	You can use this free app to take a picture, website, and so on, and add layers of animation to your original. The company provides many resources, or you can use resources you create. HP Reveal is great for getting information across in a quick, vivid, and animated way.
	Clips apple.com/clips	This free app is for creating and sharing videos. Students can create selfie videos with green-screen effects, emojis, stickers, and filters. They can also turn speech into captions and have animated titles.
	Glogster glogster.com	Create presentations you can share with this free app. You can even browse and use presentations made by others. Glogster provides images, graphics, and videos. Or upload your own. The companion website has educational pricing.
	Prezi prezi.com	You can sign up for a free educational account, and your students can create and share presentations online. Prezi has mind-mapping, zoom, and motion, and it can import files. Presentations can be downloaded. A Prezi viewer app is available.
	BaiBoard baiboard.com	This whiteboard app allows students to create, collaborate, and share—and it's free. The difference between this and other whiteboard apps is that multiple students can have real-time access to one project and collaborate.
	Google Slides google.com/slides/about	This is a simpler version of Microsoft's PowerPoint, and it's free. Students can use this for sharing projects, summarizing their work, and peer-to-peer teaching.
	Google Blogger blogger.com	This free blogging site has numerous features. Students can see other classes and can be cross-grouped with similar sections of the same course by ability or with mixed ability as needed. There is an app available.

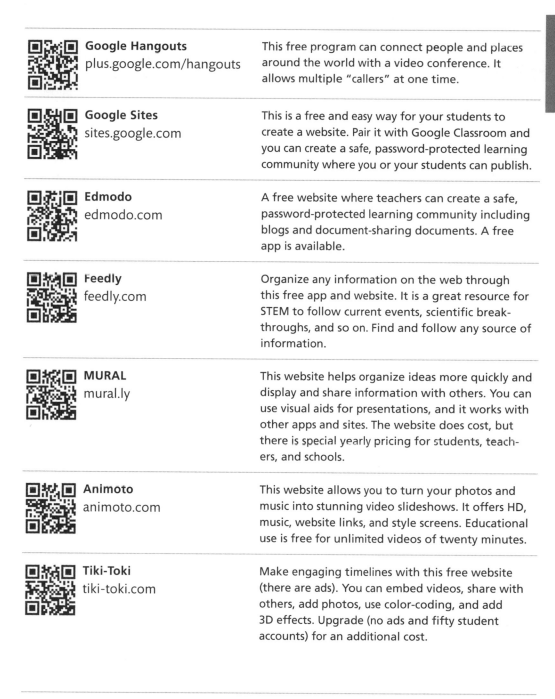

Google Hangouts
plus.google.com/hangouts

This free program can connect people and places around the world with a video conference. It allows multiple "callers" at one time.

Google Sites
sites.google.com

This is a free and easy way for your students to create a website. Pair it with Google Classroom and you can create a safe, password-protected learning community where you or your students can publish.

Edmodo
edmodo.com

A free website where teachers can create a safe, password-protected learning community including blogs and document-sharing documents. A free app is available.

Feedly
feedly.com

Organize any information on the web through this free app and website. It is a great resource for STEM to follow current events, scientific break-throughs, and so on. Find and follow any source of information.

MURAL
mural.ly

This website helps organize ideas more quickly and display and share information with others. You can use visual aids for presentations, and it works with other apps and sites. The website does cost, but there is special yearly pricing for students, teachers, and schools.

Animoto
animoto.com

This website allows you to turn your photos and music into stunning video slideshows. It offers HD, music, website links, and style screens. Educational use is free for unlimited videos of twenty minutes.

Tiki-Toki
tiki-toki.com

Make engaging timelines with this free website (there are ads). You can embed videos, share with others, add photos, use color-coding, and add 3D effects. Upgrade (no ads and fifty student accounts) for an additional cost.

Table 11.5: Speaking and Listening Resources

Binumi
binumi.com

Easily combine media from the cloud to tell a story with video, audio, pictures, animation, and so on, to create a visual narrative, or use a story template. This website is free, but it can be upgraded for a price.

Kizoa
kizoa.com

This web-based program makes and edits movies, slideshows, collages, and photos. There are templates available, along with stock video clips, photos, and music to make your presentations look and sound great. Students can also upload their own files to edit. This program is free for basic use, but you can upgrade for a price.

Powtoon
powtoon.com

This video-creating website is easy to use with ready-made templates and great content, such as music, objects, and photos. It is free for short (three minutes or less) videos, but you can upgrade for a price.

Moovly
moovly.com

This is a wonderful video-creation website for projects, portfolios, and presentations. It comes with access to the editor, unlimited videos, sounds, music, photos, and illustrations. You can even batch upload your own media. It is free for educators and their students.

Adobe Spark
tinyurl.com/yamq84lg

This free app from Adobe gives students and teachers a great way to make video presentations. Create a movie and narrate in your own voice. The app provides themes, photos, animations, and templates to organize the videos.

Shmoop
schools.shmoop.com

This site helps students build great videos for presentations and review. There are many templates included, and it uses the student's face and voice in the videos that range from ELA to math, science, social studies, test prep, and more. It can be costly for individual teachers, but school pricing is well worth it.

Flipsnack
flipsnackedu.com

This publishing tool is great for brochures, catalogs, and visual presentations. It is cross-platform and includes links, buttons, pictures, and has templates. Your work can be privately or publicly published on their website, embedded in a blog, emailed, or sent through social media. The limited version is free but can be upgraded for a price.

WebQuest
webquest.org

WebQuests are good tools to use for presentations. The WebQuest site allows students to follow an already-created, project-based lesson where information is found solely on the internet. Students can create their own WebQuest if a website-building program or a website such as SiteBuilder (sitebuilder.com) is available. WebQuest.org is the original and most popular site, but if you search the internet, you will find more sites that you can use.

Language Resources

L.9–10.4c • LANGUAGE

Consult general and specialized reference materials (e.g., dictionaries, glossaries, thesauruses), both print and **digital**, to find the pronunciation of a word or determine or clarify its precise meaning, its part of speech, or its etymology.

This standard is very straightforward. It clarifies the meaning of words at all grade levels. Students need to know how to find word meanings using not only print but digital dictionaries, glossaries, and thesauruses. In ninth and tenth grades, the standard changes slightly, adding "its part of speech, or its etymology." The technology aspect of the standard is still the same.

Bookmark these sites or add them to your website for easy access. The more students use them, the more comfortable they will become. Offer lessons and activities to learn and practice how to find parts of speech and etymology with an online dictionary.

Table 11.6: Language Resources

	Merriam-Webster merriam-webster.com	This is a free digital dictionary for all ages. It is the most commonly used digital dictionary, and it includes a thesaurus.
	Wordsmyth wordsmyth.net	This site shows three levels of a student dictionary. When looking up a word, there are also links to a thesaurus and rhyming dictionary for that word. You can sign up for an ad-free version that will not cost your school.
	Word Central wordcentral.com	This student online dictionary includes an audio pronunciation of the word as well as the definition. There are many teacher resources.
	Thesaurus.com thesaurus.com	This is a great thesaurus site with many extra features. It does have some ads, but it is available free online and as an app.
	Online Etymology Dictionary etymonline.com	This free site gives a detailed etymology for most words. There are several ways to search, from a single term to a phrase.

Math Resources

MP5 • MATH

Use appropriate **tools** strategically.

There are two main sets of standards for the Common Core math standards: processes and practices. First, you have the math targets, written similarly to ELA (Number and Quantity, Algebra, Functions, Modeling, Geometry, and Statistics and Probability). While you work with high school students on mathematical processes, such as Algebra or Modeling, you need to teach your students how to apply the SMPs (which include problem solving and precision) to those processes. One practice, the only one that includes technology, is mathematical practice 5: "Use appropriate tools strategically."

Following is the explanation CCSS provides for **MP5.**

> Mathematically proficient students consider the available tools when solving a mathematical problem. These tools might include pencil and paper, concrete models, a ruler, a protractor, a calculator, **a spreadsheet, a computer algebra system, a statistical package, or dynamic geometry software**. Proficient students are sufficiently familiar with tools appropriate for their grade or course to make sound decisions about when each of these tools might be helpful, recognizing both the insight to be gained and their limitations. For example, mathematically proficient high school students analyze graphs of functions and solutions generated using a **graphing calculator**. They detect possible errors by strategically using estimation and other mathematical knowledge. When making mathematical models, they know that technology can enable them to visualize the results of varying assumptions, explore consequences, and compare predictions with data. Mathematically proficient students at various grade levels are able to identify relevant external mathematical resources, such as **digital content located on a website**, and use them to pose or solve problems. They are able to use **technological tools** to explore and deepen their understanding of concepts.

We have provided lists of appropriate apps, websites, software, and lessons that will help translate this standard for high school.

Your students will need to begin using technology as a tool to help them strengthen their math skills. That is essentially what this math standard—the only one that explicitly includes technology—states. Using technology as a mathematical practice tool can be interpreted in many different ways. In any case, technology is a math tool students should use as much as possible. Many math programs, websites, and apps allow students to explore and deepen their understanding of math concepts. The best of them have students learning in creative ways and are not merely electronic worksheets. They automatically adapt to the students' skill levels, and they tell you where students are in their learning and what they need to advance. We list many good math resources here. Some are free. Some are not. The free resources (many with ads) are often less interesting and not as well organized. They don't give you the feedback you need. It is up to you to decide what is best for your circumstances and budget.

Table 10.1 in the previous chapter lists some websites you can use to help students meet the ninth- and tenth-grade math standards.

Literacy Lessons

Cross-curriculum planning is encouraged with CCSS by using ELA standards in history, science, and technical subjects. Getting through all of the standards you need in high school is very difficult in the time given. We highly encourage teaching more than one standard in the lesson, when you can. The key to planning is teaching multiple standards in one lesson and working with others in your department, and in other departments, if possible. We hope the following list of sample lessons in literacy for Grades 9–10 inspires you to become an effective technology lesson planner.

Gattaca

From the files of our high school friends, this assignment explores whether the movie *Gattaca* represents an accurate picture of what America will look like in the not-so-distant future. Students learn about biotechnology, DNA, and the genetics of inheritance as well as genetically engineered food (ground meat/hamburger in particular). The unit includes a lot of discussion through blogging—students are grouped across course sections for the discussion. First, students view the film

Gattaca in class. Next, students are assigned to groups (across sections of the same course). In each class, students join the blog using Google Blogger. Articles and additional resources are found on the blog. Classmates are asked to discuss specific questions on the blog and to react to comments made by other group members. A Google Form is used as a way for students to document their participation.

Because the blog is active during the entire span of the unit, it allows students to post an opinion and then revise their thinking as a result of additional knowledge or opinions of others. This is the primary focus of **W.9-10.6** and **WHST.9-10.6.** As the class is organizing a complex topic, making corrections, and using formatting, multimedia, and graphics to help in comprehension, they are satisfying **W.9-10.2.A** and **WHST.9-10.2.A.** Students make strategic use of digital media to enhance their understanding of the issues the movie presents, which satisfies **SL.9-10.5,** and they integrate multiple sources of information in diverse formats **(SL.9-10.2).**

ISTE STUDENT STANDARDS

Students will be using several ISTE Standards in this lesson.

- **Empowered Learner** by using technology to seek feedback that improves practice and learning in a variety of ways.

- **Knowledge Constructor** through evaluating information for intellectual pursuits.

- **Creative Communicator** by publishing content that customizes the message for their intended audience.

- **Global Collaborator** by connecting to other learners to broaden mutual understanding and contributing to a team project.

History of Television

A local high school tenth-grade English class spends time discussing and analyzing the television programming available to American families. After spending time discussing the history of television, students are divided into small groups and given an assignment to watch various television shows from each decade, using YouTube. Each team is assigned shows to watch so a different variety from each decade can be represented. You can generate your own list or have your students brainstorm a list with you. A list might include *The Tonight Show* (Jack Paar), *The Tonight Show*

(Johnny Carson), *The Honeymooners* with Jackie Gleason, *I Love Lucy, Bonanza,* and so on. Teams next put together a Prezi or TouchCast to depict their show (genre, plot, characters, etc.). Some may even want to include a film snippet from their show, to give their audience an opportunity to see it. Next, presentations are shown to the class.

Discuss with your students their present-day experiences with television, as well as how much they know about producing a television show. Students divide into groups for this activity. Their first task is to spend some time researching and discussing how television programs are produced. Bring the class together to have a discussion on what each group discovered about television production. Each group will then develop an idea for their own show. First, they will write a proposal, describing the plot, setting, and characters, as well as the target audience. This can easily be written and shared with you using Google Docs. Once the group is satisfied with their idea and you have given the go-ahead, they can begin writing their script for one episode of the show. It may be necessary for groups to research how television scripts are formatted.

After the script has been written, groups create a storyboard that shows the flow of the story in pictorial and written form. Use Google Storyboards for television scripts. There are a plethora of templates and examples students can use. Or, encourage them to create their own! Group members next choose actors for their show. After several rehearsals, they can begin putting their episode on video. Once all episodes have been completed, students share their creations with the entire class.

The primary focus for this lesson is **W.9-10.6** and **WHST.9-10.6,** by using the internet to produce, then update (revise) shared writing in a flexible way. They also satisfy **W.9-10.8** and **WHST.9-10.8** by researching using different sources, answering research questions, and integrating information. As the class is organizing a complex topic, making corrections, and using formatting, multimedia, and graphics to help in comprehension, they satisfy **W.9-10.2.A** and **WHST.9-10.2.A.** They also integrate multiple sources of information presented in diverse media or formats (**SL.9-10.2,** as well as **SL.9-10.5**).

ISTE STUDENT STANDARDS
Students experiencing this lesson will be using these ISTE Standards.

- **Empowered Learner** by using technology to seek feedback that improves practice and learning in a variety of ways.

- **Knowledge Constructor** through evaluating information for intellectual pursuits.

- **Creative Communicator** by publishing content that customizes the message for their intended audience.

- **Global Collaborator** by connecting to other learners to broaden mutual understanding and contributing to a team project.

Learning SAT Vocabulary Through Drama

Every freshman and sophomore has one thing on his or her mind: taking the SAT! Building a solid SAT vocabulary is essential for reading success, as well as for communicating effectively when speaking, writing, and listening. Motivation plays a big role in learning SAT vocabulary. This lesson motivates students to master SAT vocabulary words because they are using them to create and film their own teen dramas from start to finish. Student objectives include deciding how to use vocabulary appropriately and effectively by creating drama that develops real or imagined events. By creating this real or imagined drama, students use effective techniques, well-chosen details, and a well-structured event sequence, including narrative elements like dialogue, pacing, description, reflection, and multiple plot lines to develop experiences, events, and characters. Throughout this lesson, students self-assess and evaluate the creation of their drama to make sure it reflects a particular tone and outcome, including developing a sense of mystery, suspense, growth, and resolution, while effectively using technology and digital media to produce, edit, and publish a shared writing project.

Explain to students they will be writing their own teen drama to learn fifteen new words, incorporating SAT vocabulary words into their script. Using your Smart Board or **Miro (realtimeboard.com),** go over **ReadWriteThink's Rubric for Cooperative and Collaborative Learning (tinyurl.com/y77ovuy7).** This is actually a document you may wish to share electronically with your students so they each have a copy, not only for this lesson but future lessons. The final filmed drama needs to represent the whole class, and for this reason it will be necessary to work cooperatively and collaboratively with each other. Everyone should reach the goals of the rubric while working together.

Begin by showing your class **"High School Uncut: Revere High School's Teen Soap Opera to Learn SAT Words" (tinyurl.com/y8blylve).** Have a discussion about this short YouTube selection to make sure students understand the assignment. Point out how the students in the video were able to effectively incorporate the SAT vocabulary words into their drama while creating a plot. Next, have students brainstorm what topics they can use for their drama (relationships, trouble with parents, bullying, stresses in daily teenage life, peer pressure, etc.). This list will help students stay focused. To satisfy **RI.9-10.7,** have students read text of a real-life teenage drama. One example is "**Teenage Drama: Based on a True Story" (tinyurl. com/ya6hptrp).**

Have students work in small groups. Their first task is to choose whether they would like to be writers, actors, or costume and set designers. There only needs to be one set and costume designer, but more writers and actors are needed. You should be the director until everyone has a grasp of the project. You can choose a director when the small groups are on a good path with the task.

Use ReadWriteThink's **Story Map (tinyurl.com/ykqgbob)** to meet with the writers, instructing them to identify characters, setting, conflict, and resolution. Writers also use the **Plot Diagram (tinyurl.com/yampr4z)** to write the story. Consider sharing all of these documents with every student, so others not directly involved in the writing can help the writers formulate ideas, etc. Students should plan to make their drama about four-to-eight minutes long with about three or four scenes. Also, share with your students the article *How to Write a Screenplay* **(screenwriting.info).** Students will also need a copy of **Vocabulary.com's 100 Top SAT words (vocabulary. com/lists/23400).** Choose how many words students should include in their initial episode. Fifteen words is a nice place to start. This is a great project to continue throughout the year. Students can extend their drama by adding another episode, as well as fifteen more vocabulary words. By the end of the school year, students will have a nice, full-length drama!

Review with the class how to write sentences using the SAT vocabulary words. Do the sentence and situation adequately provide clues as to the meaning of the word? Again, students not yet involved with a task can also write sentences with vocabulary words and share with the writers. When they are involved in their tasks, the writers can be asked to help.

After the stories have been written, they need to be shared amongst the group. Everyone needs a copy of the **Readers Theater Rubric (tinyurl.com/2d5hp72)** to make sure everything in their assignment meets the criteria. Costume and set designers, as well as well as camera people and actors need to work together on staging. Again, if writers are finished with their task, they can also help out. Writers can also work with the actors on learning their lines, and helping the dialogue to run smoothly. When the writers and actors are satisfied, they can begin learning and practicing the next scene.

When everyone is ready, begin filming the scenes. Have students use a tablet or smartphone camera. Filming may require several attempts, but should improve with each take. This is another reason why scenes should be no longer than five minutes. As scenes are finished, students can work directly from their tablets or smartphones. This is also something students can do if there is only one camera and it needs to be shared. Students use the presentation tool you have chosen or choose one of their own (if applicable). There are many presentation tools to choose from. **Animoto (animoto.com)** and **iMovie (apple.com/ios/imovie)** are some of the more popular choices. Encourage your students to try some of the new presentation tools available: **Powtoon (powtoon.com), Moovly (moovly.com), Shmoop (schools. shmoop.com)** or **Adobe Spark (tiny.cc/mvix3y)**. These are only a few examples. There are many presentation tools available. Some are free, while some do have a cost.

Students use the editing software of their presentation tool to edit the scenes and add titles. Don't forget to add the SAT vocabulary words as they appear in each scene! Students may also need to watch "**High School Uncut: Revere High School's Teen Soap Opera to Learn SAT Words**" **(tinyurl.com/y8blylve)** again, especially if they need a refresher on how their final product should look. Although most students are pretty adept at editing, you may need to offer some assistance and/or have your school's media instructor on hand in your classroom to help.

When your students finish their dramas, have a sharing session. These presentations can also be saved to their digital portfolios or published on your website for others to see. As mentioned earlier, this lesson can also be used throughout the year.

W.9-10.2.A, WHST.9-10.2A, W.9-10.6, WHST.9-10.6, W.9-10.8, and **WHST.9-10.8** are satisfied when students research and write about their topic using technology, and when students write, produce, and publish their writing, presenting their information clearly and efficiently. You may even wish to publish their writing on your website. **SL.9-10.2** and **SL.9-10.5** are satisfied when students contribute to class discussions and present their plot diagrams, story maps, and final projects to the class. **L.9-10.4c** is also satisfied in this lesson, when students use dictionaries, glossaries, and thesauruses, not only to search for words to bolster their writing, but to clarify the precise meaning of SAT vocabulary.

ISTE STUDENT STANDARDS

This lesson uses these ISTE Standards.

- **Knowledge Constructor** by curating information using a variety of tools to create a collection of artifacts that demonstrate learning.

- **Creative Communicator** by creating original work and communicating complex ideas using effective digital tools.

- **Global Collaborator** by working as a team member and connecting to other learners to broaden mutual understanding.

Science/Social Studies Lessons

The following sample lessons address CCSS ELA standards and teach lessons based on national standards in social studies and science.

World Religions

The students in a ninth-grade high school class compare the six major religions of the world. In this unit, you, as teacher, outline the major research questions. Students break into groups. Your class then completes research on the different religions using internet sites and school/public library databases. Next, students are asked what questions they still have, now that they have done the research. Their questions are sent to a representative for each religion (this particular high school found them through the school's career counselor). Each representative then is scheduled for a thirty-minute presentation time to present to the class and answer the questions your class posed. Representatives either come to the classroom or are connected via a virtual meeting using Google Hangouts. Finally, your students compare and contrast the religions and revise their research for a better understanding.

The primary focus of this lesson is organizing a complex topic, making corrections, and using formatting, multimedia, and graphics to help in comprehension, so students are satisfying **W.9-10.2.A** and **WHST.9-10.2.A.** Also, **W.9-10.6** and **WHST.9-10.6** are satisfied by using the internet to produce, then update (revise) shared writing in a flexible way. They also satisfy **W.9-10.8** and **WHST.9-10.8** by researching using different sources, answering research questions, and integrating information. They also integrate multiple sources of information presented in diverse media or formats **(SL.9-10.2).**

ISTE STUDENT STANDARDS

Students will be using a variety of ISTE Standards in this lesson.

- **Digital Citizen** by demonstrating respects for rights in using and sharing intellectual property.

- **Knowledge Constructor** by employing research, evaluating and building knowledge, developing ideas and pursuing solutions to real-world issues using digital resources.

- **Creative Communicator** by communicating complex ideas effectively through creation of new resources using a variety of media and publishing for an intended audience.

- **Global Collaborator** by using collaborative technologies to work with experts and community members and connecting to other learners to broaden mutual understanding and contributing to a team project.

World Social Issues

Each year a nearby high school has their tenth-graders grapple with world social issues to help students better understand political, religious, and economic issues. To complete this series of lessons, you might choose to have your students research countries that are participating in the Olympics. This knowledge then transfers to a larger unit during the fourth quarter, which requires your students to have a more extensive knowledge of a single country. The essential question for the fourth quarter learning would be, "Why do countries have hostility/resentment toward the United States?" Your students are assigned a country to research, compare, and contrast. This is done under the umbrella of the Olympics. You would share overarching questions, which your students discuss, comment on, and then rethink.

The class can use apps such as Feedly to obtain current events about their country. Print media, videos, internet links, political cartoons, and so on are provided as source materials. When doing this, you fulfill **RI.9-10.7,** to analyze various accounts of a subject told in different mediums. Students must also compare and contrast text and other sources to note pros and cons and thus satisfy **RST.9-10.9.** Students in your class can use Evernote, iAnnotate, or similar apps to help organize their sources and resources. That satisfies **WHST.9-10.6** by using technology, including the internet, to produce, publish, and update individual or shared writing products, taking advantage of technology's capacity to link to other information and to display information flexibly and dynamically, and **WHST.9-10.8** by gathering relevant information from multiple authoritative print and digital sources. Then your students can summarize their learning by using Google Docs or Slides, TouchCast, HP Reveal, MURAL, or other great sites and apps to create a presentation that is electronically posted for all to view, and review. This meets **SL.9-10.2** by integrating multiple sources of information presented in diverse media or formats and **SL.9-10.5** by making strategic use of digital media.

ISTE STUDENT STANDARDS

Students will be using a variety of ISTE Standards in this lesson.

- **Empowered Learner** through use of technology to seek feedback that informs and improves their learning.

- **Digital Citizen** by demonstrating respects for rights in using and sharing intellectual property.

- **Knowledge Constructor** by employing research, evaluating and building knowledge, developing ideas and pursuing solutions to real-world issues using digital resources.

- **Creative Communicator** through choosing the appropriate platform and publishing and presenting customized content

- **Global Collaborator** by working as a team member and connecting to other learners to broaden mutual understanding.

Math/Technical Subjects Lessons

Many teachers have embraced WebQuests as a way to make good use of the internet while engaging their students in a technology-rich environment for problem solving, information processing, collaboration, and the kinds of thinking that the digital age requires. There are many WebQuests available for any high school subject: simply do a Google search. WebQuests can be used all year. Once students are familiar with WebQuests, have them write their own!

Baseball Activities

A neighboring high school starts the year with a WebQuest titled "Can You Buy a Winning Baseball Team?" You can find several versions of this WebQuest (already written) by searching the web with the title. Students work in teams and are presented with the problem: Major league baseball players are paid millions of dollars by team owners. Fans are questioning whether their favorite teams can compete with other teams. Is it possible for a team with a minimal payroll to win the World Series?

To answer these questions, students will need to collect the following data:

- The number of wins each professional baseball team had during the regular season in (pick a year).

- The total team payroll for each professional baseball team in (pick the same year as above).

- The population of each city with a professional baseball team (same as the year above).

Next, teams must put all data in a chart (Google Sheets, TouchCast, Glogster, etc.). Data should include the following:

- City population

- Attendance

- Team Payroll

- Number of regular-season wins

For this lesson, students will need a straightedge and graph paper, as well as access to the internet. Google online graph paper to check out the many options available. You can also use the Desmos website for graphing. You may want to give students sites that will be helpful to access the information they will need. See our website for this book **(tinyurl.com/y9dfltpr).**

After teams have completed their research, they start to work on the following process.

- Plot the numerical data on a coordinate plane three times:

  o Plot I: payroll versus wins

  o Plot II: population versus wins

  o Plot III: population versus payroll

- Find a line of "best-fit" so most of the points are close to the ruler for each of the three graphs.

- Plot the line, and then write an equation in slope-intercept form.

When all data has been plotted and graphed, students answer the following evaluation questions and submit to you via Google Docs or a similar program.

- How much would you expect to pay a major league baseball team if you wanted them to win 100 games?

- How many people would you expect to find in a city if the major league baseball team in that city won only fifty games?

- Describe each of the three plots as having a positive correlation, negative correlation, or no correlation.

- In Plot I, what does m value in the slope-intercept form represent?

- In Plot II, what does the b value in the slope-intercept form represent?

- What does the line on Plot I say about the relationship between the payroll of a major league baseball team and the number of games you can expect them to win?

- What does the line on Plot II say about the relationship between the population of a major league baseball team's city and the number of games you can expect them to win?

- What does the line on Plot III say about the relationship between the population of a major league baseball team's city and payroll of the major league baseball team in that city?

- Examine your answer to #6 above. Some people are upset by this. Why?

- Do you think all teams have an equal chance at getting to, and winning, the World Series? Why or why not?

- *Extra Credit:* Do a team payroll versus wins versus population analysis of a different professional sport. You will need to answer all questions and complete all plots from above.

When all student teams have finished, come together as a class. Have a discussion and see if a consensus can be reached. Fans may be upset. They might know ahead of time that their team doesn't have a chance to win it all. At least that is the perception. Solutions to this problem are thrown around often (salary caps, removal of free agency), but because professional sports have become big business, the issue is becoming more complicated each year. What conclusion did your student team come up with? This would also be an excellent topic for a class blog discussion (Google Blogger, etc.).

In addition to **MP5,** using appropriate tools strategically, primary standards satisfied are **RI.9-10.7, RH.9-10.7,** and **RST.9-10.7,** as quantitative and technical analysis is needed to understand and determine the results for the teams. Also, **W.9-10.6** and **WHST.9-10.6** are satisfied when students share their data and debate the conclusion. These two standards are also addressed when students write, share, and publish their own WebQuests. Students are making strategic use of digital media to enhance their understanding of the data discovered in the WebQuest task, which satisfies **SL.9-10.5,** as well as integrating multiple sources of information in diverse formats **(SL.9-10.2).** Gathering relevant information from multiple digital sources, as well as assessing the usefulness of each resource to help plot the data and answer the research questions, satisfies **W.9-10.8** and **WHST 9-10.8**.

ISTE STUDENT STANDARDS

Students will be using a variety of ISTE Standards in this lesson.

- **Knowledge Constructor** by employing research, evaluating and building knowledge, developing ideas and pursuing solutions to real-world issues using digital resources.

- **Computational Thinker** by formulating problem definitions suited to technology solutions and through data collection, breaking problems into component parts, and developing models to help facilitate problem solving.

- **Global Collaborator** by working as a team member and connecting to other learners to broaden mutual understanding.

Income Tax Activities

From the files of a local high school math coach, this lesson has students apply percentages to real-life situations by figuring the amount of income tax (federal, state, and local) that will be withheld from a salary for their "dream" job. Students will learn about credit and credit scores. They will learn what will hurt their scores and what will help their scores. Students will learn about all the aspects of credit, and that they will be able to make informed decisions regarding credit. The concept of interest and how to analyze interest will also be addressed.

Students will use the internet to research salary information, as well as tax percentages for their area. This may be information you wish to provide for them, ensuring that all students have the same, accurate information. Math Standard **MP5** has students use appropriate tools strategically. You will need to decide if a calculator is appropriate for your students to use during this lesson. Most computers, laptops, tablets, and smartphones are equipped with a calculator. There are also free online calculators available.

Start the discussion with a survey of how many students (or their parents) have a credit card and if they understand how credit cards work. You may even want to consider doing a quick check of vocabulary, which will be addressed during the lesson. Terms like *credit, credit card, credit risk, credit score, interest, APR,* and *credit limit* are a few suggestions to include in your lesson. You may wish to find videos to help you with this discussion (Virtual Nerd, Khan Academy, MathPickle, etc.).

Next, have students research and report to you (using Google Forms, Google Docs, or even a blog) by answering the following questions.

- How do credit cards work?

- How does credit card interest work, especially if you do not pay off the balance when the payment is due?

- What are the differences among credit cards, debit cards, and cash, and how does each work?

- What role do banks play in offering you credit?

- What is a credit score? How do you get one? What makes up an individual's credit score? How do lenders use credit scores? How do private businesses use the scores?

- Who calculates credit scores? The bank? Government? Private organizations? Give examples.

Once students have a solid foundational knowledge of salaries and taxes, they should think about their "dream" job. Explain they will have to pay taxes on that salary to the local, state, and federal government. They can research the tax percentages, or you can give the rates to them. Have them calculate how much each week, month, and year they will pay in taxes. Record the amount in a manner of their choice (Google Sheets, TouchCast, Glogster, Desmos, etc.). Once they have graphed the different amounts, have students draw conclusions about the taxes people pay. This can be written and submitted to you in a variety of ways (e.g., Google Docs, Google Blogger, or GoToMeeting **[AU: Should GoToMeeting appear in a list?]**).

Finally, your students can summarize their learning by using Google Docs, Prezi, TouchCast, HP Reveal, MURAL, or other great sites and apps to create a presentation that is electronically posted for all to view, and review.

This meets **SL.9-10.2,** to integrate multiple sources of information presented in diverse media or formats, and **SL.9-10.5,** by making strategic use of digital media. Also, primary standards satisfied are **RI.9-10.7, RH.9-10.7,** and **RST.9-10.7,** as quantitative and technical analysis is needed to understand and determine the results for the teams.

Gathering relevant information from multiple digital sources, as well as assessing the usefulness of each resource to help plot the data and answer the research questions, satisfies **W.9-10.8** and **WHST.9-10.8. RI.9-10.6** is also satisfied when students analyze various accounts of a subject told in different mediums. Students in your class can use Evernote, iAnnotate, or similar apps to help organize their sources and resources. That satisfies **WHST.9-10.6** by using technology, including the internet, to produce, publish, and update individual or shared writing products, taking advantage of technology's capacity to link to other information and to display information flexibly and dynamically.

ISTE STUDENT STANDARDS

Students will be using multiple ISTE Standards in this lesson.

- **Digital Citizen** by demonstrating respects for rights in using and sharing intellectual property.

- **Knowledge Constructor** by employing research, evaluating and building knowledge, developing ideas and pursuing solutions to real-world issues using digital resources.

- **Computational Thinker** by formulating problem definitions suited to technology solutions and through data collection, breaking problems into component parts, and developing models to help facilitate problem solving.

- **Creative Communicator** by communicating effectively using a variety of media and publishing for an intended audience.

Savvy Buyer

This lesson is a very important application of math and a great unit for high school students who are novice consumers. It satisfies many of the standards in high school statistics such as interpreting data and making inferences. But it can also be used in any grade in middle or high school. The students will be comparison shopping for groceries at three different stores and analyzing the data to compare and draw conclusions.

You can use local stores or select them from a collection of online grocery sites. If you aren't sure which stores in your area provide online shopping services, assign students to find out as a homework assignment! If you want a wider variety of choices, use Google to search online groceries. There are other educational resources about grocery shopping and consumer shopping in general at this great site by the **Utah Education Network (tinyurl.com/y7syckdq).** Or maybe you'll find your own favorite resources for this lesson. There are many out there.

There can be a great deal of variation in how you set this up. You could provide a list that all the students price at three different stores, or the list could be student generated. The grocery list could be part of a weekly menu plan they need to create, if you want to bring in nutrition and budgeting to the lesson. Also, you might want them to work individually or in teams.

Students should first create a spreadsheet using **Microsoft Excel (office.com), Apple Numbers (apple.com/numbers),** or **Google Sheets (google.com/sheets/about),** or some other database to record the items, brand, quantity, size of their items, price, and unit price. Discuss unit price, that is, total cost divided by total quantity. (e.g., if apples are 4 for $1, then they are $.25 each; if juice is $1.65 for 10 ounces, then it is $.165 per ounce.). Also talk about price per serving which is different than cost per unit.

During the time they are shopping, students should be recording their observations in a note-taking document such as **Simplenote (simplenote.com), Evernote (evernote.com),** or **Penzu (penzu.com).** This will help them later when they share their findings with the class.

Students should complete their comparison shopping by going to the checkout area and seeing their totals with tax. Is there a price for delivery? Once the prices have been recorded, students should begin to do their comparison.

1. Students need to compare costs five ways:

2. Different brands, grades of quality

3. Foods in different forms, such as canned, frozen, fresh, dried

4. Different stores

5. Built-in convenience versus made-from-scratch

6. Similar foods as different varieties of the same fruit, or types of similar bread

The class will then begin to work on what they want to share of their shopping experience. This should include the following:

- Essential questions:

- What choices did they have?

- What food selections did they make and why?

- Is there an advantage to seasonal foods?

- Did they take advantage of sales?

- Did they price store brands?

- Did they buy larger quantities than they needed? Why?

- Did they consider cost per serving?

- Do stores have strengths and weaknesses?

- Which store is their choice to shop?

Students will then write using a word-processing program such as **Microsoft Office (office.com), Apple Pages (apple.com/pages),** or **Google Docs (google.com/docs/about)** and present their project to the class in two parts using a slideshow program such as PowerPoint, **Google Slides (google.com/slides/about)** or **Apple Keynote (apple.com/keynote).** The first will consist of the shopping data, which includes the computation of the prices and a comparison of the different store prices. They should include the data in graphs or charts. The second part is a presentation of analysis of what the data shows including their observations and evaluation of the best grocery store at which to shop and why.

As well as satisfying **MP5,** by using appropriate math tools (databases-generating charts and graphs) in solving a problem, they are fulfilling **RH.9-10.7** and **RST.9-10.7,** which is translating and integrating quantitative or technical analysis with qualitative analysis in digital text by writing their presentation. Of course they will also be using the skills of writing on a topic in an organized fashion and using multimedia, so satisfying **W.9-10.2.a** and **WHST.9-10.2.a.** If they publish their finding on the class website they will also be practicing standards **W.9-10.6** and **WHST.9-10.6.** In gathering the data from digital sources, they have fulfilled **W.9-10.8** and **WHST.9-10.8.** The

D uring my time in high school, many of my classes utilized a broad range of technology. We were all given tablets to use, and many teachers made good use of them. The biggest help for me were course websites. It was extremely helpful to have all the required information in one place. As well, the course websites were organized well, so navigating them was very helpful. While in elementary school, I remember being very comfortable using technology in many settings. I believe this to be a result of using technology frequently and because of my familiarity with it, I was able to successfully use technology as a tool to help me in further education. Specifically, I recall doing many projects that involved searching for valid, accurate information online. Learning this skill early on in my education allowed me to use it well even now, in my sophomore year of college.

—**Andy Christiansen, student**

presentation of the material also satisfies the speaking and listening standard **SL.9-10.5** by using presentation software to share their findings.

This activity can also be used for other shopping, such as clothes (example: a pair of jeans or shoes).

ISTE STUDENT STANDARDS

Students will be using a variety of ISTE Standards in this lesson.

- **Empowered Learner** by leverage technology to reflect on the learning process and improve learning outcomes and demonstrating learning in a variety of ways.

- **Knowledge Constructor** by employing research, evaluating and building knowledge, developing ideas and pursuing solutions to real-world issues using digital resources.

- **Innovative Designer** by using a design process for testing theories and solving authentic problems, including selection and use of the most appropriate digital tools.

- **Computational Thinker** by formulating problem definitions suited to technology solutions and through data collection, breaking problems into component parts, and developing models to help facilitate problem solving.

- **Creative Communicator** by communicating effectively using a variety of media and publishing for an intended audience.

- **Global Collaborator** by working as a team member and connecting to other learners to broaden mutual understanding.

A Final Note

As students progress through the grades, they establish their baseline of proficiency in technology. This will definitely enhance their experiences with technology in high school, as well as satisfy the CCSS performance standards at the 9–10 levels. We hope that you find the resources and lesson ideas presented in this chapter useful and that they are easy to adapt to your class.

You will find more resources online at our website **(tinyurl.com/y9dfltpr),** which may be helpful to you as you look to differentiate your instruction. Visit our site for updated information about this book. To learn more about applying technology found within the standards for other grades, look for our additional title.

12 Practical Ideas for Grades 11–12

W e realize that you will want to focus on your particular grade or subject when you are planning your lessons and implementing the standards, so we have organized the Practical Ideas chapters by grade level and subject. Each grade starts with an overview followed by ELA technology standards with accompanying apps, software, and websites that you can use to help your students succeed with that standard. We then continue with the math standard for the grade level and review appropriate resources. Finally, we have included sample lessons for each grade level in various subject areas. Although we have organized the book so you can find your specific grade and subject easily, please do not disregard other sections of this chapter. It is often helpful to see what the standards require before and after the grade you teach. To see grades other than 6–12, look for our other title in this series, as it could provide information to help you differentiate for students at all levels of your class.

The standards have been set up to encourage cross-curricular work in ELA for Grades 6–12. It standardizes the writing process through all classes in freshman through senior years by bringing the same writing standard into history, science, and technical subjects. The CCSS in high school are divided in two ranges: Grades 9–10 and Grades 11–12. As a high school teacher, you understand the difficulty of working with colleagues in other departments. There are systemic roadblocks that make communication with other departments difficult in most high schools. But, co-designing lessons between the language arts teachers and the history, science, and technical teachers will be a significant step in helping to create a strong foundation for your students before they enter college. It is also important to work with your administrators to ensure that you have time to plan. Planning can take place during a school- or districtwide professional development day or during staff meetings. Of course, the best option is to build collaboration time into the regular schedule.

Junior and senior students are the culmination of the mission that aligned the standards with college and career expectations. This is where the real test of success takes place. Are they ready for college? If they are not college bound, are they ready to explore a career? Of course, it takes a decade of implementing the standards, from kindergarten on, before they reach their junior year. Complete success will most likely be harder to measure. In time, students coming to you will have had to measure up to the standards each year, and they should be coming to you more prepared every year.

Math is also a subject area where technological tools become more varied and complex as students advance. The math standards are meant to be embedded in, and a natural part of, the units your students study. Choosing the correct math tools is an important part of your students' learning. There are wonderful new math resources available to help students become proficient in the standards, especially in the area of technology. We list some of our favorites later in this chapter.

Resources for Reading Literature

RL.11-12.7 • READING LITERATURE

Analyze multiple interpretations of a story, drama, or poem (e.g., **recorded** or live production of a play or recorded novel or poetry), evaluating how each version interprets the source text. (Include at least one play by Shakespeare and one play by an American dramatist.)

This standard begins in kindergarten with comparing illustrations and text and is developed through the grades using all types of media to compare, support, and analyze a story's meaning. So, the standard is essentially to get meaning from more than text; it can come from the accompanying media, even the format of the writing or media. The standard for Grades 11–12 differs somewhat from the same standard in Grades 9–10. As in this standard, freshmen and sophomores analyzed two things (art), but the end result was different. In Grades 9–10, they had to analyze what is emphasized and absent in each. In Grades 11–12, they need to analyze and then evaluate the different versions in relation to the source text.

The standard also requires that one of the studied plays is written by Shakespeare and another is written by an American dramatist. There are several sites with excellent resources for Shakespeare and the complete collection of his plays. There are also free resources for American plays. Of course, many movies, novels, songs, and poems are based on Shakespeare's plays, either directly or indirectly. Moreover, many American plays have been made into movies. So, there are plenty of resources in which to immerse your students.

Your school district may subscribe to **Gale Literature Resource Center** or other Gale products **(tinyurl.com/o47ydvs).** These are fine sources for thousands of frequently studied works. Your public library may have digital resources that are free to your school district. **Table 12.1** also contains some excellent media resources.

Table 12.1: Reading Literature Resources

APPS

	Genius genius.com	This free website can be used to annotate everything from rap songs to Shakespeare. There is even an annotated Common Core to help teachers understand it better. You must sign up to post and add writing.
	Folger Shakespeare Library folger.edu	This free, easy-to-search digital collection of online texts of the classics brings Shakespeare and other works into the digital age. Students can read them anywhere they have digital access.
	Open Source Shakespeare tiny.cc/t2at3y	This free, easy-to-search, digital online text brings Shakespeare's works into the digital age. Students can read them anywhere they have digital access.
	The Complete Works of William Shakespeare shakespeare.mit.edu	This is another free, easy-to-search, digital online text with all of Shakespeare's works. Students can read them anywhere they have digital access.
	Internet Archive archive.org	This free site has more than twelve million books, films, audio files, photos, songs, and documents. They come from libraries worldwide, TV stations, radio stations, and many other for-profit and non-profit groups. Books include plays by Shakespeare and American classics.

Table 12.1: Reading Literature Resources

 Read Print
readprint.com

This website with ads has thousands of poems, essays, stories, and plays, many of the classics from Dickens, Shakespeare, Twain, and so on. It is a great free literature resource. Keep track of books you have read and books you'd like to read. Discover new books and get recommendations. Discuss books and join online book clubs and groups.

 Edmodo
edmodo.com

A free website where teachers can create a safe, password-protected learning community, including blogs and document-sharing. This is a great way to get students to write daily. A free app is available.

 YouTube
youtube.com

There are many free videos that your students can view, including literature, reviews of art, and endless other topics that might fit your curriculum. There is also a free app. ·

 iTunes U
tinyurl.com/lbjbarh

As stated on Apple's website, "Choose from more than 750,000 free lectures, videos, books, and other resources on thousands of subjects from Algebra to Zoology." Access it free through iTunes. A free iTunes U app is also available.

 SchoolTube
schooltube.com

This educators' best free source for a video sharing community where students can watch or post videos.

 Netflix
netflix.com

Find films based on classic literature, more current literature, and Shakespeare can be found at this site. A subscription is required.

 Open Culture
tinyurl.com/d8ww8ez

This free website is a one-stop shop for audio-books, ebooks, and movies. There are even courses for teachers! They do not create the media. They just compile it so we can find it easier.

NeoK12
neok12.com

There are many science experiments, simulations, and videos on all sorts of topics on this website, and they are guaranteed to be kid safe. As an added bonus, it is free.

PBS LearningMedia
pbslearningmedia.org

This site is a great source for classroom-ready, free digital resources at all grades and in all subjects. This includes Masterpiece Theatre with accompanying lessons.

Resources for Reading Informational Text

RST.11-12.9 • READING HISTORY, SCIENCE, AND TECHNICAL SUBJECTS

Synthesize information from a **range of sources** (e.g., texts, experiments, simulations) into a coherent understanding of a process, phenomenon, or concept, resolving conflicting information when possible.

In the Reading Standard 9, the anchor standard is to analyze theme similarities in two or more texts. Although the Grades 11–12 standard does not state the actual digital sources, the anchor standard does, so it is implied that some of the sources must be videos and other media. In Grades 9–10, students were to compare and contrast; the Grades 11–12 standard demands a bit more thought and a different process. But the differences do not end there. The Grades 9–10 RST standard 9 also required that students note their support and contradictions in their comparison. In the Grades 11–12 version, as part of the synthesis, they must resolve any conflicting information. By this point in their studies, your students has already read history, social studies, science, and other disciplines extensively. They come to this standard with a good foundation of knowledge. The digital resources in **Table 12.2** are good jumping-off points in all areas of science, technical subjects, and history, including current events.

Table 12.2: Reading Informational Text Resources

The Learning Network
tiny.cc/gebt3y

This free website by the New York Times has many intriguing questions on current affairs that makes students think and analyze. The site contains multimedia and links to help students find more about issues, and it includes prompts for writing. There are ads.

APPS & WEBSITES

Table 12.2: Reading Informational Text Resources

	CNN cnn.com	The Cable News Network site is free but includes ads. It has trending news events and access to text, pictures, and video of current events.
	The Washington Post washingtonpost.com	This is the official site of the leading newspaper in the U.S. capital. There is access to current events in the nation and world. The site is free, but it does have ads.
	NPR npr.org	This site from National Public Radio is government sponsored and is free with no ads. There are links to current stories with media. Students can watch the most current NPR News Now.
	MSNBC msnbc.com	Another cable news site from NBC Universal, this free site does contain ads. You can find all the day's national and world news including video, photos, and text.
	Newsmap newsmap.jp	Using visual mapping to focus on the hottest current issues makes this site like a "word cloud" for news. Each map has links to the story behind the headlines. Articles provided by top news outlines around the world on this free site.
	Library of Congress tinyurl.com/2knoku	This free site, as part of the Library of Congress' website, offers easily searchable access to thousands of digital resources from the history of the United States.
	Feedly feedly.com	Organize any information on the web with this free app and website. It is a great resource for STEM to follow current events, scientific breakthroughs, and so on. Find and follow any source of information.
	Flipboard flipboard.com	Similar to Feedly, but with more constraints, and it draws from some different resources. A free app that provides a wide range of information in a magazine format.

WatchKnowLearn
watchknowlearn.org

The site has free educational videos that allow access to everything from frog dissection simulations to earthquake destruction. It organizes content by age range and provides reviews.

PBS LearningMedia
pbslearningmedia.org

This site is a great source for classroom-ready, free digital resources at all grades and in all subjects. This includes Masterpiece Theatre with accompanying lessons.

Explain Everything
explaineverything.com

This app uses text, video, pictures, and voice to help students present a variety of possible creations. Students can animate, draw, or import almost any file and share multiple ways. The company offers educational pricing.

HP Reveal
hpreveal.com

You can use this free app to take a picture, website, and so on and add layers of animation to your original. They provide many resources, or you can use resources that you create. It is great for getting information across in a quick, vivid, and animated way.

Corkulous
corkulous.com

This free app allows you to collaborate with friends and colleagues, manage project assignments, brainstorm, prepare or teach a lesson, take notes, and more. You can also export as a PDF. Upgrade to Pro for a price.

Glogster
glogster.com

Create presentations you can share with this free app. You can even browse and use presentations made by others. Glogster provides images, graphics, and videos. Or upload your own. The companion website has educational pricing.

Gooru
gooru.org

This is a free, K–12 website with a supportive app. The site is a place to share information and make resources globally available. It covers math, science, social studies, and language arts by providing videos, worksheets, assessments, and other resources for students, broken out by standard. Great for flipping the classroom.

Table 12.2: Reading Informational Text Resources

 **MURAL**
mural.ly

This website helps organize ideas more quickly and display and share information with others. You can use visual aids for presentations, and it works with other apps and sites. The website does cost, but there is special yearly pricing for students, teachers, and schools.

 TouchCast
touchcast.com

This free software and app video creator lets you embed linkable websites, pictures, photos, and more into your video. There is some concern about privacy. TouchCast does have the EduCast channel, which is geared to education, with teacher tutorials and other resources.

 Binumi
binumi.com

Easily combine media from the cloud to tell a story with video, audio, pictures, animation, and so on, to create a visual narrative, or use a story template. This website is free, but it can be upgraded for a price.

Resources to Integrate and Evaluate Information

RI.11-12.7 • READING INFORMATIONAL TEXT

Integrate and evaluate multiple sources of information presented in **different media** or formats (e.g., visually, quantitatively) as well as in words in order to address a question or solve a problem.

RH.11-12.7 • READING HISTORY

Integrate and evaluate multiple sources of information presented in **diverse formats** and media (e.g., visually, quantitatively, as well as in words) in order to address a question or solve a problem.

RST.11-12.7 • READING SCIENCE AND TECHNICAL SUBJECTS

Integrate and evaluate multiple sources of information presented in **diverse formats and media** (e.g., quantitative data, video, **multimedia**) in order to address a question or solve a problem.

RI.11-12.7, RH.11-12.7, and **RI.11-12.7** are essentially the same standards and again focus on integration and evaluation when reading historical and technical texts. This standard begins in kindergarten with comparing illustrations and text and is developed through the grades to use all types of media to compare, support, and analyze a story's meaning. By freshman and sophomore year students analyze various accounts of a subject told in different mediums. In Grades 11–12, the next step is to integrate and evaluate that information. Of course, they must put into practice their analytical skills from Grades 9–10 to master the integration and evaluation of information, which are higher-level thinking skills.

Integration and evaluation need to be taught through argumentation and teaching key questioning techniques. **Odell Education (odelleducation.com)** can help a great deal with techniques. Students and teachers can link examples to specific text lines in published works.

An overwhelming amount of what we hear and read today comes from people speaking and writing without proper support. There are many unsubstantiated opinions out there, and the standards attempt to force a speaker or writer to support what they say. Students can use text, embed images, links, and videos in their writing, integrating media not simply as an illustration, but as an integral part of their overall argument.

In the next section, we offer some useful apps, programs, and websites to help students become proficient at integrating and evaluating information.

There are many tools students can use to improve their reading skills. **Table 12.3** includes some of our favorites.

Table 12.3: Reading Resources

WEBSITES		
	Feedly feedly.com	Organize any information on the web with this free app and website. It is a great resource for STEM to follow current events, scientific breakthroughs, and so on. Find and follow any source of information.
	Google Scholar scholar.google.com	When your students conduct research, have them use Google Scholar by typing "google scholar" into the Google search engine. This will bring up research, legal documents, academic articles, and more on the topics they research.
	Diigo diigo.com	With this free browser add-on, you can highlight, add a note or sticky, annotate, embed a website, and keep and organize everything you want. It is great for research and writing.
	SpicyNodes spicynodes.org	This is an interesting three-dimensional mind-mapping website. Some services are free, while others are paid. It is great for organizing and very effective for student memory retention. Nodes can contain links to URLs, links to other nodes, sound, pictures, and so on, for students to support their analyses.
	Have Fun with History havefunwithhistory.com	This free website offers many short videos about historical events. There are ads.
	PBS LearningMedia pbslearningmedia.org	This site is a great source for classroom-ready, free digital resources at all grades and in all subjects.

 **SimpleMind**
tinyurl.com/y7ualejm

This cross-platform mind-mapping app can have multiple mind-maps with unlimited page sizes. You can add photos, video, and images to make your mind-map stand out. Free version that can be upgraded for a price.

The Current
tiny.cc/t2bt3y

This website is free, supported by the Educator Innovator Fund. The Current is working to change the educational process by making connections among students, their peers, the real world, student's interests, and education. This website is full of great resources and ideas. Each month they take on a new task to research.

 Digital Public Library of America
dp.la

A free website that provides innovative ways to search and scan through the united collection of millions of items. You can search by timeline, map, virtual bookshelf, format, subject, and partner libraries.

 Newsmap
newsmap.jp

Using visual mapping to focus on the hottest current issues makes this site like a "word cloud" for news. Each map has links to the story behind the headlines. Articles provided by top news outlines around the world on this free site.

 Odell Education
odelleducation.com

This site is great for ELA teacher resources. Everything is free and sharable. Teachers can find well-researched step-by-step ways to implement standards in the area of student research.

 WebQuest
webquest.org

WebQuests are good tools to use for presentations. The WebQuest site allows students to follow an already-created, project-based lesson where information is found solely on the internet. Students can create their own WebQuest if a website-building program or a website such as SiteBuilder (sitebuilder.com) is available. WebQuest.org is the original and most popular site, but if you search the internet, you will find more sites that you can use.

Table 12.4

	Notability gingerlabs.com	This note-taking app allows your students to draw, using handwriting, typing, and importing text and other media. It allows markup of PDFs, too. It includes a word processor for essays, outlines, and forms. There is a cost.
	Evernote evernote.com	This free app allows you to create freeform notes, upload images, and make checklists. It is great for note-taking. It can then sync your data across platforms.
	Flipboard flipboard.com	Similar to Feedly, but with more constraints, and it draws from some different resources. A free app that provides a wide range of information in a magazine format.
	Inspiration Maps inspiration.com/inspmaps	This app helps students organize, plan, and build thinking skills as well as create and analyze charts and other data by producing a mind-map that can include text, video, photos, audio, and so on. Volume discounts are available. The web-based version is called Webspiration Classroom (tinyurl.com/bmop3nh) and is subscription based.
	Explain Everything explaineverything.com	This app uses text, video, pictures, and voice to help students present a variety of possible creations. Students can animate, draw, or import most any file and share multiple ways. They can link to other resources for supporting information. Educational pricing is available.
	TouchCast touchcast.com	This free software and app video creator lets you embed linkable websites, pictures, photos, and more into your video. There is some concern about privacy. TouchCast does have the EduCast channel, which is geared to education, with teacher tutorials and other resources.

Writing Resources

W.11-12.2.A • WRITING

WHST.11-12.2.A • WRITING HISTORY, SCIENCE, AND TECHNICAL SUBJECTS

Introduce a topic; organize complex ideas, concepts, and information so that each new element builds on that which precedes it to create a unified whole; include formatting (e.g., headings), graphics (e.g., figures, tables), and **multimedia** when useful to aiding comprehension.

W.11-12.6 • WRITING

WHST.11-12.6 • WRITING HISTORY, SCIENCE, AND TECHNICAL SUBJECTS

Use technology, including the Internet, to produce, publish, and update individual or shared writing products in response to ongoing feedback, including new arguments or information.

W.11-12.8 • WRITING

WHST.11-12.8 • WRITING HISTORY, SCIENCE, AND TECHNICAL SUBJECTS

Gather relevant information from multiple authoritative print and **digital sources, using advanced searches effectively;** assess the strengths and limitations of each source in terms of the task, purpose, and audience; integrate information into the text selectively to maintain the flow of ideas, avoiding plagiarism and overreliance on any one source and following a standard format for citation.

The standards have students experiencing informative or explanatory writing with **Standard 2** beginning in kindergarten. But, as they reach the high school level, they need to become college and career ready. In Grades 9-10, students had to make important connections and distinctions when satisfying Standard 2. Students in Grades 11-12 must construct the written piece so that each element contributes to a unified whole. As with Grades 9-10, outlining programs are wonderful ways for students to organize their ideas, concepts, and information so they can lay them as building blocks of the unifying whole that is required. Several fine software programs have been used for mind-mapping and outlining for many years. However, there are also free sites available.

Students from kindergarten to Grade 12 need to become proficient in **Standard 6**, which involves using technology to collaborate with others when writing. In ninth grade, for the first time, they were required to update their writing and to display information flexibly and dynamically. Updating their writing requires students to revise, react, and, in the case of argument, to rethink their positions when more information about the topic is discovered. As juniors and seniors, they need to learn how to update, in an ongoing way, by including new arguments and information gathered as they view, hear, and read more about the subject of their product. Updating is made easy with blogging and instantaneous feedback through technology. From this ongoing assessment of information, they may make a more informed decision, see it from other viewpoints, and sometimes draw different conclusions.

Writing Standard 8 starts in Grade 3 and continues through Grade 12. This writing standard keys in on the gathering of information, analyzing the information, and avoidance of plagiarism using multiple sources, digital as well as text, when writing informative or explanatory works. The standard changes significantly between Grades 10 and 11. Juniors and seniors will assess not only the usefulness of a source, but its strengths and limitations based on specific criteria (task, purpose, and audience.) Therefore, students will need to use techniques they have been honing, in both reading and writing, to identify the type of writing, audience, and its purpose, and then assess it. Juniors and seniors also have a higher standard regarding overreliance on any one source. They may have listed many sources in the past but only primarily used one or two. Now they must pull information from all of their sources—if not equally, at least more equitably.

Table 11.3 in the previous chapter features some well-designed products that will help your students become more effective in the writing standards for these grades.

Google Drive (featured in the previous chapter) offers many free and useful tools. **Table 12.5** shares some other useful websites to help students become proficient in writing and note-taking.

Table 12.5: Writing Resources

	Genius genius.com	This free website can be used to annotate everything from rap songs to Shakespeare. There is even an annotated Common Core to help teachers understand it better. You must sign up to post and add writing.
	The Current tiny.cc/t2bt3y	This website is free supported by the Educator Innovator Fund. The Current is working to change the educational process by making connections among students, their peers, the real world, student's interests, and education. This website is full of good resources and ideas. Each month they take on a new task to research.
	Feedly feedly.com	Organize any information on the web through this free app and website. It is a great resource for STEM to follow current events, scientific breakthroughs, and so on. Find and follow any source of information.
	Gooru gooru.org	This is a free, K–12 website with a supportive app. The site is a place to share information and make resources globally available. Its covers math, science, social studies, and language arts by providing videos, worksheets, assessments, and other resources for students, broken out by standard. Great for flipping the classroom.
	Folger Shakespeare Library folger.edu	This free, easy-to-search collection of online texts of the classics brings Shakespeare and other works into the digital age. Students can read them anywhere they have digital access.
	Open Source Shakespeare tiny.cc/t2at3y	This free, easy-to-search, online text brings Shakespeare's works into the digital age. Students can read them anywhere they have digital access.
	The Complete Works of William Shakespeare shakespeare.mit.edu	This is another free, easy-to-search, digital online text with all of Shakespeare's works. Students can read them anywhere they have digital access.

Table 12.5: Writing Resources

	Edmodo edmodo.com	A free website where teachers can create a safe, password-protected learning community, including blogs and document-sharing. This is a great way to get students to write daily. A free app is available.
	EasyBib easybib.com	Students can use this free website and app to generate citations in MLA, APA, and Chicago formats. Just copy and paste or scan the book's barcode.
	Edublogs edublogs.org	A free website built for students where teachers can create a safe, password-protected learning community, including blogs and document-sharing. There are free apps for blogging on the go. Upgrade for a price.
	The Learning Network tiny.cc/gebt3y	This free website by the New York Times has many intriguing questions on current affairs that makes students think and analyze. The site contains multimedia and links to help students find out more about issues and includes prompts for writing. There are ads.
	Citation Machine citationmachine.net	This is another free website students can use to generate citations in MLA, APA, Turabian, and Chicago formats. Just copy, paste, and the website does the rest.
	Purdue Online Writing Lab tinyurl.com/n8r94uf	This free website was developed for college students but is available to all. It has resources for any kind of writing, grammar, spelling, and mechanics.
	CAST UDL Book Builder bookbuilder.cast.org	Use this nonprofit website to create, share, publish, and read digital books that engage and support diverse learners according to their individual needs, interests, and skills. The site is free.
	Lulu lulu.com	This site allows you to create real books and publish them online. Parents and students can purchase the books. The site is free to use, but a fee is required to publish.

	Wix wix.com	This online website creator is drag-and-drop easy and includes templates. The basics are free. An app version is available.
	Webs webs.com	This online website creator allows you to choose a template and then drag-and-drop elements onto webpages. Basic functionality is free, and an app is available.
	SiteBuilder sitebuilder.com	This is an online website creator that is drag-and-drop easy and includes templates. The website is free. With a domain name included, there is a cost.
	Weebly weebly.com	This is an online website creator that is drag-and-drop easy and includes templates. The basics, which include five pages, are free. There is even an app available.
	Digital Public Library of America dp.la	A free website that provides innovative ways to search and scan through the united collection of millions of items. You can search by timeline, map, virtual bookshelf, format, subject, and partner libraries.
	Newsmap newsmap.jp	Using visual mapping to focus on the hottest current issues makes this site like a "word cloud" for news. Each map has links to the story behind the headlines. Articles provided by top news outlines around the world on this free site.
	Naviance naviance.com	Students can use this web-based service for college or career planning, personal-learning plans, and getting their college documents organized and sent. Schools can use this service for family connections, help with admissions, and career guidance. The cost is per student, but there is a minimum; it can be expensive.
	Odell Education odelleducation.com	This site is great for ELA teacher resources. Everything is free and sharable. Teachers can find well-researched step-by-step ways to implement standards in the area of student research.

Table 12.5: Writing Resources

iAnnotate
iannotate.com

Similar to Notability, this app is primarily for note-taking and markup of PDFs, PPT, and Docs. It is a bit easier to import other formats than it is in Notability. See the website for pricing.

iThoughts
toketaware.com

Students can use this mind-mapping app to organize their writing and presentation ideas. It has good import and export capabilities (PDF, PowerPoint, and other formats). This app can also be used as an interactive whiteboard. See the website for current pricing.

Pixton
pixton.com

This intriguing site is great for creating sophisticated comics where you can flexibly pose characters and change expressions and backgrounds, all while creating great dialog in story form. There is individual, school, or district pricing.

APPS

Speaking and Listening Resources

SL.11-12.2 • SPEAKING AND LISTENING

Integrate multiple sources of information presented in **diverse formats and media** (e.g., visually, quantitatively, orally) in order to make informed decisions and solve problems, evaluating the credibility and accuracy of each source and noting any discrepancies among the data.

SL.11-12.5 • SPEAKING AND LISTENING

Make strategic use of **digital media (e.g., textual, graphical, audio, visual, and interactive elements)** in presentations to enhance understanding of findings, reasoning, and evidence and to add interest.

Speaking and listening standard 2 expects the use of technology from kindergarten through Grade 12. In today's world, we listen to all kinds of diverse media and constantly need to analyze and make decisions about its content. We also use multiple kinds of technology to speak to others. The idea behind speaking and listening standard 2 changes between sophomore and junior years. Specifically added is the need to integrate multiple sources of information to make informed decisions and solve problems. The Grades 9–10 standard in speaking and listening did not have students use sources to make decisions and solve problems. Students in Grades 11 and 12 will need to analyze their sources and determine which is more valid, informed, opinionated, and so on. Taking everything into consideration, they must also make decisions about the issue or problem, where they stand, why, and what might be done to solve the problem.

Also different is Standard 2 in speaking and listening, from Grades 9–10 to Grades 11–12. Students must evaluate the sources, noting any discrepancies among the data. Students will need to use close-reading skills **(tinyurl.com/pk5ea7x),** have a deep knowledge of their topic, and understand the data to find discrepancies. They will need to judge the pros and cons of each source and decide what weight to give the data, even with discrepancies, depending on the importance of the source.

Speaking and Listening Standard 5 is unchanged from Grades 9 and 10. Learning to use media to help in presentations is critical for college and career readiness. Your students need to make strategic use of digital media to enhance understanding for them and their audience. This highlights using technology effectively, not just using it because it is something "awesome."

Microsoft PowerPoint has been the presentation program of choice, but it can be expensive. There is now a free educational version called **Microsoft 365 (tinyurl. com/zsfogge)** that includes PowerPoint. While this still a great program, other presentation tools are just as useful. Apple offers **Keynote (apple.com/keynote)** as part of its computer software package. Its features are very similar to PowerPoint's, but it does require a purchase. Another program that has emerged is **Google Slides (google.com/slides/about).** There are other resources that help with presentations, such as **Microsoft Paint 3D (tinyurl.com/zsfogge)** and **Google Drawings (tiny.cc/5gfs3y).** Although Office 365 is free to schools, Google Drive products such as Slides and Drawings are free and web-based. Google Slides makes it very easy to share a project that multiple users can work on at once, which makes it an especially good program to use when interacting and collaborating remotely. Students can also add audio recordings to their slides, as well as visual displays, such as pictures and short video clips. Consider having your students use the digital tools featured in **Table 12.6** below in addition the those shared in **Table 12.1**.

Table 12.6: Speaking and Listening Resources

APPS	**Magisto** magisto.com	It is surprising how easy it is to create a movie with this free app for all platforms. Create movies with photos and videos. Add sound from your songs or theirs, and it does the rest.
	Tiki-Toki tiki-toki.com	Make engaging timelines with this free website (there are ads). You can embed videos, share with others, add photos, use color-coding, and add 3D effects. Upgrade (no ads and fifty student accounts) for an additional cost.
	Doceri doceri.com	This app combines an interactive whiteboard, screen-casting, and desktop control in one resource. Create a lesson or presentation, insert images, save and edit your project, and record a screen-cast video. Pricing for the app varies. There is a desktop app for both Mac and Windows with educational pricing.

 **BaiBoard**
baiboard.com

This whiteboard app allows students to create, collaborate, and share—and it's free. The difference between this and other whiteboard apps is that multiple students can have real-time access to one project and collaborate.

 Clips
apple.com/clips

This free app is for creating and sharing videos. Students can create selfie videos with green-screen effects, emojis, stickers, and filters. They can also turn speech into captions and have animated titles.

Google Blogger
blogger.com

This free blogging site has more numerous features. Students can see other classes and can be cross-grouped with similar sections of the same course by ability or with mixed ability as needed. There is an app available.

 Google Slides
google.com/slides/about

This is a simpler version of Microsoft's PowerPoint, and it's free. Students can use this for sharing projects, summarizing their work, and peer-to-peer teaching.

 Animoto
animoto.com

This website allows you to turn your photos and music into stunning video slideshows. It offers HD, music, website links, and style screens. Educational use is free for unlimited videos of twenty minutes.

 Kizoa
kizoa.com

This web-based program makes and edits movies, slideshows, collages, and photos. There are templates available, along with stock video clips, photos, and music to make your presentations look and sound great. Students can also upload their own files to edit. This program is free for basic use, but you can upgrade for a price.

 Flipsnack
flipsnack.com

This publishing tool is great for brochures, catalogs, and visual presentations. It is cross-platform and includes links, buttons, pictures, and has templates. Your work can be privately or publicly published on their website, embedded in a blog, emailed, or sent through social media. The limited version is free, but can be upgraded for a price.

WEBSITES

Table 12.6: Speaking and Listening Resources

WEBSITES

Binumi binumi.com		Easily combine media from the cloud to tell a story with video, audio, pictures, animation, and so on, to create a visual narrative, or use a story template. This website is free, but it can be upgraded for a price.
Feedly feedly.com		Organize any information on the web with this free app and website. It is a great resource for STEM to follow current events, scientific breakthroughs, and so on. Find and follow any source of information.
Paper.li paper.li **Scoop.it** scoop.it		Publish your own newspaper with these websites' access to sources, print as well as video. Then customize it for your audience. Share it to Facebook, Twitter, and so on. Free, but you can upgrade to Pro version for a price.
SpicyNodes spicynodes.org		This is an interesting three-dimensional mind-mapping website. Some services are free, while others are paid. It is great for organizing and very effective for student memory retention. Nodes can contain links to URLs, links to other nodes, sound, pictures, and so on, for students to support their analyses.
SimpleMind tinyurl.com/y7ualejm		This cross-platform mind-mapping app can have multiple mind-maps with unlimited page sizes. You can add photos, video, and images to make your mind-map stand out. Free version that can be upgraded for a price.
Slideful slideful.com		This is a basic slideshow website. All it does is slideshows, but it does them well. You can upload your own photos, graphics, and charts (up to ten) free. They include transitions, text, zoom, and frames. Then you can share or download.

Movie-Making Programs, Apps, and Websites

Video-editing programs and apps are numerous. **Table 12.7** includes a few that we recommend for students in Grades 11–12.

Table 12.7: Movie-Making Resources

iMovie and iMovie Trailer apple.com/ios/imovie	This powerful program is also available as an app. Students can use it to create presentations, movies, documentaries, and motion slideshows. Students can also create short trailers that focus on important points about issues and events studied.
AndroVid tinyurl.com/puuc8qr	Create a movie on an Android device. The free app is limited. The pro version has a cost. Make a movie or slideshow, add effects, trim, cut, and add music. This app does most of what you want in a movie editor and is fairly intuitive.
Magisto magisto.com	It is surprising how easy it is to create a movie with this free app for all platforms. Create movies with photos and videos. Add sound from your songs or theirs, and it does the rest.
Green Screen by Do Ink doink.com/support	Create a green-screen effect to put yourself or students in the story, video, photo, artwork, and so on, with this app from Do Ink. Great for presentations. There is a timeline feature to edit presentations and mix audio and video layers. Saves to iPad. It does cost.
Microsoft Photos tinyurl.com/y7wcwxma	Buried deep within Microsoft Windows is the successor to Movie Maker called Photos. It is an easy-to-use and powerful video-creating and video-editing software application, designed for the latest Windows 10. You can import, edit, add music, and share your newly created video with others.
Adobe Spark Video tiny.cc/6lby3y	This free app from Adobe gives students and teachers a great way to make video presentations. Create a movie and narrate in your own voice. The app provides themes, photos, animations, and templates to organize the videos.

APPS & WEBSITES

239

Table 12.7: Movie-Making Resources

 Movavi
movavi.com

Make movies using your photos and videos or create slideshows, video blogs, or screen-capture tutorials. It's easy to enhance, edit, and tell your story, and it's a lot of fun! Check the website for educational pricing.

 Shmoop
schools.shmoop.com

This site helps students build great videos for presentations and review. There are many templates included, and it uses the student's face and voice in the videos that range from ELA to math, science, social studies, test prep, and more. It can be costly for individual teachers, but school pricing is well worth it.

 **TouchCast**
touchcast.com

This free app video creator lets you embed linkable websites, pictures, photos, and more into your video. It is also available on PC. There is some concern about privacy. TouchCast does have the EduCast channel, which is geared to education, with teacher tutorials and other resources.

 Moovly
moovly.com

This is a wonderful video-creation website for projects, portfolios, and presentations. It comes with access to the editor, unlimited videos, sounds, music, photos, and illustrations. You can even batch upload your own media. It is free for educators and their students.

 Powtoon
powtoon.com

This video-creating website is easy to use with ready-made templates and great content, such as music, objects, and photos. It is free for short (three minutes or less) videos, but you can upgrade for a price.

Language Resources

L.11-12.4C • LANGUAGE

Consult general and specialized reference materials (e.g., dictionaries, glossaries, thesauruses), both print and digital, to find the pronunciation of a word or determine or clarify its precise meaning, its part of speech, its etymology, or its standard usage.

This standard is very straightforward, clarifying the meaning of words in all grade levels. Students need to know how to find word meanings using not only print but digital dictionaries, glossaries, and thesauruses. The standard changes slightly between Grades 9-10 and Grades 11-12, adding "or its standard usage." The technology aspect of the standard is still the same.

Digital Dictionary and Thesaurus Websites

Digital dictionaries and thesauruses are updated more often than their print versions, and they are very convenient to use. The more students use them, the more comfortable they will become. Offer lessons and activities to learn and practice how to find parts of speech, standard usage, and etymology with an online dictionary. Table 11.5 in the previous chapter includes useful tools. Bookmark or add them to your website for easy access.

Math Resources

MP5 • MATH

Use appropriate **tools** strategically.

There are two main sets of standards for the Common Core math standards: processes and practices. First, you have the math targets, written similarly to ELA (Number and Quantity, Algebra, Functions, Modeling, Geometry, and Statistics and Probability). While you work with high school students on mathematical processes, such as Algebra or Modeling, you need to teach your students how to apply the SMPs (which include problem solving and precision) to those processes. One practice, the only one that includes technology, is mathematical practice 5: "Use appropriate tools strategically." Following is the explanation CCSS provides for **MP5.**

Mathematically proficient students consider the available tools when solving a mathematical problem. These tools might include pencil and paper, concrete models, a ruler, a protractor, a calculator, **a spreadsheet, a computer algebra system, a statistical package, or dynamic geometry software**. Proficient students are sufficiently familiar with tools appropriate for their grade or course to make sound decisions about when each of these tools might be helpful, recognizing both the insight to be gained and their limitations. For example, mathematically proficient high school students analyze graphs of functions and solutions generated using a **graphing calculator**. They detect possible errors by strategically using estimation and other mathematical knowledge. When making mathematical models, they know that technology can enable them to visualize the results of varying assumptions, explore consequences, and compare predictions with data. Mathematically proficient students at various grade levels are able to identify relevant external mathematical resources, such as **digital content located on a website**, and use them to pose or solve problems. They are able to use **technological tools** to explore and deepen their understanding of concepts.

We have provided lists of appropriate apps, websites, software, and lessons that will help translate this standard for high school.

Your students will need to begin using technology as a tool to help them strengthen their math skills. That is essentially what this math standard—the only one that explicitly includes technology—states. Using technology as a mathematical practice tool can be interpreted in many different ways. In any case, technology is a math tool students should use as much as possible. Many math programs, websites, and apps allow students to explore and deepen their understanding of math concepts. The best of them have students learning in creative ways and are not merely electronic worksheets. They automatically adapt to the students' skill levels, and they tell you where students are in their learning and what they need to advance. We list many good resources here. Some are free. Some are not. The free resources (many with ads) are often less interesting and not as well organized. They don't give you the feedback you need. It is up to you to decide what is best for your circumstances and budget.

Table 12.8 shares a few tools that you can use to help meet the eleventh- and twelfth-grade math standards. Additional resources can be found in **Table 10.1** in Chapter 10 of this book.

Table 12.8: Math Resources

	Shmoop shmoop.com	Students can work on math, language, SAT and ACT test prep, GED, STEM, and so on, with this free website. It does have ads, but the site is appealing to teenage students and keeps track of their progress. Also, for a fee, you can upgrade and access more.
	IXL Math ixl.com/math	This site features adaptive, individualized math through gameplay, including data and graphing problems. It gives students immediate feedback and covers many skills, despite its emphasis on drills. Levels go to Algebra 2. There is a limited free version.
	Algodoo algodoo.com	This free app is a virtual sandbox tool that helps students play with the concepts of physics to design, construct, and explore. It allows you to model geometry and physics. Students and teachers can create 2D simulations and can interact with their objects. They can add physics in the simulation, such as fluids, springs, hinges, motors, thrusters, light rays, tracers, optics, and lenses. Create graphs and visualize forces and momentum.

Literacy Lessons

Cross-curriculum planning is encouraged with CCSS by using ELA standards in history, science, and technical subjects. Getting through all of the standards you need in high school is very difficult in the time given. We highly encourage teaching more than one standard during a lesson when you can. The key to planning is by teaching multiple standards in one lesson and working with others in your department, and in other departments, if possible. We hope the following list of sample lessons in literacy for Grades 11–12 inspires you to become an effective technology lesson planner.

Classroom Example

Our first example is more a model of a classroom style than a particular lesson. At our local high school, the English Composition class in 11th and 12th grades is a paperless composition class, which uses peer editing to a great degree. Assignments in this class are made using the Google Drive add-on Doctopus to distribute tasks, writing prompts, and other assignments. Students open the prompt or a blank sheet in Google Docs and share the assignment with their teacher. They then begin their work. If research is required, they use a variety of sources online or through the library. Students are able to access library databases through the internet. Students also access Google Scholar for some assignments.

The ability to peer edit each other's work using the share option in Google Docs is very important. Once completed, the assignment is checked for authenticity with Turnitin. The teacher is able to check progress throughout and use the comment feature to make suggestions. All work is graded online in Google Drive.

The primary focuses of this lesson are organizing a complex topic, making corrections, adding appropriate sources, and using formatting, multimedia, and graphics to help in comprehension, so students are satisfying **W.11-12.2.A, W.11-12.6,** and **W.11-12.8.** Of course, the class satisfies all the technology Reading standards **RI.11-12.7/RH.11-12.7/RST.11-12.7,** Speaking and Listening **SL.11-12.2/ SL.11-12.5,** and Language **L.11-12.4c** standards through their strategic use of digital resources to read, write, present, collaborate, and consult digital reference materials.

ISTE STUDENT STANDARDS

Students will be using a variety of ISTE Standards in this lesson.

- **Empowered Learner** by understanding fundamental concepts of technology operations, demonstrating the ability to choose, use, and troubleshoot current technologies.

- **Digital Citizen** by demonstrating respects for rights in using and sharing intellectual property.

- **Knowledge Constructor** by employing research, evaluating and building knowledge using digital resources.

- **Creative Communicator** by communicating complex ideas effectively through creation of new resources using a variety of media and publishing for an intended audience.

- **Global Collaborator** by connecting to other learners to broaden mutual understanding.

Literature WebQuest

Many teachers have embraced WebQuests as a way to make good use of the internet while engaging their students in a technology-rich environment for problem solving, information processing, collaboration, and the kinds of thinking that the digital age requires. Many WebQuests are available for any high school subject; locate them simply by searching Google. WebQuests can be used all year. Once students are familiar with WebQuests, have them write their own!

A local high school literature class starts the year with a WebQuest titled "All Quiet on the Western Front." You can find several versions of this WebQuest (already written) by searching the web for the title. Students work in teams of four. Teams will answer the essential question: What was it like to be a part of World War I? Next, teams are given the task of researching how different groups of people were affected by the Great War.

Students create an electronic presentation (with a program of their choosing: PowerPoint, Keynote, Google Slides, etc.) and share it with you. This presentation will incorporate the information learned and draw conclusions about what it is like to experience war. Once groups have been chosen, teams must choose roles: a soldier, an officer, a civilian, or a woman involved in war work. Each member must choose a different role and follow the directions for that chosen person. Questions and answers for each role must be submitted electronically by individual team members. Once this step has been completed, teams may begin their presentations.

Following is a list of questions the students will need to consider.

1. Each team member needs to participate. How many slides should each team member create?

2. In what person should the slides be written? First? Third?

3. Should each slide contain information representing all four roles?

4. Do you want graphics or illustrations for each slide?

5. What information should the slides contain? For example, social status, living conditions, job during the war.

6. What else would you like students to explain about each role? A typical day in the life of their role?

7. Do you want a title slide? What should it contain?

8. Do you want students to include a resource slide that lists where images and information for the presentation were found?

Next, students work on tasks for their individual roles. Encourage students to use the links provided, search for additional material on their own, and find print material from the library to use, citing sources used. Speaking and Listening **SL.11-12.2/ SL.11-12.5,** and Language **L.11-12.4c** standards are satisfied through students' strategic use of digital resources to read, write, present, collaborate, avoid plagiarism, and consult specialized reference materials.

Following are the four roles students have to choose from along with questions specific to each role.

ENLISTER

You are about to enlist to fight in World War I as a soldier. You can use the links provided by us on our website (tinyurl.com/y9dfltpr), search on your own, and look for print sources to help you answer the following questions.

1. What country are you from? Why did you enlist?

2. What branch of the military are you in?

3. What is an average day like?

4. What are your assigned duties?

5. How did your assigned role change people who lived during World War I?

6. How did your role change the war?

7. What are some good things about your job? World War I?

8. What are some bad things about your job? World War I?

PILOT

You are about to be called up as an officer and will be sent overseas to fight in World War I. You can use the links provided on our website (tinyurl.com/y9dfltpr), search on your own, and look for print sources to help you answer the following questions.

1. What country are you from? What is your rank?

2. What branch of the military are you in?

3. What is an average day like?

4. What are your assigned duties?

5. How did your assigned role change people who lived during World War I?

6. How did your role change the war?

7. What are some good things about your job? World War I?

8. What are some bad things about your job? World War I?

9. Have you been in any battles? Which ones?

PRIVATE CITIZEN

You are a private citizen caught in the middle of the war. You can use the links provided on our website (tinyurl.com/y9dfltpr), search on your own, and look for print sources to help you answer the following questions.

1. Where do you live?

2. What do you (and your family) do for a living?

3. Have any battles been fought near your home?

4. What is an average day like for you and your family?

5. Did your country assign you and your family any duties? What are they?

6. What are some good things about World War I?

7. What are some bad things about World War I?

8. How has your life changed during the war?

9. How else are you helping the war efforts?

10. How do you feel about the war?

NURSE

World War I saw many medical personnel involved in the war effort. You volunteered to help the war effort as a nurse. You can use the links provided on our website (tinyurl.com/y9dfltpr), search on your own, and look for print sources to help you answer the following questions.

1. What organization do you work for?

2. Why did you choose to join the service?

3. Where are you stationed?

4. What country are you from? Why did you enlist?

5. What branch of the military are you in?

6. What is an average day like?

7. What are your assigned duties?

8. How did your assigned role change people who lived during World War I?

9. How did your role change the war?

10. What are some good things about your job? World War I?

11. What are some bad things about your job? World War I? Have you been aiding people in any battles? Which ones?

Students should refer to their research throughout the reading of the book. The goal of this WebQuest is to help students understand what it would have been like to be involved in the Great War. Students gain an understanding of what life was like for people involved in all sides of the conflict. While reading the book, continue the idea through class discussions and debates on the topic "What is the legacy of World War I?" Once students are familiar with WebQuests, have them write and publish their own!

In addition to **SL.11-12.2**, **SL.11-12.5**, and **L.11-12.4c**, all informational reading standards **RI.11-12.7/ RH.11-12.7/RST.11-12.7** are satisfied by reading information using diverse media formats, as well as integrating and evaluating multiple sources of information in diverse formats. Organizing a complex topic, making corrections, adding appropriate sources, and using formatting, multimedia, and graphics to help in comprehension satisfy **W.11-12.2.A**, **W.11-12.6**, and **W.11-12.8**. These standards are also addressed when students write, share, and publish their own WebQuests. Gathering relevant information from multiple digital sources, as well as citing to avoid plagiarism and assessing the usefulness of each resource to help answer the research questions, satisfies **W.11-12.8** and **WHST 11-12.8**.

ISTE STUDENT STANDARDS

Students will be using several ISTE Standards in this lesson.

- **Empowered Learner** by understanding fundamental concepts of technology operations, demonstrating the ability to choose, use, and troubleshoot current technologies.

- **Digital Citizen** by demonstrating respects for rights in using and sharing intellectual property.

- **Knowledge Constructor** by employing research, evaluating and building knowledge using digital resources and using a variety of tools to create a collection of artifacts that demonstrate learning.

- **Creative Communicator** by communicating complex ideas effectively through creation of new resources using a variety of media and publishing for an intended audience.

- **Global Collaborator** by working as a team member and connecting to other learners to broaden mutual understanding.

Fun with Children's Books

This lesson can be adapted in many ways. This idea will also work with graphic novels. Students will plan, write, illustrate, and publish their own children's picture book, using technology. With their team, students will review picture books from their childhood to gain an understanding of the creative process, as well as the elements that make a children's book successful. Share with your students ReadWriteThink's **Tips for Writing A Children's Picture Storybook (tinyurl.com/lwmq2v4).**

Arrange students into teams of three. Team members takes turns reading aloud their favorite picture book from their childhood, making sure (at the end) to share three reasons why the book is their favorite. On their own (for homework), students should be encouraged to evaluate various accounts of their story, told in different mediums. For example, students can read the original Maurice Sendak's *Where the Wild Things Are*, read the online version of this book, and then watch the movie. They should be prepared to discuss what is emphasized or absent from each medium. This, in turn, satisfies **RI.11-12.7, RH.11-12.7,** and **RST.11-12.7.**

Have students use **Go Conqr (goconqr.com), Coggle (coggle.it), MindMup (mindmup. com), Bubbl.us (bubbl.us),** or **Mindomo (mindomo.com),** to create a mind-map of concrete examples of how their book was or was not effective with plot, characterization, and illustrations. Students should be encouraged to develop their own guidelines for what makes effective plots, characterizations, and illustrations. This can be done on a separate mind-map, or use a note-taking app such as **Simplenote (simplenote.com), Evernote (evernote.com),** or **Penzu (penzu.com).** Have students refer to their "Tips for Writing A Children's Picture Storybook." Did their book include many of these elements?

Once this research is complete, use your Smart Board or **Miro (realtimeboard.com)** to have students present their findings. Encourage the audience to ask clarifying questions of the student who is presenting. When all information has been shared, students will need time to update their findings. They should save their guidelines to use when they create their own children's book.

Next, share with your students ReadWriteThink's "**Children's Book Review Guide" (tinyurl.com/d9cf5r9),** as well as ReadWriteThink's list of "**Recommended Children's Picture Books" (tinyurl.com/y7w47z8v).** Students pick a picture book to read and review. Of course, if there is a children's book not on the list, encourage students to consult with you about doing their review on that book. Many websites offer digital copies of books. Have students use **Internet Archive (archive.org), Readbookonline (readbookonline.net), The Children's Literature Web Guide (people.ucalgary.ca/~dk-brown),** or **Internet Public Library (ipl.org)** to find and read their book.

Students should read through as many picture books as timing permits. During this time, they should explore the general characteristics of children's books. In their small groups, have students (using their preferred note-taking site) identify all of the similarities among the books reviewed by the group. Once this task is complete, come together and have all groups share their findings. Their lists should be compared to the original list of characteristics generated in an earlier class. This list should be revised so all students have the same list to consult when writing their own children's book.

Also, brainstorm a list of themes central to the books they read. Have students think about these themes and how they were dealt with in the books they read. Once the list is compiled, review it as a class, making any additions or revisions. Some themes may include:

- Acceptance of others

- Concern of family dynamics

- Physical growth (size)

- Fear of the unknown

Explain the entire task to your students. They will need to write their own children's book, complete with text and illustrations. At this time, go over your grading expectations. You may wish to share ReadWriteThink's **Grading Rubric for the Children's Picture Storybook (tinyurl.com/y78damrk).** Now is a good time for the class to ask clarifying questions about the project. Students will gather details about their stories, develop plots, plan their stories on a storyboard, write and illustrate their stories, and finally publish their books.

Have students use ReadWriteThink's interactive **Story Map (tinyurl.com/ybmpwpz)** to work though their planning stages. This story map leads students through planning and mapping out characters, conflict, resolution, and setting. Remind students they will need to constantly refer to **Tips for Writing A Children's Picture Storybook (tinyurl.com/lwmq2v4),** as well as the guidelines they come up with in class.

Students should next complete ReadWriteThink's **Brainstorming the Conflict Chart (tinyurl.com/y87335qn)** to test their potential conflicts. They will need to identify the complications that may or may not arise when trying to resolve them. Students should also be encouraged to seek advice from peers in the classroom. They want to work through any possible problems now, before they write. As students listen to each other, encourage them to ask questions and take notes on characteristics of effective plots, characterizations, and illustrations.

Next have students work though ReadWriteThink's **Plot Pitch Template (tinyurl. com/jpcvvnq);** they can develop a basic layout and then focus on the details for their stories. Once again, encourage students to collaborate and share ideas, always allowing time for students to rework their Plot Pitch Template.

Once the templates are complete, have students graph their plots using Read-WriteThink's **Plot Diagram (tinyurl.com/y92qjsc).** Students should also be working on sketches for their main character and setting. Encourage them to use lots of colors and labels (to identify certain characteristics or details that might only be revealed in the text of their stories). Once again, encourage students to share their Plot Pitch, Plot Diagrams, and sketches with their peers. Allow time for students to work on updating everything. The more students share their works-in-progress and get feedback, the stronger their stories will be.

Using **Storyboard That (storyboardthat.com)** or **Storyboarder (storyboarder.com),** have students begin their storyboards. Remind them they should have enough boxes to represent each page of their books, starting with the cover. Students should also sketch their illustrations in the corresponding boxes. The goal for students is to create a balance of text and illustrations. They will need to experiment with location, size, as well as amount of illustrations and text for each page. Also remind them that these are rough sketches, not final sketches. Getting the idea across is the main goal in storyboards. Once storyboards have been completed, have the students meet in small groups or come together as a class to share their planned layout for their books.

Students have many choices to publish their electronic books. **Book Creator (red-jumper.net/bookcreator)** allows students (for a fee) to create an ebook with pictures, text, audio, and music! **iBooks Author (apple.com/books-author)** is another great, free app that is complex enough for your high school students to use. **Storybird (storybird.com)** is another free site that students will find easy to use. It also has very interesting graphics for younger students. **Flipsnack (flipsnack.com)** is yet another free app students can use.

As students finish their books, encourage them to share with the entire class, using your Smart Board or **Miro (realtimeboard.com).** Finished stories should be saved to students' digital portfolios: **Edmodo (edmodo.com), eBackPack (ebackpack.com), Evernote (evernote.com),** or **LiveBinders (livebinders.com),** to name a few.

Consider visiting prekindergarten, kindergarten, or first-grade classes to have your students share their ebooks. Students might also consider printing hard copies of their books to give to students when you visit.

As we have discussed earlier, **RI.11-12.7**, **RH.11-12.7**, and **RST.11-12.7** is satisfied if students read and watch different mediums of published children's books. **W.11-12.2.A**, **WHST.11-12.2A**, **W.11-12.6**, **WHST.11-12.6**, **W.11-12.8.8**, and **WHST.11-12.8** are also satisfied when students research and write about their topic using technology, and when students write, produce, and publish their writing, presenting their information clearly and efficiently. **SL.11-12.2** and **SL.11-12.5** are also satisfied when students contribute to class discussions, and present their plot diagrams, story maps, and final projects to the class. **L.11-12.4c** is also satisfied by this lesson, when students use dictionaries, glossaries, and thesauruses, not only to search for words to bolster their writing but to clarify the precise meaning of words they wish to use.

ISTE STUDENT STANDARDS

Students will be using many ISTE Standards in this lesson.

- **Empowered Learner** by understanding fundamental concepts of technology operations, demonstrating the ability to choose, use, and troubleshoot current technologies.

- **Digital Citizen** by demonstrating respects for rights in using and sharing intellectual property.

- **Knowledge Constructor** by employing research, evaluating and building knowledge using digital resources and using a variety of tools to create a collection of artifacts that demonstrate learning.

- **Innovative Designer** by using a design process for testing theories and solving authentic problems, including selection and use of the most appropriate digital tools.

- **Creative Communicator** by communicating complex ideas effectively through creation of new resources using a variety of media and publishing for an intended audience.

- **Global Collaborator** by connecting to other learners to broaden mutual understanding and contributing to a team project.

> I use technology daily to complete school assignments and to prepare for
> tests. My tech tools are an essential part of my daily life as a high school
> student. Fulfilling school academic standards has allowed me to reach my
> goal to attend college.—**Helene Fogel, student**

Science/Social Studies Lessons

The following sample lessons address CCSS ELA standards and teach lessons based
on national standards in social studies and science.

Research Activity

In our local high school's AP environmental science class, students select a topic of
interest, but this could be a model for any research in history, science, or technical
writing (e.g., Should water be sold in plastic bottles? Should public transportation in your hometown be increased?). Students conduct research by collecting
data from a survey that uses Edmodo or another survey site such as Google Form.
The students also speak with local experts (if feasible) and conduct more global
research using internet resources such as The Learning Network, The Current, or
Google Scholar and their library's databases.

The final product is presented using digital media, such as iMovie or Explain Everything. The presentation includes a statement of their belief after the research and a
plan of action, and it includes live survey results, graphs, and research to support
their points of view. Edmodo is also used to post links and videos that presenters
wish to share.

The main standards driving this project are **WHST.11-12.2.A, WHST.11-12.6,** and
WHST.11-12.8, to produce and publish a STEM writing project using digital technology. But, in Grades 11 and 12, students must also "update individual or shared
writing products in response to ongoing feedback, including new arguments or
information." Using surveys and flexible apps and programs such as Edmodo can
assist ongoing feedback and make it easy to update on the fly. Students are also fulfilling **RI.11-12.7, RH.11-12.7,** and **RST.11-12.7** by integrating and evaluating multiple

sources of information to address a problem. **SL.11-12.2** and **SL.11-12.5** are satisfied by making the presentation of their findings using digital media.

ISTE STUDENT STANDARDS

Students will be using all ISTE Standards in this lesson.

- **Empowered Learner** through use of technology to seek feedback that informs and improves their learning.

- **Digital Citizen** by demonstrating respects for rights in using and sharing intellectual property and engaging in safe behavior when using digital technology.

- **Knowledge Constructor** by employing research, evaluating and building knowledge, developing ideas and pursuing solutions to real-world issues using digital resources.

- **Innovative Designer** by using a design process for testing theories and solving authentic problems, including selection and use of the most appropriate digital tools.

- **Computational Thinker** by formulating problem definitions suited to technology solutions and through data collection, breaking problems into component parts, and developing models to help understanding.

- **Creative Communicator** by communicating complex ideas effectively through creation of new resources using a variety of media and publishing for an intended audience.

- **Global Collaborator** by connecting to other learners to broaden mutual understanding and contributing to a team project and using collaborative technologies to work with experts and community members.

Consumer Education

Our local students complete this is a lesson, called the Apartment Project, in consumer education class during the final years of high school. Several high schools in our area do this as a paperless project, using only tablets.

Student typically complete this activity as a group project where students select "roommates." Students choose their careers after high school, additional training, or college. They then research their career, including future workplace projections, tasks, work environment, location, and estimated beginning salary, using free resources such as the school's career counselor and websites such as the government's **Career One Stop (careeronestop.org),** or paid services such as Naviance.

After this research is complete, and with teacher assistance, a realistic beginning salary is determined. Taxes are discussed and deducted from income. Ten percent savings are calculated. Then using Google Sheets and the internet (Zillow, Kelley Blue Book, automobile websites) as well as primary interviews with adults, a budget is devised. Pie charts are created with Google Sheets to visually represent the percentage of income for items. (Teachers explained parameters to students, for example, comfortable percentages of income for housing, transportation, food, utilities, etc.) Adjustments are made to live within the student's income. Presentations are made with Explain Everything.

This lesson meets many of the technology standards. Primary standards satisfied are **RI.11-12.7, RH.11-12.7,** and **RST.11-12.7,** as quantitative and technical analysis is needed to understand and determine the economic realities for your students. Also, **WHST.11-12.2.A, WHST.11-12.6,** and **WHST.11-12.8** are satisfied by writing a shared product and analyzing different sources. Making informed decisions from the sources and presenting them to others in a natural outcome satisfies **SL.11-12.2** and **SL.11-12.5.** Finally, using Google Sheets, pie charts, analyses of budgets and taxes is an effective way to bring in the math standard **MP5.**

ISTE STUDENT STANDARDS

Students will be using all ISTE Standards in this lesson.

- **Empowered Learner** by leverage technology to reflect on the learning process and improve learning outcomes and demonstrating learning in a variety of ways.

- **Digital Citizen** by engaging in safe behavior when using digital technology.

- **Knowledge Constructor** by employing research, evaluating and building knowledge, developing ideas and pursuing solutions to real-world issues using digital resources.

- **Innovative Designer** by using a design process for testing theories and solving authentic problems, including selection and use of the most appropriate digital tools.

- **Computational Thinker** by formulating problem definitions suited to technology solutions and through data collection, breaking problems into component parts, and developing models to help facilitate problem solving.

- **Creative Communicator** by communicating complex ideas effectively through creation of new resources using a variety of media and publishing for an intended audience.

- **Global Collaborator** by connecting to other learners to broaden mutual understanding and contributing to a team project and using collaborative technologies to work with experts and community members.

Math Lessons

Measurement

This next lesson comes from the files of the math coach at a local high school. Students use hands-on, real-life activities to practice measuring square footage, taking into account varying factors and making adjustments for them. This activity can be performed individually, in partners, or teams, and it gets students out of the classroom!

Students will need tape measures or laser measurement devices. Math standard **MP5** has students use appropriate tools strategically. You will need to decide if it is appropriate for your students to use a calculator during this lesson. Most computers, laptops, tablets, and smartphones come equipped with a calculator. There are also free online calculators available. Next, share with students (Google Docs, Google Blogger, Google Hangouts, etc.) the problems they will be working to solve. Following are some examples.

1. Have students calculate the amount of concrete necessary to put a four-foot walkway from one specific point on the school grounds to another.

2. Have students calculate the amount of carpet needed to cover a classroom, leaving a three-foot band of tile all the way around.

3. Have students calculate the amount of fencing needed to surround an Olympic-size swimming pool, with a three-foot deck all around.

Have students keep track of their calculations and notes, recording what they discover in a manner of their choice (Google Sheets, TouchCast, Glogster, Desmos, etc.). Once all students have finished their calculations, have them summarize their learning by using Google Docs, Prezi, TouchCast, HP Reveal, MURAL, or other good sites and apps that let students create presentations that are electronically posted for all to view and review. You may even wish to ask students for suggestions of things to measure!

In addition to **MP5,** the presentation portion of this lesson meets **SL. 11-12.2** (integrating multiple sources of information presented in diverse media or formats) and **SL.11-12.5** (making strategic use of digital media). Students may need to gather relevant information (such as equations specific to their given question) from multiple digital sources, to help them complete calculations related to their given questions (e.g., How big is a swimming pool? What is the common width of a sidewalk?).

They will also need to assess the usefulness of each resource to help record their data and answer the research question. When doing this, standards **W.11-12.8** and **WHST.11-12.8** are satisfied. They are also fulfilling **RI.11-12.7, RH.11-12.7,** and **RST.11-12.7** by integrating and evaluating multiple sources of information to address a problem. In addition, **RST.11-12.9** is satisfied, as students need to synthesize information from many sources to resolve conflicting information. Students in your class can use Evernote, iAnnotate, or similar apps to help organize their sources and resources. That satisfies **WHST.11-12.6** by using technology, including the internet, to produce, publish, and update individual or shared writing products, taking advantage of technology's capacity to link to other information and to display information flexibly and dynamically.

ISTE STUDENT STANDARDS

Students will be using the following ISTE Standards in this lesson.

- **Empowered Learner** by understanding fundamental concepts of technology operations, demonstrating the ability to choose, use, and troubleshoot current technologies.

- **Knowledge Constructor** by employing research, evaluating and building knowledge, developing ideas and pursuing solutions to real-world issues using digital resources.

- **Computational Thinker** by formulating problem definitions suited to technology solutions and through data collection, breaking problems into component parts, and developing models to help facilitate problem solving.

- **Creative Communicator** by communicating complex ideas effectively through creation of new resources using a variety of media and publishing for an intended audience.

Real-World Problem Solving

This math lesson, again from the files of one of our high school friends, is used to teach real-world problem solving, involving any math concept. Students make a word-problem video similar to those found at Virtual Nerd or Khan Academy, of real-world mathematical problems. If students prefer, they can also make a presentation involving a word problem. Working in pairs, students use a video or digital camera (a smartphone or tablet works as well) to take video or pictures of interesting objects around the school that have mathematical implications. Some suggested ideas include:

1. Tiles in the cafeteria or classroom.

2. A stone or brick wall.

3. Paper folding.

4. Field of dandelions.

5. Rate of acceleration.

6. Testing gravity from a balcony.

Using iMovie, Movie Maker (any other movie-making software), or PowerPoint, Keynote, Google Slides, and so on, teams make their word-problem videos or presentations. Teams may wish to research ideas and examples from Virtual Nerd or Khan Academy before beginning. Next, students write their real-life word problem to go along with their pictures or video.

At the appropriate time, have students project their movies and "teach" the class. "Learning" students solve the problems and/or take necessary notes using Evernote, Diigo, Explain Everything (in which they can use written and voice recorded notations), and so on. Teams present (BaiBoard, Doceri, etc.) to the class, making sure they save time for asking and answering any questions, as they are "the experts" on the problem. These movies and presentations can then be uploaded to YouTube or your favorite posting site to share with absent students and/or parents. They can then be revisited any time during the year. Encourage students to continue looking for examples throughout their daily lives, writing problems, and posting them for others to solve. This is a good idea for flipping the classroom as well.

In addition to math standard **MP5,** students are also fulfilling **RI.11-12.7, RH.11-12.7,** or **RST.11-12.7** by integrating and evaluating multiple sources of information to address a problem. Students are introducing, producing, and publishing writing, as well as working together to present their ideas clearly and efficiently, so **W.11-12.2A/WHST.11-12.2A, A, W.11-12.6/WHST.11-12.6,** and **W.11-12.8/WHST.11-12.8** are also met. **RI.11-12.7** and **W.11-12.7** are also satisfied when students gather, integrate, and present their information in an original way. Using diverse media and formats (including music, graphics, voiceovers, etc.) to present and clarify information is definitely a part of this project, so **SL.11-12.2** and **SL.11-12.5** are also fulfilled.

ISTE STUDENT STANDARDS

Students will be using all ISTE Standards in this lesson.

- **Empowered Learner** by leverage technology to reflect on the learning process and improve learning outcomes and demonstrating learning in a variety of ways.

- **Digital Citizen** by engaging in safe behavior when using digital technology.

- **Knowledge Constructor** by evaluating accuracy, perspective and credibility of media and digital resources and evaluating information for intellectual pursuits.
  and pursuing solutions to real-world issues using digital resources.

- **Innovative Designer** by using a design process for testing theories and solving authentic problems, including selection and use of the most appropriate digital tools.

- **Computational Thinker** by formulating problem definitions suited to technology solutions and through data collection, breaking problems into component parts, and developing models to help facilitate problem solving.

- **Creative Communicator** by communicating complex ideas effectively through creation of new resources using a variety of media and publishing for an intended audience.

- **Global Collaborator** by connecting to other learners to broaden mutual understanding and contributing to a team project and using collaborative technologies to work with experts and community members.

Game Theory

One of the areas that juniors and seniors need to study in math is probability and statistics. Game theory is a great way to go into depth in this area of math and keep your student's interest! Specifically, game theory covers the areas of conditional probability and the rules of probability, and, of course, using probability to make decisions. This lesson was modified and adapted from several online game-theory lessons and resources. You can use it as is or create your own from the resources below.

Begin with students learning about game theory and understanding what it is; use these sites to help broaden students' knowledge base:

- **Wikipedia, Game Theory (tinyurl.com/85qdcs4)**

- **Game Theory Explained in One Minute (tinyurl.com/y7e9vhq3)**

- **Mathematics Illuminated (tinyurl.com/ybtzepll)**

- **Cornell, Game Theory (tinyurl.com/y7dyrot6)**

- **Random (tinyurl.com/y9qhb732)**

Have students write down important new terms and note their meanings, using a digital dictionary such as Word Central, Merriam-Webster, or Wordsmyth. They also should journal their progress in understanding game theory using apps like Explain Everything or Doceri. This will be part of their presentation of their understanding of game theory and their game solution at the end of the project.

Have students discuss the chance that a fair coin will land on heads if it's flipped. After a discussion about how this fits game theory, present the students with another game theory question, "What is the probability you will share a birthday with someone in this room?" Have students use this resource from the **University** of Illinois (tinyurl.com/y77fryzx) to help them with the problem, having them show any work they did to solve. They should continue to use their app to journal their discussions, math work, and reasoning as they solve the problem.

After giving the students time to figure out the problem, discuss the solution as a whole class. Split the class into groups of two or three for the next activity, telling them that they are going to learn about different types of probabilities and how they relate to game theory.

Have them review proportionality with the following exercise. Students should use their apps or a database such as Google Sheets, Apple Numbers, or Microsoft Excel to record their results. Create groups of four-to-five students and give the class M&Ms. Count the M&Ms in their bag by color. Also, record the total number of M&Ms. Have students draw sixty M&Ms with replacement and record the results by color. After they finish, ask them to calculate the proportion of M&Ms drawn of each color. Then use the activity from this site to have students practice proportionality: (tinyurl.com/y74nunf5). They can also explore conditional proportionality using this site: (tinyurl.com/y8bsek8z).

Essential Questions:

1. Does each combination have the same probability?

2. Which combinations have a smaller chance and why?

Discuss formal definitions of notation for the probability of an event, the probability of its complement, and its conditional probability—the probability that event A will occur based on the fact that event B has already occurred.

Continue to discuss how game theory allows your students to make decisions based on all alternative outcomes. Use rock, paper, scissors as a way to demonstrate. Have students record the trends they notice in their digital journals. After explaining how the activity uses Bayes Theorem to predict your next move, allow students to play the rock-paper-scissors game with this game generator: (tinyurl.com/y7vm7uuc). Again, students should note any trends they notice while playing the game. Finally, have them watch the video "How To Win Scissors, Paper, Rock Using Math" (tinyurl.com/yauqyek6). Then explain Bayes Theorem and present how it applies to game theory. Have students play rock, paper, scissors with a partner keeping track of their results. How often do they win? Change partners. Do results differ? Run through the Bayes Theorem activity **(tinyurl.com/y8jcgc7y)** with the class to illustrate the theory.

Next discuss the Prisoner's Dilemma scenario. Define basic probability notation and discuss it. There are many sites that have information and examples such as: **(tinyurl.com/ybsw3gls).** Discuss the idea of game theory as optimization of strategies. Then allow students to play through the scenario a few times using one of the sites below. They should keep their work in their digital journal.

Prisoner's Dilemma:

- **Game Theory 101 (tinyurl.com/ybxpvopn)**

- **Game Theory (tinyurl.com/y9x9dhbg)**

- **Iterated Prisoner's Dilemma (tinyurl.com/ybqwnx4b)**

Finally, have students work in pairs and choose a game in which to practice game theory; they should track, through digital journaling, the different strategies their team used.

- **Marbles: (tinyurl.com/yhkuzu)**

- **Monty Hall (Let's Make A Deal) Game**

- **Simple Monty Hall: (tiny.cc/2oiy3y)**

- **Advanced Monty Hall: (tinyurl.com/3ycz9f)**

- **Dice Roll: (tlnyurl.com/gmtbonu)**

- **Adjustable Spinner: (tinyurl.com/2awqr4)**

- **Dice Table: (tinyurl.com/ma93s4m)**

- **Racing Game: (tinyurl.com/38cpu3v)**

- **Toads and Vines: (tinyurl.com/y96x8x8o)**

At the end of this project students should prepare a slideshow or video presentation of their findings to the class using Moovly, Clips, Shmoop, Animoto, Keynote, PowerPoint, Google Slides, or any other appropriate program. After the presentations, it would be great to publish your students' work, either the entire presentation, or maybe just their solutions to the games they chose on your class website using Wix, SiteBuilder, or another web design product of your choosing. They could then update their work as they come across more or different variables in their games, or have feedback from other students about their solutions.

This should include:

3. A definition of game theory.

4. New mathematical terms learned.

5. Examples of what they feel are the most important concepts of game theory.

6. What they learned during the project from a review of their journals, which includes illustrations or video demonstrations of key points.

7. Materials they used and online resources cited.

8. The final game they worked on, what strategies they used, and what they learned from it about game theory.

9. Their opinion about how they can use game theory in their lives.

As well as satisfying **MP5** by using appropriate math tools in solving a problem, they are fulfilling **RH.11-12.7** and **RST.11-12.7,** which is integrating multiple sources presented in diverse media in order to solve a problem. And they will be synthesizing information from a range of sources to understand a concept, so satisfying **RST.11-12.9.** Of course they will also be using the skills of writing on a topic in an organized fashion and using multimedia, so satisfying **W.11-12.2.a** and **WHST.11-12.2.a.** If they publish their finding on the class website they will also be practicing standards **W.11-12.6** and **WHST.11-12.6,** especially if they are updating their work after feedback from other students. In gathering the data from digital sources, they have fulfilled **W.11-12.8** and **WHST.11-12.8.** Also using digital dictionaries, to clarify meanings of new terms they have learned, satisfies **L11-12.4.c.** The presentation of the material, and integrating multiple sources into that presentation, also satisfies the speaking and listening standards **SL.11-12.2** and **SL.11-12.5.**

ISTE STUDENT STANDARDS

Students will be using many ISTE Standards in this lesson.

- **Empowered Learner** by leverage technology to reflect on the learning process and improve learning outcomes and demonstrating learning in a variety of ways.

- **Digital Citizen** by engaging in safe behavior when using digital technology.

- **Knowledge Constructor** by employing research, evaluating and building knowledge, developing ideas and pursuing solutions to real-world issues using digital resources.

- **Computational Thinker** by formulating problem definitions suited to technology solutions and through data collection, breaking problems into component parts, and developing models to help facilitate problem solving.

- **Creative Communicator** by communicating complex ideas effectively through creation of new resources using a variety of media and publishing for an intended audience.

A Final Note

As students progress through the grades, they establish their proficiency in technology, finally culminating in their readiness for college or a successful career. There are many good ideas in this chapter that you may be able to adapt to your class. Satisfying the performance standards at the Grades 11–12 levels gives our students a greater chance of success as adults in the "real" world.

You will find more resources online at our website **(tinyurl.com/y9dfltpr),** which may be helpful to you as you look to differentiate your instruction. Visit our website for updated information about this book. To see grades other than 6–12, look for our additional title in this series.

References

Bray, B. (1999, May 1). *Ten steps to effective technology staff development: Getting teachers on board.* Retrieved from edutopia.org/ten-steps-effective-technology-staff-development

Darling-Hammond, L., Hyler, M. E., Gardner, M. (2017, June). Effective Teacher Professional Development. Palo Alto, CA: Learning Policy Institute. Page 12-13. Found online at: https://www.teacherscholars.org/wp-content/uploads/2017/09/Effective_Teacher_Professional_Development_REPORT.pdf

DeWitt, P. (2013, July 7). Take a risk . . . Flip your parent communication! [Blog post]. Retrieved from blogs.edweek.org/edweek/finding_common_ground/2013/07/take_a_risk_flip_your_parent_communication.html

Devaney, L. (2016, May 6). Survey: Teachers now use twice as much gaming and video in the classroom. *eSchool News.* Retrieved October 5, 2018, from eschoolnews.com/2016/05/06/survey-teachers-now-use-twice-as-much-gaming-and-video-in-the-classroom/

Education Weekly. (Updated September 18, 2017) Map: Tracking the Common Core State Standards. Found online at: https://www.edweek.org/ew/section/multimedia/map-states-academic-standards-common-core-or.html?cmp=cpc-goog-ew-dynamic+ads&ccid=dynamic+ads&ccag=common+core+dynamic&cckw=&cccv=dynamic+ad&gclid=Cj0KCQjw1pblBRDSARIsACfUG13KQYIBOwHWbddp65eUNT2qvZczhTcn0Njb1ORuMM1G0AArW8CCsh0aApQTEALw_wcB

Edutopia. (2007, November 5). What is successful technology integration? *Technology Integration Professional Development Guide.* Retrieved from edutopia. org/technology-integration-guide-description

Games and Learning Publishing Council. (2014). Teachers surveyed on using digital games in class: A games and learning research report. Retrieved from gamesandlearning.org/2014/06/09/teachers-on-using-games-in-class

Gazzaley, A, and Rosen, L (2016, Sep 16) The Distracted Mind: Ancient Brains in a High-Tech World. MIT Press.

Gerwitz, C. (2019, March 5). What Does Each State Require? *Education Week.* Retrieved April 1, 2019 https://www.edweek.org/ew/section/multimedia/ what-tests-does-each-state-require.html

Henderson, A., & Mapp, K. (2002). *A new wave of evidence: The impact of school, family, and community connections on student achievement.* Retrieved from sedl. org/connections/resources/evidence.pdf

LEAD Commission. (2012). Parents' and teachers' attitudes and opinions on technology in education [PDF]. Retrieved from leadcommission.org/sites/ default/files/ LEAD Poll Deck.pdf

Meador, D. (2018). The pros and cons of allowing cell phones in schools. *Thought Co.* Retrieved from thoughtco.com/ embrace-or-ban-cell-phones-in-school-3194571

Meeuwse, K. (2013, April 11). Using iPads to transform teaching and learning [Blog post]. Retrieved from iteachwithipads.net/2013/04/11/ using-iPads-to-transform-teaching-and-learning

National Governors Association Center for Best Practices, Council of Chief State School Officers. (2010). *Common core state standards.* Washington, DC.

New York University. (2007) *National symposium on the millennial student.* Retrieved from nyu.edu/frn/publications/millennial.student/Millennial.index.html

Partnership for 21st Century Skills. (2004). The partnership for 21st century skills— Framework for 21st century learning. Retrieved from p21.org/about-us/ p21-framework

Sammons, L. (2009). *Guided math: a framework for mathematics instruction.* Huntington Beach, California: Shell Education (2011, September 21). *Guided math: a framework for math instruction* [PowerPoint slides]. Retrieved from slideshare.net/ggierhart/guided-math-powerpointbytheauthorofguidedmath

Sparks, S. D. (2017, January 24). Common core revisions: What are states really changing? *Education Week (36).* Retrieved October 5, 2018 from edweek.org/ew/articles/2017/01/25/clarifying-common-core.html

Strategic Learning Programs. (n.d.). Retrieved from iste.org/lead/professional-services/strategic-learning-programs

Sun, Liping & Siklander, Pirkko. (2018). How to trigger students' interest in digital learning environments A systematic literature review. Retrieved March 28, 2019 from https://www.researchgate.net/publication/326682783_How_to_trigger_students'_interest_in_digital_learning_environments_A_systematic_literature_review

Swanson, K. (2013, October 1). Five tips for explaining common core to parents. *THE Journal.* Retrieved from thejournal.com/2013/10/01/how-to-explain-common-core-to-parents.aspx

Szybinski, D. (2016). –Teaching a new generation of students. *NETWORK: A Journal of Faculty Development.* Retrieved from facultyresourcenetwork.org/publications/teaching-a-new-generation-of-students

United States Congress. (2010) Section 1015c. Chapter 28: Higher education resources and student assistance. In *Title 20–Education* (2010 ed.). Retrieved from gpo.gov/fdsys/pkg/USCODE-2010-title20/html/USCODE-2010-title20-chap28.htm

U.S. Department of Education, National Center for Education Statistics. (2018). Student Access to Digital Learning Resources Outside of the Classroom (NCES 2017-098) Retrieved March 20, 2019 from https://nces.ed.gov/pubs2017/2017098/index.asp

Appendix A
ISTE Standards

ISTE Standards for Students

The ISTE Standards for Students emphasize the skills and qualities we want for students, enabling them to engage and thrive in a connected, digital world. The standards are designed for use by educators across the curriculum, with every age student, with a goal of cultivating these skills throughout a student's academic career. Both students and teachers will be responsible for achieving foundational technology skills to fully apply the standards. The reward, however, will be educators who skillfully mentor and inspire students to amplify learning with technology and challenge them to be agents of their own learning.

1. Empowered Learner

Students leverage technology to take an active role in choosing, achieving and demonstrating competency in their learning goals, informed by the learning sciences. Students:

    a.   articulate and set personal learning goals, develop strategies leveraging technology to achieve them and reflect on the learning process itself to improve learning outcomes.

    b.   build networks and customize their learning environments in ways that support the learning process.

    c.   use technology to seek feedback that informs and improves their practice and to demonstrate their learning in a variety of ways.

d.   understand the fundamental concepts of technology operations, demonstrate the ability to choose, use and troubleshoot current technologies and are able to transfer their knowledge to explore emerging technologies.

2. Digital Citizen

Students recognize the rights, responsibilities and opportunities of living, learning and working in an interconnected digital world, and they act and model in ways that are safe, legal and ethical. Students:

a.   cultivate and manage their digital identity and reputation and are aware of the permanence of their actions in the digital world.

b.   engage in positive, safe, legal and ethical behavior when using technology, including social interactions online or when using networked devices.

c.   demonstrate an understanding of and respect for the rights and obligations of using and sharing intellectual property.

d.   manage their personal data to maintain digital privacy and security and are aware of data-collection technology used to track their navigation online.

3. Knowledge Constructor

Students critically curate a variety of resources using digital tools to construct knowledge, produce creative artifacts and make meaningful learning experiences for themselves and others. Students:

a.   plan and employ effective research strategies to locate information and other resources for their intellectual or creative pursuits.

b.   evaluate the accuracy, perspective, credibility and relevance of information, media, data or other resources.

c.   curate information from digital resources using a variety of tools and methods to create collections of artifacts that demonstrate meaningful connections or conclusions.

d.   build knowledge by actively exploring real-world issues and problems, developing ideas and theories and pursuing answers and solutions.

4. Innovative Designer

Students use a variety of technologies within a design process to identify and solve problems by creating new, useful or imaginative solutions. Students:

a.   know and use a deliberate design process for generating ideas, testing theories, creating innovative artifacts or solving authentic problems.

b.   select and use digital tools to plan and manage a design process that considers design constraints and calculated risks.

c.   develop, test and refine prototypes as part of a cyclical

design process.

d.   exhibit a tolerance for ambiguity, perseverance and the capacity to work with open-ended problems.

5. Computational Thinker

Students develop and employ strategies for understanding and solving problems in ways that leverage the power of technological methods to develop and test solutions. Students:

a.   formulate problem definitions suited for technology-assisted methods such as data analysis, abstract models and algorithmic thinking in exploring and finding solutions.

b.   collect data or identify relevant data sets, use digital tools to analyze them, and represent data in various ways to facilitate problem-solving and decision-making.

c.   break problems into component parts, extract key information, and develop descriptive models to understand complex systems or facilitate problem-solving.

d.   understand how automation works and use algorithmic thinking to develop a sequence of steps to create and test automated solutions.

6. Creative Communicator

Students communicate clearly and express themselves creatively for a variety of purposes using the platforms, tools, styles, formats and digital media appropriate to their goals. Students:

    a.   choose the appropriate platforms and tools for meeting the desired objectives of their creation or communication.

    b.   create original works or responsibly repurpose or remix digital resources into new creations.

    c.   communicate complex ideas clearly and effectively by creating or using a variety of digital objects such as visualizations, models or simulations.

    d.   publish or present content that customizes the message and medium for their intended audiences.

7. Global Collaborator

Students use digital tools to broaden their perspectives and enrich their learning by collaborating with others and working effectively in teams locally and globally. Students:

    a.   use digital tools to connect with learners from a variety of backgrounds and cultures, engaging with them in ways that broaden mutual understanding and learning.

    b.   use collaborative technologies to work with others, including peers, experts or community members, to examine issues and problems from multiple viewpoints.

    c.   contribute constructively to project teams, assuming various roles and responsibilities to work effectively toward a common goal.

    d.   explore local and global issues and use collaborative technologies to work with others to investigate solutions.

Index